THE GOVERNMENT AND POLITICS OF BRITAIN

Politics

Editor

PROFESSOR W. A. ROBSON
B.SC.(ECON.), PH.D., LL.M.

Professor Emeritus of Public Administration
in the University of London

THE GOVERNMENT AND POLITICS OF BRITAIN

John P. Mackintosh

HUTCHINSON UNIVERSITY LIBRARY

LONDON

HUTCHINSON & CO (*Publishers*) **LTD**
3 Fitzroy Square, London W1

London Melbourne Sydney Auckland
Wellington Johannesburg Cape Town
and agencies throughout the world

First published 1970
Second edition 1971
Third, revised, edition 1974

This book has been set in Times type, printed in Great Britain
on smooth wove paper by Anchor Press, and
bound by Wm. Brendon, both of Tiptree, Essex

ISBN 0 09 118480 0 (cased)
0 09 118481 9 (paper)

CONTENTS

PREFACE TO THIRD EDITION

In preparing the third edition, I was grateful for the advice and aid of my former research assistant, Miss Norma Percy, who showed me material she had collected for a most stimulating series of Granada Television programmes on the reform of Parliament.

John P. Mackintosh
House of Commons

PREFACE

This book was suggested to me by Professor W. A. Robson, and I am most grateful to him and to Hutchinson University Library for giving me this opportunity. The opportunity came towards the end of the 1966–70 Parliament when I had had time to acquire some general views as to how British government works. The book is not intended to provide a factual guide—many of these already exist—nor is it to lead the student towards the more detailed studies that have been written about specialised aspects of our government and politics. The book is an interpretation, an extended essay trying to explain how the system works and what it looks like to someone in one of the best spectator seats. As such I have referred to those major controversies which need to be dealt with in order to establish or explain my views, but academic or political controversies which have no bearing on my theme are not mentioned.

I must thank Miss Louise McAdam for her great kindness and incredible accuracy and speed in typing the book, and my wife and family for putting up with me during the period when it was being written. I dedicate it to my daughter Deirdre Victoria Una whose birth occurred to cheer me up and speed the writing of the last chapter.

April 1970

John P. Mackintosh
House of Commons

I

DESCRIBING THE BRITISH CONSTITUTION

It is often said that Britain has an unwritten Constitution, but this is true only in the sense that there has never been any attempt to give the major rules guiding the system a special validity by putting them all in a single document as was done in the United States. But a great number of these rules are written and embodied in Acts of Parliament such as the Representation of the People Act, 1948, which prescribes the arrangements for holding elections, or the Parliament Acts of 1911 and 1949 which set out some of the relations between the House of Lords and the House of Commons. Other aspects of the system which are not laws but are established practices (such as the convention that the Queen asks the leader of the majority party after an election to form a government) are written down in many books on British politics. The difference is that it is not illegal to break these rules but if a serious attempt to avoid them occurred, it would indicate that profound changes were taking place in the whole system. Again, there is another category of practices, examples being the way the Cabinet is organised or parliamentary candidates selected, which are neither law nor established conventions but are simply convenient methods of procedure whose change would involve no major shake-up in the process of government. It might even be some time before such changes were noticed.

The difficulty in producing an accurate and comprehensive account of these laws, conventions and practices is partly that they are scattered over the history of the country from the Habeas Corpus Act of 1679 which prevents people being held in prison without trial and the convention that the Queen will not veto legislation, which has been built up since 1708, to recent changes in parliamentary procedure dealing with the control of public expenditure. In part,

the difficulty is that situations which call for the application of
certain conventions may be few and far between. Thus how far a
convention would apply today may not be absolutely clear while
some conventions (such as 'the collective responsibility of ministers')
may have changed their actual content or meaning though the
words used remain the same. As a result, to try and describe the
British Constitution is like trying to explain the working of an
ancient university with its old statutes, more recent regulations,
traditions begun for one purpose but still useful for another where
new students and teachers are continually altering current practice.

There is yet a further problem in that so many developments of
all kinds in Britain and in the rest of the world have some effect on
the working of the institutions that it is hard to know where to stop
the account. For example, changes in voters' attitudes are likely, in
time, to alter the responses of the political parties and to have an
influence on the kind of people who are prepared to go into politics.
In 1955, a combination of forces inside and outside Parliament led
to the end of the BBC's monopoly of broadcasting and the creation
of commercial television which has probably had some effect on the
public's responses. On the other hand, Acts of Parliament insisting
on political balance in television have meant that the public receives
much of its political news without the slant and editorialising which
is normal in newspapers. At a different level, British membership of
the Common Market has already altered the tax system and has begun
to change the methods by which agriculture is supported. Further
afield, a wave of isolationism in the United States and the withdrawal
of her forces in Europe could force Britain to return to conscription
and to forge closer defence links with her European partners.

It is because of the ancient origins of many of the laws and conventions of the Constitution that books on British government often
start with an historical section. However, it is not essential to go far
back into history because most of the conventions, practices and
maxims which have been inherited either date from the late nineteenth century or were in operation then. Also it is important not
just to list the various acts or to describe how Parliament or the
Civil Service developed, but to show their interconnections. Each
part of the machinery of government can only be understood in
terms of the other cog wheels with which it must intermesh and
many of the maxims or descriptions are only meaningful if they can
be seen in relation to the whole system in operation at the time when
the conventions became established.

It so happens that the pattern of government which evolved in

Britain between 1870 and 1914 was regarded then (and by many since then) with particular satisfaction. Not only were a large number of books written about it, but most of the commentators assumed that there could scarcely be any improvement. There were several reasons for the belief that the system prevailing at that time was almost the end of the road. In those years Britain was particularly powerful and successful, the dominating mood being one of confidence that progress would continue and that Britain's peculiar and powerful position in the world would always remain. Looking back it seemed clear to the Victorians that Britain had been through the social and political phases or overcome the difficulties then besetting most other nations. Personal liberty and equality before the law had been established. A respected monarchy gave continuity and an aura of authority to the government, yet all personal or arbitrary rule had been eliminated. The aristocracy had never been marched to the guillotine, yet their powers had been tempered and shared with the other classes in the community. As late as the 1860s, there had been serious worries that any move towards democracy would introduce class warfare and political instability but, by the 1880s, these fears had faded. It was accepted that Britain had managed, apparently with unique success, to combine a proper degree of governmental authority with responsiveness to popular opinion, that patriotism, property and stability had been fortified rather than endangered by bringing all sections of the population into a continuing debate about public policy.

Exemplifying this self-confidence, late nineteenth-century historians tended to regard all aspects of British history as stages in an inevitable march towards this happy conclusion. They thought they had discovered that the Anglo-Saxon tribes, even before coming to Britain, had always proceeded by open decisions at 'folk moots' and that these albeit rudimentary democratic practices had tempered the Norman autocracy introduced into England after 1066. Any further attempts at despotic rule were countered by baronial revolts which forced respect for basic liberties upon recalcitrant sovereigns. These concessions and rights were embodied in Magna Carta. Then the practices of presenting grievances, of agreeing to grants of taxation and of making proclamations clarifying ancient custom, were all brought together in periodic Parliaments dating from the time of Simon de Montfort and Edward I. The Lancastrian kings, it was alleged, were involved in a 'constitutional experiment' of rule with Parliament while even the Tudor despotism only served to strengthen the House of Commons since it was used to carry through the

Reformation and to show patriotic support for Queen Elizabeth. From this point of view, Charles I may have had a tragic history but he was guilty of attempting to halt the country's steady progress towards Constitutional monarchy and the emergence of the House of Commons as an essential partner in government. Charles II and James II had the same failings and the English genius for non-violent progress was revealed when the latter monarch was allowed to escape. A new monarch was installed and what these historians dubbed as 'the Glorious Revolution of 1688' established simply that Parliament could not be set aside or overruled. Next, it was argued that the late seventeenth century saw the invention of the two-party system, the descendants of the Roundheads and Cavaliers becoming the Whigs and Tories who were content to fight it out at the hustings and in the House of Commons. According to this version of British history, George III's great error was to try and restore a measure of personal rule but luckily this was abandoned by his successors. The Reform Bill of 1832 created a uniform right to vote for men of property who were thus brought into the political system without any sharp break with tradition. Then the Reform Acts of 1867 and 1884 carried the process further and gave all established male householders a voice and a vote.

This, known as 'the Whig theory of history', viewed the system of government in practice in Britain between 1880 and 1914 as virtually the last word. The pattern then established was regarded as not only the culmination of fifteen hundred years of progress but was itself so simple, so logical, so effective and satisfactory, that the accounts of it had great force. These accounts filled the books and the minds of students of British government long after much had changed and were still regarded as largely correct until the 1940s. Thus the conventions and practices of the late Victorian period were not considered as merely true for that time, they were regarded as proper or normal. When further changes occurred, they were noticed with reluctance and tended to be regarded as departures from the norm, the main features of this system which may be called 'the Westminster Model', still dominating the textbooks in use after the Second World War. It then became the basis of the constitutions which were carefully written up for emergent nations of the Commonwealth on the grounds that if this system was the most advanced yet produced, why not hand it on in its complete form to the new states of Africa and Asia? It is also not surprising that many of the conventions and much of the language of this system are still used by British politicians and commentators.

For these reasons, to understand the meaning and original relevance of much that is said about current British government and politics, it is worth considering 'the Westminster Model' as it was supposed to work at the end of the last century. Those describing it at the time neglected to note that, as with all periods, social, political and legal conditions were changing. They did not think of this as a stage but as an end-product and thus their account may not have been true of any one precise moment, since practices they thought essential may have been declining and trends they had failed to notice may have been starting. But the account was broadly correct for the 1880–1914 period and relevant for this book in that it explains what is still for many British politicians and informed observers, the proper state of affairs and one which still underlies many of the maxims used to describe the British political system.

2

THE WESTMINSTER MODEL

The key feature of the British system of the 1880–1914 period, according to its exponents, was the Cabinet. This body of some sixteen senior political leaders, presided over by the Prime Minister, had two functions. On the one hand, the Cabinet governed the country and on the other, it sat in, led, was maintained, criticised and influenced by the House of Commons. As Bagehot put it in 1865, the 'Cabinet is a combining committee—a *hyphen* which joins, a *buckle* which fastens, the legislative part of the state to the executive part of the state'. In the Cabinet, which operated totally informally without officials present or minutes taken, all the major policy issues were thrashed out. The Prime Minister might, like Peel or Gladstone, have a commanding presence or, like Lord Aberdeen, might act essentially as a chairman taking no major part in discussions himself. While Prime Ministers advised the Crown as to who should be appointed to the Cabinet, the House of Commons played a background role in the selection. Some men had such a reputation that they could not be omitted and, conversely, to be a failure in the House was a serious disqualification for high office. Also, leaving a powerful man on the back benches might expose the Cabinet to dangerous attacks. Most of those likely to be appointed were men of wealth, usually with a considerable social or commercial reputation which gave them a position which was not solely derived from politics. For these reasons, the relationship between the Prime Minister and his colleagues was said to be that of a *primus inter pares*; he could lead and suggest but his fellow ministers had to be persuaded. Sacking ministers was scarcely proper but they were usually ready to resign if they had major doubts on policy issues, though no Prime Minister or Cabinet wanted to face the parliamentary problems that would be created by pointed criticisms from ex-ministers.

The source of the Cabinet's strength and its ultimate responsiveness to criticism came alike from the ministers' position in the House of Commons. There they normally enjoyed the support of a majority held together by party loyalty. MPs were returned at elections largely because of their views which indicated the party they supported, though many MPs had a personal hold on their constituencies. Once in the House, they wanted to see the leaders of their party succeed and were likely, other things being equal, to provide the Cabinet with fairly steady support. On the other hand, if the policies of the government failed, if it seemed to run counter to the principles espoused by its followers or if the Opposition seemed to be winning the argument, MPs might become restive and vote against their own leaders. The Cabinet, sensing such dangers, could then agree to modify its policies. Thus ministers enjoyed considerable power in the House so long as their policies were successful and were arousing both public acclaim and the enthusiasm of their own supporters. But a dispirited leadership, external setbacks, an impression of incompetence or of internal disagreements could lead to heavy pressure on the government to change its policies. If this yielded no results, the Commons might go on to dismiss a government, a general election only being necessary if the Parliament was near the end of its life or if MPs were not prepared to support another combination of ministers.

Because of the pressure of the House of Commons, all administration had to be handled by ministers answerable to Parliament. In the early nineteenth century, some administrative functions had been allocated to commissioners or boards (e.g. the administration of the Poor Law) simply because it was feared that the monarch might use appointments to such posts as a method of influencing the House of Commons. After the 1830s, these fears ceased and Parliament began to insist on its right to question all policies. MPs demanded that every aspect of central government should be allocated to one or other minister who could then be held responsible for all the actions of his department. This was the doctrine of 'ministerial responsibility' which had reality in two senses. First, the departments were small enough for the minister to have been seen and to have endorsed every decision likely to arouse outside comment and, secondly, if there was comment, the House of Commons would insist on holding the minister personally responsible. A further doctrine of 'collective responsibility' arose also in the face of parliamentary pressure. Ministers found that they had to support each other, for if one of them voiced doubts, it made the position of the entire Cabinet too precarious. This convention seemed reasonable in that all major decisions were taken collectively by the Cabinet.

Little was said about the process of administration because it was relatively simple. If the Cabinet proposed something and the House of Commons agreed, then the senior civil servants had merely to write the appropriate letters. There was no problem of the relations between officials and ministers as the distinction between political decisions and the execution of policy was so clear. Civil servants were, after the reforms of 1870, all recruited by open competition, the administrative class from the universities, the executive class from those who had completed a full school education and the clerical grade from those with a suitable, more elementary education. The Civil Service was not supposed to have views on politics or on policy issues or to have contact with outside interests. They were protected from parliamentary criticism and were allowed to serve one government after another on the assumption that they loyally carried out whatever policy was determined by the Cabinet. The small amount of local, as opposed to central, administration was placed in the hands of elected county and borough councils.

The primary tasks of the House of Commons in this period have been explained; each party evolved a leadership which it supported while the House as a whole commented on and criticised the performance of those leaders who were in office at that time. The House exercised these functions through the traditional forms of the power to legislate, to grant money and to debate. The process of legislation was designed to let the House know what the Cabinet or the private members sponsoring the Bill intended (1st reading), to give MPs ample time to debate the principles involved (2nd reading), to amend the proposal in detail (Committee of the whole House) and to have a look at the final result (3rd reading). In financial matters, the House worked on the same annual programme as the government. It scrutinised civil and defence estimates in the spring, and could amend or alter them. Then from April to July both the detailed expenditure proposals and the methods of raising revenue were debated and determined. In the autumn, the Public Accounts Committee (set up in 1860) scrutinised the accounts for the previous year to see that every penny had been spent as authorised by Parliament. The responsibility for raising the money and watching over its expenditure within the government lay with the Treasury which thus acquired a central and commanding position inside the government. Finally, with the Commons controlling the use of two or three days' time each week and with the government reluctant to close or curtail debate (powers to do so were taken in 1882), there was little need for a special Question Time or methods of getting at ministers. The House could and did debate any issue as it arose, private members could call for papers (that is for official documents), they could propose Select Committees of investigation, move and carry bills and go on and on talking about the Cabinet's proposals until they had arrived at a conclusion. Ministers had to attend the House on every sitting day and explain and defend their policies with the Prime Minister (if he was in the Commons) acting as Leader of the House and chief spokesman for the Cabinet.

The House of Lords was of secondary importance but it had powers to amend and reject Bills passed by the Commons though its leaders usually accepted that a measure clearly demanded by that House and by the country had to be passed. If the mass of peers looked like holding out against the Commons on a serious issue, the Cabinet could in the last resort ask the Crown to create sufficient peers to alter the balance. The Lords could also do much useful tidying up of legislation and its members contained sufficient men of talent to provide about a third of the ministers in nineteenth-century cabinets.

In such a system, there was little room for royal initiative. The Crown provided an impartial or non-political focus of loyalty, an embodiment of national feeling. The political functions of the Crown were to provide continuity, particularly when a Cabinet was defeated either in the Commons or at a general election. Then the King or Queen had the task of initiating consultations to find out which new leader was most likely to command the confidence of the majority in the Commons. In nine cases out of ten, the answer was obvious and in the tenth was soon established. Apart from this, the Crown could, under very special circumstances, refuse to grant a dissolution (if it was thought that the existing House of Commons was ready to maintain another Prime Minister without an election being held). The Sovereign could also, as Bagehot put it, insist on being consulted and then encourage or warn his ministers but, in the last resort, the views of the Cabinet had to prevail.

Little was said in most descriptions of 'the Westminster Model' about the electorate or the electoral system. There were discussions of the transferable vote or proportional representation (tried in a limited form in certain three-member seats after 1867) but on the whole it was accepted that either single or double-member seats (which largely disappeared after 1884) were an adequate way of allowing public opinion to express itself. There was also little emphasis on the party machines outside Parliament for these were only growing up in the 1880s. In general, it was still assumed that elections were for the purpose of choosing a House of Commons and were not a means of selecting a government. Thus the laws designed to diminish the influence of money in elections set limits not on expenditure in the national campaigns but on the costs of standing in individual constituencies. Party leaders did, from the 1870s, tour the country and candidates explained which principles they favoured. General and even by-elections were contested with considerable partisanship creating, on occasion, great excitement. Under these circumstances, a division into two wide-ranging groups or parties was accepted as natural and proper. This led the satirist W. S. Gilbert to inquire:

> How Nature always does contrive
> That every boy and every gal,
>   That's born into the world alive,
> Is either a little Liberal,
>   Or else a little Conservative!

The great virtues of this model were its efficiency and its beneficial effect on the community. The interdependence of the Cabinet and the Commons meant that when the country and MPs agreed that action was needed, the Cabinet's powers could be enormously augmented. When the political leadership began to falter, it could at once be checked, stopped, questioned, made to provide full explanations and then, if necessary, altered or dismissed. The good effect was that the system emphasised government by discussion, by argument with the assumption that the best case wins in the end. No single class swamped Parliament. The aristocracy were most numerous but even the landed interest could be defeated by an unanswerable argument, as happened when Peel felt he had no reply to the case put by the Anti-Corn Law League in the House. Such a system drew the ablest and those most desirous of serving their country into politics. It provided a great public spectacle and educated the entire community by exposing the facts and the arguments. The nightly battles in the Chamber attracted the attention of all who were interested in current affairs and in the great moral and political issues of the day.

Because, in this way, power lay in the interaction of the Commons and the Cabinet, anyone with a case or a special interest concentrated on the Commons. The Anti-Slavery Society, the Anti-Corn Law League and the Factory Reformers all sought to penetrate the House while the Railway Companies and the Churches had their back-bench spokesmen. But there were other interests involved and because landed and industrial wealth could clash, there was little evidence of the 'haves' uniting to exploit the 'have nots'. After Parliament had reached its decision, the administration of the laws was entrusted to a small group of non-political, upper middle class but highly able officials, their actions being given extra authority by the fact that they were technically acting in the name of a King or Queen revered as the figurehead and exemplar of the nation.

One reason for the strength of this system was that while this fairly simple pattern of administration remained constant, any social and political changes, such as the further development of an urbanised, industrialised society and of demands for a wider distribution of political power, could easily be accommodated by a refashioning of the institutions of control. As a result of such pressures, the Commons found its membership refurbished, the constituencies reformed, party organisations outside Parliament established, the Crown and the Lords relegated and the Civil Service reorganised to permit control through the relevant minister.

Although there is no evidence of conscious planning, the enthusiasm for representative institutions was such that the gradual growth of the administration was matched, for most of the period, by the increasing watchfulness of politicians and effectiveness of the House of Commons. It is true, as a general proposition, that systems of control must alter and adapt to follow changes in the system they are trying to monitor. The act of checking by a legislature must be based on relevant information of what ministers and officials are doing and must come at the moment when decisions are still open to influence. In this, the House of Commons was reasonably successful in the last decades of the nineteenth century and up to 1914.

One of the main problems of recent years has been that while the pattern of government has been adapted at an ever increasing pace to the needs of society, including, for instance, the administration of hospitals, the stimulation of decaying industries, the promotion of tourism, the preservation of the countryside and so on, little has been done to adapt the machinery of control to keep pace with this new network of government. This is because the British have been prepared to tackle practical problems of administration and management but, since the Westminster Model was supposed to be the most advanced method of democratic control, there was thought to be no need for equivalent alterations in its form or approach. A further reason is that the late nineteenth-century enthusiasm for democratic control has waned but no other coherent political philosophy has taken its place.

3

FORCES OF CHANGE

Since the 1880–1914 period, the organisation of life in Britain and the factors in society affecting the political superstructure have been altering very rapidly. Even in the period when the Westminster Model was supposed to have been working perfectly, there were many changes, but these were barely noticed since they could all be described by the same maxims and, if any comment was necessary, they could be regarded simply as extensions of the right to vote or as improvements in administrative methods.

But the changes taking place were significant and their effects cumulative and lasting. The change that led to the most far-reaching consequences was the rapid move towards a mass electorate. Before 1832 it is hard to estimate the number of voters but there were some 500 000. With the first Reform Act of that year, the vote was given to men only on a restrictive property qualification and in 1867 it was extended to all male householders in borough constituencies. In 1884 the same general principle was applied to the county seats. The 1918 Act enfranchised all men over 21 and all women over 30, the younger women being included in 1928. Finally in 1969 the age for voting was lowered to 18.

The effects of this mass electorate were pervasive, altering the whole political life of Britain and deeply affecting the institutional structure. It was assumed that because the Westminster Model was essentially democratic, this vast increase in the electorate could be accommodated without any profound alterations, but this was not true. For instance, a mass electorate, in 1972 averaging 63 000 voters in each constituency, has totally altered the relationship between the MP and his constituents. Before 1867 and even up to 1884, many candidates could hope to speak personally to most of the electors during an election campaign but soon after this ceased to be possible. And when the voters, instead of merely choosing someone they trusted, wanted to find out what was happening in Parliament, this magnified the role of the press and the most exciting

	Electorate	Total central government non-industrial civil servants	Central government gross-income (£ million)
1833	717 224	—	50·2
1868	2 225 692	16 000	70·8
1886	4 937 204	—	88·0
1900	6 730 935	280 000	140·2
1918	21 392 322	380 693	889·0
1945	33 240 000	575 274	3401·2
1966	35 964 684	690 400	9144·4
1972	40 036 504	—	17141·0

reports in the papers were not about the local MP but about the leaders in Parliament. So the mass electorate began to look past the member they voted for directly to the men who were governing the country or leading the opposition.

Facing this new situation, the senior politicians found that general elections were becoming too important to leave local contests merely to anyone who happened to be interested in that constituency. So long as this had been the case, some constituencies were contested but others went by default. To remedy this, the Conservatives built up, and the Liberals adopted, organisations which linked the constituencies, and these in time hardened into party machines which in their turn affected the working of the political system. The party organisations were composed of associations of enthusiasts in the constituencies who could be asked to put pressure on the local MP if he was proving troublesome at Westminster. They also retained a degree of independence in their selection of candidates and were thus in a position to affect the kind of members being returned to Parliament. On the other hand, the national gatherings of these local associations could show some life of their own and have, on occasion, tried to influence the government's choice of policies or personnel. While the main source of a politician's power has remained his standing in the parliamentary party, popularity among constituency activists as revealed at the annual conferences or, in the case of the Labour party, in the votes for the National Executive, has assumed some importance.

With a mass electorate who could only be reached through meetings or the press, the party leaders began to campaign not merely in their own constituencies but also by touring the country elaborating their policies. Either by virtue of the criticisms of the existing government or directly because of the proposals put forward, these campaigns set out programmes of action to which the political leaders became committed. At the same time as the transition to a mass electorate, the political philosophy of the electorate changed as new voters were brought into the system and began to put forward demands which had not hitherto been voiced, at least by those who had had votes. The small, largely propertied electorate of the 1850s and 1860s had accepted that the government's task was confined to foreign affairs, defence, internal law and order and raising the very limited amount of money needed to pay for these services. A certain degree of regulation of social and industrial practices was also possible, such as specifying a minimum age for children or maximum hours for women who were working in difficult conditions, and some elementary services could be provided, such as free primary education. But it was not thought proper to extend regulations to cover the hours of work of adult men; they were best left to look after themselves—a view taken by the Trades Union Congress until the late 1880s. Nor was it considered proper or possible for the government to act in any way which influenced the activity of industry or the rates of wages that were paid. When Keir Hardie was elected in 1892 as the first independent Labour member he was deeply offended, not so much by political attacks, as by the assumption on all sides that unemployment and poverty were not issues which should concern Parliament.

But with the growth of a mass electorate, voters gradually came to expect more from the political machine, the politicians soon sensing and responding to these demands. First there was the call for legal protection for trade unions, then for regulation of hours of work in dangerous trades and then a demand for relief for the unemployed, for the indigent in old age and for those who fell sick or were injured at work. These demands began in the 1890s and then flourished after 1906 with the passage of the first spate of interventionist legislation, a further milestone being marked by the bitterly contested Budget introduced by Lloyd George in 1909. This was the first Budget which proposed to use taxation as a means of social policy, taking money from one section of the community to give it to another, thus opening up a whole new vista of governmental activity for the mass electorate to demand and for political leaders to offer.

The First World War saw a great increase in the government's activities, with intervention in industry, food rationing, the conscription of manpower and the expenditure of vast sums of money. In the election at the end of the war, the Labour party emerged as the second largest party in the House of Commons (though it was not recognised as the official opposition till 1922) with a policy of state ownership of the basic industries and of state action to ensure a reasonable standard of life for all sections of the community, policies which were endorsed by the trade union movement. The predominantly Conservative post-war coalition created a Ministry of Health, admitting the principle that the government should help to build houses if those provided by private landlords and builders were inadequate.

There was a fierce debate between the Labour and Conservative parties in the 1920s as to how much the government could or should do to revive the basic industries, alleviate unemployment and provide for those in difficulty, though there was little difference between their actual policies when in office. The major changes came in the 1930s after the world-wide slump of 1929–33, the National Government (Conservative in all but name) turning to aid industry by pushing through reorganisations of the coal, cotton, shipbuilding and steel industries. Britain left the gold standard and abandoned free trade, adopting a system of industrial protection, the government thus becoming steadily more involved in the task of holding the ring for private industry, and in creating suitable conditions for private activity.

The Second World War again led to a major increase in the government's activities but this time with more lasting effects. In 1944 a White Paper, *Employment Policy* (Cmd 6527), for the first time recognised that the government could, by overall management of the economy, ensure full employment and accepted that this was a proper concern for any administration. Earlier, in 1942, Sir William (later Lord) Beveridge had published a Report which received great publicity. Its principle was that the government should create a pattern of welfare payments (in sickness, injury, accident, unemployment, old age and exceptional circumstances) which were supposed to ensure that no one in the community was ever destitute. The Labour Government, elected at the end of the war in 1945, put all these proposals into force and added a National Health Service paid for by a combination of weekly payments and a contribution from the Treasury. Unlike what happened after the First World War, many wartime controls were retained. This was partly in order to concentrate investment in certain fields, partly to meet balance of payments problems, partly to ensure fairness in time of scarcity and partly because these methods had worked well in the war and seemed compatible with the ideology of the Labour party. The Attlee Government went on to take the coal, gas and electricity industries, the railways, the Bank of England, and parts of the road haulage and steel industries into public ownership. Certain enterprises ranging from the London Port Authority to the London Passenger Transport Board and the British Broadcasting Corporation had been started or taken over by the State before the war, but the post-1945 series of Nationalisation Acts was the first large-scale take-over of sectors of private industry. When the Conservatives came to power in 1951, they accelerated the dismantling of controls begun by the Labour Government in its last years and ended rationing, but of the nationalised industries, only steel was returned to private ownership.

By the end of the 1950s or the early 1960s the government was being asked to do even more in providing higher education, in building motorways, protecting the countryside, stopping the congestion of the cities and supporting the regions of Britain which had lower rates of growth, lower wages and higher rates of unemployment and emigration than the rest of the country. The Conservatives had responded to this shift in mood in their last years of office. Then the Labour party, returned to power in 1964 (by a 6-seat majority) and in 1966 (by a majority of 96), went a stage further by preparing an elaborate National Plan. This failed because the Government decided to meet severe balance of payments problems by a policy of deflation. In practice, by the end of the 1960s it was generally accepted that regional imbalance, the prevention of environmental pollution and the preservation of amenities were all tasks for the government.

Thus, in the period under consideration, the demands of a mass electorate, uninhibited by any notions that governmental action was inherently undesirable or inappropriate, all led in the direction of greater government involvement in the life of the community. The number of civil servants in Whitehall, which had stood at 280 000 in 1900 (see p. 23), rose to 575 274 in 1945 and to 827 049 in 1966, while at the same time, the Civil Service's conception of its task altered. In the mid-nineteenth century, officials were simply the clerks for the ministers, ministers who could and sometimes did personally dictate every important dispatch or letter leaving their department. By the end of the century some formidable figures were emerging such as Sir Robert Morant and Alfred (later Lord) Milner, who clearly put up suggestions on matters of policy and gave their departments a distinctive outlook. Lloyd George's social reforms required much more positive administration, though after the First World War there was a swing back to the view that civil servants ought not to be actively forming policy—a view which coincided with a somewhat negative or defensive attitude in all aspects of public life. By the 1940s, because of the Second World War and the consequent social reforms and post-war economic problems, officials had to act in a much more positive capacity and it became accepted that a major task for civil servants from the level of Assistant Secretary upwards was to advise on policy. But the traditionally cautious approach was still common in the early 1960s. Then the Fulton Committee on the Reform of the Civil Service reported in 1968 wanting an even more definite turn towards the concept of civil servants as managers whose skill and inventiveness would have a major effect on the rate of growth of the entire economy.

The point to notice is that while the Westminster Model has never lost its appeal, the actual tasks of administration, the continuation of existing trends (such as the extension of the right to vote) and the development of British society, all quietly affected the system, introducing new elements and finally altering the balance between the major institutions. As regards new elements, the tremendous increase in government intervention in the economy meant that many sectors of private industry formed pressure groups to put their case to the government. At the same time, the growth of a mass electorate and of a fairly rigid party system so reduced the power of the House of Commons, that these pressure groups preferred to deal directly with Whitehall. Under the Westminster Model, all direction on matters of policy was supposed to come from politicians so that civil servants in the 1860s and 1870s thought it improper for them to see pressure group representatives—everything had to go through the House of Commons and the appropriate minister. The executive committee of the Trades Union Congress was originally called the Parliamentary Committee because the point of unions coming together was to press for favourable legislation and this, in turn, meant lobbying Parliament. Likewise the various groups of industrialists dealt primarily with favourable MPs. By the end of the century, this attitude was changing and pressure groups have found it increasingly worth while to deal directly with Whitehall. On the Civil Service side, inhibitions about such contacts have declined and since the 1940s, it has been accepted that departments should always consult with recognised pressure groups, most items of legislation being worked out in this way before they are ever placed before the legislature. (A fascinating example of the hangover of the old proprieties is that it is thought to be 'unconstitutional' to show the draft of a clause in a Bill to the spokesman for a pressure group. They can be told the content of the clause and can bargain as to whether it is acceptable or not, but they are not allowed to see the final wording because of the old conventions of the Westminster Model which require that Parliament must be the first to see the actual words of the government's legislative proposals.)

But the cardinal virtue of British government in its classic period had been the delicate balance between authority and popular control, between the Cabinet and the House of Commons. And it was here that the responses to new political demands and to new administrative tasks produced the most important and perhaps least appreciated changes; least appreciated because the words used and the outward forms remained the same. Yet the trends and their effects can be clearly discerned. While governments in the 1850s and 1860s could rely on something approaching a consensus of backbench support and only faced defeat if they seriously antagonised distinct bodies of MPs, by the 1890s the opposition was indulging in systematic attacks and governments had to rely much more exclusively on their own backbenchers. The number of party divisions in the House (defined as cases where nine-tenths of each major party voted together) rose from around 30 per cent in the early 1860s to 60 per cent in the early 1870s to over 90 per cent in the 1890s. Because of this 'state of bloodless civil war', as Lord Salisbury put it, governments were able to rely on their supporters and used this to assume full control of the House of Commons. This was achieved by stages between 1882 and 1902 when Mr Balfour carried his procedural reforms or 'parliamentary railway timetable', so called because it was possible under his revised Standing Orders to know just what station along the road to enactment any item of legislation would have reached by a given date.

These changes all increased the power of the executive so that by the turn of the century, the government could rely on voting down any undesirable motions in the House. This enabled the government to cut down the flow of information to MPs, stopping, for instance, the nineteenth-century practice of regularly publishing sets of documents (Blue Books) explaining or revealing the recent conduct of foreign policy. Detailed scrutiny of the financial estimates ceased. Question Time was developed in these years as a substitute for the right to raise debates, whenever a member so desired, on motions to go into committee and on other procedural opportunities. Forty years later, after the Second World War, Question Time began to lose its value as so many members wanted to ask questions in the same limited period of time that the Speaker decided to limit each member to one supplementary question and the whole process was so speeded up that any reasonably competent minister has little difficulty in withholding information. Also, Question Time became less of an occasion for backbenchers to press ministers on specific, often constituency, matters. Instead, the frontbench opposition spokesmen took a larger part and questions became increasingly part of the party political mêlée between the two sides of the House.

The complexity of legislation and the practice of prior consultation with pressure groups, already referred to, had the same effect as did the very large extension in the Prime Minister's patronage in the form of ministerial appointments. Governments in the 1880s had some 35 ministers in the House of Commons. By 1918 the figure had risen to 60; in 1945 it reached 71, while Mr Wilson in 1970 had 89 jobs to distribute among his backbench supporters. At the same time, the outlook of members had altered in that many came into politics in order to have some influence on public life and could see no way of achieving their objective unless they held office. Being an MP does not in itself confer sufficient opportunities or satisfaction on the more ambitious and capable members. Also few MPs have the wealth or social prestige of their nineteenth-century predecessors so that they have fewer satisfying alternatives to the quest for political advancement and ministerial office.

Thus though so many outward features of the Cabinet and of the House of Commons remain the same, the balance between them, which was such a central and admired feature of the Westminster Model, has been steadily altered in a way which was not intentional but which was the product of the trends that have been described. Whatever is thought of the virtues and failings of British government today, it cannot be denied that relations between the executive and the legislature are quite different from the relations existing a hundred years ago. The capacity of the Commons to remove one government and install another, to amend major legislation, to pick off individual ministers who have failed and to push the government into changes of policy, has largely disappeared. While this may or may not be a desirable development, the mistake is to go on talking as if these powers existed or, and this is a more sophisticated modern twist, to admit the present situation but then to assert that the use of these powers in the last third of the nineteenth century has been greatly exaggerated or misunderstood; in short, that there has been little change.

The reader may wonder why it is necessary to spend so much time explaining that the Westminster Model, the idealised version of British government in the 1880s–1914 period, has changed in the last sixty years. This is partly because, as has been explained, its language is still used and misleads current observers and its maxims are still quoted either to cover up or to try to accommodate current practice. But there is a further point. The pace of development of the two sides of government, one being the executive or the administration, and the other the system of supervision or control, seems to alternate. Up till the late eighteenth century, there had been almost no administrative reform, no innovation or renovation in government. The process began in the 1780s under the Younger Pitt at a time when all reform of Parliament or local government was anathema. It was resumed in the 1820s and 1830s, under the influence of Bentham, the radical reformers and the free traders, many of the old cobwebs being swept aside. Administration was grouped in a few departments all under ministerial control, urban local government was reformed, the legal system was tidied up and financial organisation was focused on annual accounting of all that flowed into and out of one Consolidated Fund.

Political reform was begun in 1832 and accelerated after 1867, the distinctive feature of the late nineteenth century being that, apart from the reorganisation of the Civil Service and its recruitment by open competition (1870), there were no further extensive changes in the practical operation of government. The new departures were not administrative or organisational but political. What was carefully elaborated was the system of popular control based on the moral doctrines of equality of respect for the individual and of the individual's right to make his own judgment of political issues. As Gladstone put it in 1864 when he 'set the Thames on fire', 'I venture to say that every man who is not presumably incapacitated by some consideration of personal unfitness or of political danger, is morally entitled to come within the pale of the Constitution'. This doctrine underlay the extension of the right to vote in 1867 and 1884. the introduction of the secret ballot in 1872, the Corrupt Practices Act of 1883, much of the intense battle over Irish Home Rule and the final adjustment of relations between the House of Commons and the House of Lords in the Parliament Act of 1911.

Since the turn of the century, however, the pendulum has swung the other way and the vast administrative developments noted at the opening of this chapter have altered the whole shape of British government, but there has been no new political theory and almost no new machinery of scrutiny or control to match the increased scope and power of the executive. Ostensibly Britain still adheres to the democratic doctrines enunciated by the late-nineteenth-century liberals, but with flagging conviction. There are strong undercurrents which, though not often brought to the surface in public discussion, run strongly in favour of keeping decisions in the hands of limited groups of experts, men chosen for their knowledge, training or existing authority.

The curious result was that by the 1960s, when it began to be recognised that the political control system was out of date and when some of the forms of government built into the Westminster Model began to prove administratively inadequate, there was no strong ideology to provide guide lines for the necessary reforms. For instance, local government of the old county and borough pattern had become quite incapable of carrying on the tasks assigned to it by the central government and demanded by the voters, so the structure had, by common consent, to be changed. But there was no agreement as to whether a reformed system should involve more devolution or more central control, whether it should be based on the doctrine of genuine local democracy or whether the role of elected members should be largely advisory. Similarly the Treasury found the House of Commons' system of annual provision of part of the money needed for government (which the Treasury had abandoned in 1962 in favour of a five-year rolling programme covering the whole of public expenditure) a nuisance and sometimes so misleading to foreign financial circles as to be positively damaging. But this dissatisfaction did not mean that there was any agreement about the nature of a reformed system; that is whether it should lead to a restoration of the House of Commons' former power to scrutinise public expenditure effectively or whether this should remain a formality. Again the public sensed that the role of backbench MPs had altered to such an extent that reforms of parliamentary procedure were necessary and ministers found some of the older aspects of procedure tedious; but there was no doctrine which gave a ready answer to the fundamental question of what backbench MPs were supposed to do, how much influence they should have or

whether the object was to make it easier or harder for the executive
to manage the House of Commons.

In all these cases, the governments (Mr Wilson's Labour Government, for most of this period) either handed the task over to a Royal
Commission or began piecemeal pragmatic changes in the hope
that such difficult and unanswered questions would resolve themselves. Needless to say this did not happen and while most of the
value judgments still repeated the old slogans of democratic control,
the actual effect of the reforms proposed usually left these issues
open. A good example is the effort to reform local government which
was examined by the Mallaby Committee (restricted to staffing) and
the Maud Committee (restricted to management), the Redcliffe-
Maud Commission (restricted to existing functions of English local
government), the Wheatley Commission (same for Scotland), the
Seebohm Committee on Local Authority and Allied Personal
Services and in two White Papers on Welsh local government and in
Green Papers on the Administrative Reorganisation of the Scottish
and of the English and Welsh Health Services. The problem of what
was most suitably settled in Whitehall and which decisions were
better devolved to other authorities was belatedly put to a separate
Royal Commission under Lord Crowther (later, when he died, under
Lord Kilbrandon) which reported in late 1973. But in the meantime,
the Labour Government published a White Paper (Cmnd 4276) in
early 1970 accepting those aspects of the Redcliffe–Maud Report
which made for a more efficient pattern of local authorities and
which permitted easier and more effective control by the central
government. When the Conservatives came to office, they passed a
Local Government Reform Bill in 1972 which reverted to a two-tier
pattern of authorities but was entirely similar to the Labour party's
proposals in that it did nothing to clarify the functions of or to
extend the freedom of action of local authorities.

Similarly the Select Committee on Procedure of the House of
Commons poured out reports and proposals from 1966 to 1970,
those favouring an increase of backbench control, particularly the
establishment of specialist or investigatory committees of backbenchers running into trouble, while virtually all the proposals
enabling the government to push its business more readily through
the House were adopted. The Fulton Commission investigated the
central Civil Service but was restricted to its 'structure, recruitment
and management', so that its Report (published in 1968) was not
able to deal with the key question of how far and in what way
Parliament should supervise the machinery of government and of

how far ministers themselves can and should control their departments.

So while governmental systems can always be said to be 'in
transition' in that change never stops, British government is in a
peculiar state of transition and indecision. The administrative requirements of a government which spends a half of the total gross
national product and the demands of an electorate which expects
the government to provide a rising standard of living, reasonable
social welfare and the preservation of the overall level of amenities,
are both being met. In doing so, there has had to be a process of
administrative adaptation and development. But while this has been
proceeding, there has been confusion, inaction and a drift away from
the old principles of democratic scrutiny and supervision whenever
that aspect of institutional renewal has come up for decision.

In the next chapter, there is an attempt to give a brief overall
picture of the working of the current system of government (in 1973)
which is then explained and elaborated in the following chapters,
the last chapter returning to this question of the attitudes to changes
in the institutions of democratic control and to the likely directions
these changes might take in the next decade.

4

BRITISH GOVERNMENT TODAY

In analysing a system of government, the student of politics is seeking
to find out who wields power, how the machinery for the exercise of
power operates, what are the constraints on those with power and
why society is prepared to accept these arrangements. Some, particularly those who exercise considerable power, have tended to cast
doubt on the idea that power can be located in this way and it is true
that in no political system is there that crock of gold at the end of
the politicians' rainbow, untrammelled power. This is the correct
comment on the anecdote told by the late Aneurin Bevan in the
House of Commons. Explaining his quest for the source of authority
in this country, he recounted how his father had said to him, 'You
see that man walking along the other side of the street, Aneurin.
That's Mr Davies. You should observe him. He's a member of the
Urban District Council and he has power.' So Bevan, in due course,
got himself elected to the Urban District Council and some months
later complained to the Clerk that he had not found any power.
'Ah,' said the Clerk, 'things have changed. Since those days the
power has gone to the County Council.' On the County Council,
Bevan was told that 'because of the new local government legislation . . . the power is now with the government and Parliament'.
But when he became a backbench opposition MP, he found he
was still powerless. 'It is all monopolised by the Treasury Bench
over there,' Bevan declared, pointing to the Prime Minister and the
other senior ministers.

In fact, Bevan was wrong in several senses. On the one hand,
neither the Prime Minister nor the Cabinet have complete power.
On the other, in each of the posts Bevan had occupied, he had
exercised more power than the average citizen, though Bevan can be

excused some frustration as he was at that time occupying one of the least influential positions in British government, that of the rank and file elected Member of Parliament. In practice there are several senses in which power can be located in certain persons or institutions. President Harry Truman had a sign on his desk in the White House, 'The buck stops here', and bucks of different sizes stop at different levels throughout the governmental machine in the sense that at this point a decision has to be taken. But to find out where a governmental decision is taken or what influences have been brought to bear only partly solves the question 'who has power?' and 'how much does he have?' There are two rather different issues involved. The first deals with what happens if different individuals in the executive of institutions want different decisions and concludes that the man or body who triumphs, who wins the vote or gets his ideas or candidate accepted, has most power. The second approach concentrates not on the decision to take a certain line but on whether the objective of the policy is achieved. It is important to distinguish between these two sides of the question 'who has power?' as concentration on one rather than the other produces very different answers.

For example, an author who dwells chiefly on the second aspect, on the outcome of policies, is Mr Ian Gilmour in *The Body Politic*. In his chapter on the Prime Minister, he notes that successive governments failed to reform the economy in the 1920s, to strengthen defence policy in the 1930s; refused 'to join the discussions on the European Coal and Steel Community' and 'to join Europe in the 1950s'; failed 'to bring local government into the twentieth century' and 'to reform the Trade Unions'. He concludes that 'these incidents or evasions do not suggest the presence of great power'. But these failures were either due to lack of solutions, to lack of political will or to positive decisions not to act. They are not guides to the balance of power between the Premier and his colleagues or between the Cabinet and Parliament. In terms of estimating which persons or institutions are most powerful within the government, the issue is who decides what the government *tries* to do, irrespective of whether satisfactory or sensible results are achieved.

But this does not mean that there is no connection between the two. To set certain goals and then frequently fail to achieve them does weaken the total position of even the most powerful elements in the political system. It may also cast doubt on the effectiveness of the system itself.

Nevertheless, the first objective for a student of politics is to try and discover where power lies within the system. The task is to set out the principles, methods and machinery according to which a society arranges that some of its members lead, organise and, if necessary, coerce others. The problem in such a study is that there is an endless amount of information which could be deployed. Much of it, however, can be omitted as there are countless almost identical traffic offences, many very similar minor items of legislation and building one school is much like building another. An account that tries to decide which institutions or persons really matter has to look at the rather special cases where there is conflict, where one body has overridden another or, where there is no conflict, has to try and determine where the final decisions are actually made. Moreover, most of the important cases have special features and it is hard to be sure what cases are normal or typical. Facing this difficulty, the only solution is to describe numbers of occasions when the same type of case has occurred so that even though each one is different, some general picture will emerge of how the system operates.

Considered in this way, contemporary British government is highly complex with many power centres, many institutions which cannot be coerced and persons who cannot be removed or pressurised; but the main flow of power is between the leadership and the people. At intervals, at least once every five years, the public choose their leadership, the choice being narrowed down to one man and a number of lieutenants by the two-party system. Directly the choice is made, power within the system concentrates on the Prime Minister, though he may share part of it with one or two senior colleagues and with his Cabinet, this team then dominating British government till the next election. During these years, the chief limitation on the leadership's power is a combination of the House of Commons, the parties, the Civil Service and the pressure groups with the actual problems to be faced and the reactions of the electorate. In the last resort, what matters to the Prime Minister and the Cabinet is their standing with the public as revealed in the opinion polls, in by-election results and in their general sense of success and popularity or of failure and public disparagement. But in the short run what matters may be, for example, getting an anti-inflation policy to work and obtaining the cooperation of the unions and of management.

The purely political institutions through which the leadership operates have an influence on what is done, but relatively little actual power to stop the Prime Minister and his team once they have made up their minds to act. The chief obstacles, when such decisions have been made, do not lie in Parliament, where the government has an almost watertight grip on the Commons and on a subservient and timid House of Lords, or in the Civil Service which can be ordered and regrouped. The chief obstacles are usually external institutions over which the government has little direct control though such resistance may lead to a more active opposition in the Commons. For instance, Mr Wilson and his Cabinet were able to force a Prices and Incomes Policy through the House of Commons against the bitter opposition of a large section of the Labour majority and in the teeth of resolutions adopted by the Labour Party's Annual Conference but they were not able to carry the Trades Union Congress and the policy was ultimately abandoned, the whole episode having weakened Labour's hold over its traditional supporters. Similarly Mr Macmillan was able to commit his party to an application to join the Common Market in 1961 despite considerable internal opposition. The ultimate failure when the French veto was applied did not materially alter Mr Macmillan's power as against his colleagues in the Cabinet, his party or the House of Commons. Nor were the voters disappointed, but the effect was to leave the government policyless and dispirited. In 1972, Mr Heath's policy of controlling wages by defeating union claims as they arose was not lost in Parliament (where its legislative counterpart was the Industrial Relations Bill) but was defeated when the Government had to capitulate to a series of strikes, the chief one being by the miners. Then, when the Government turned to a statutory limitation of wages, the real trial was in the field and success became evident when the Ford workers, the miners and the dockers accepted wage settlements within the prescribed limits.

Within the political machine, the Prime Minister dominates. He chooses his colleagues and while he is sometimes limited by the need to take in or to retain certain popular or impressive figures, his own position is almost totally secure and the position of his lieutenants is open to change. They can, with only a few exceptions, be demoted or dismissed. Prime Ministers occupy a lonely pinnacle and if the government's fortunes are low, there will be criticisms of their leadership from within the ranks of their party in Parliament. There were serious criticisms of Mr Macmillan in 1963 and attempts to remove Mr Wilson in 1969 but though these attempts came at times of maximum weakness for these two Prime Ministers, in neither case was there any serious chance of success. The Prime Minister is the embodiment of the government in the eyes of the public, appearing in far more news stories than either the Leader of the Opposition or any other member of the Cabinet. He can, to a large extent, manage his own public relations by careful release of news at the appropriate moments. Given success, British Prime Ministers receive great acclaim, though equally they are subject to severe personal attacks if the tide sets against them. The Prime Minister has the Cabinet Secretariat to brief him and to coordinate the work of the various departments and an order from No. 10 Downing Street outranks any other instruction. The Civil Service Department controlling the staffing of Whitehall works directly to the Prime Minister. Moreover, if the Prime Minister wants to curb a department such as the Treasury, he can set up a second economics ministry or reallocate powers in a way which alters the balance between the various ministries.

While the Leader of the Opposition derives certain powers from the fact that he may one day be Prime Minister, his position out of office is far weaker because he lacks patronage, he lacks the backing of the Whitehall machine and his service to his party is incomplete so long as he has failed to carry it through to victory and office. In this situation, the Leader has less freedom to choose his front-benchers (in the Labour party, they are imposed on him by an annual election in the parliamentary party). Attempts to remove the Leader of the Opposition have sometimes been successful, Sir Alec Douglas-Home resigning in 1965, while the attacks on Mr Gaitskell in 1960–1, though unsuccessful, were more dangerous than anything Mr Wilson had to face as Prime Minister.

In the present system, the work of government is performed by the senior Civil Service in constant cooperation and consultation with the mass of local government councils, public and privately owned industries and other pressure groups. This complex of organisations cannot be easily separated into public and private sectors and the government's area of influence extends far beyond the bodies which it actually controls by law. But, at the same time, this means that the area of manoeuvre open to any government is limited. It inherits a large number of on-going policies and commitments and a public with certain expectations. Thus public expenditure is planned for five years ahead and departmental sub-heads are fixed for three years ahead. A new government can alter the atmosphere, the context and, to some extent, the priorities but it has no clean slate on which to write. Within these limitations, there has been some controversy about how far the established long-term views of the departments are imposed on ministers, but the minister is not left on his own and defenceless. He can be reinforced by the Prime

Minister and the Cabinet. Departmental views and capacity for action may be a limiting factor, but the limits can also come from the politicians. For example, Mr Wilson prevented any serious discussion of devaluation from 1964 to November 1967 although the Treasury was perfectly willing to examine this option and Mr Heath ruled out an incomes policy for the first two years of his ministry.

The government also operates through Parliament, the chief function of the House of Commons being to support the government of the day, to defend its policies and carry its legislation. Thus the House of Commons is the place where the government explains its policies and intentions and the opposition makes its counter case. Politicians often prefer to make their announcements direct over television to the electorate but, because the enactment of laws requires three readings in the House and MPs can be touchy if they are ignored, it is usually used for this purpose.

In the hey-day of the Victorian era, Parliament had a certain corporate feeling as against the executive. Backbenchers controlled part of the timetable which enabled them to extract information from the government and to force issues on to the floor of the House. Also, political leaders accepted that government was by discussion in the parliamentary forum with public attention focusing on the House of Commons. Now that the government controls the entire timetable of the House, information can be denied and many ministers prefer not to proceed by means of public discussion but to act first and then explain and defend their policies later. This has reached the pitch that policies can be operated and charges levied from the announcement of the government's intention to act rather than from the time when the legislation is passed.

Similarly the role of the parties outside Parliament has altered. These bodies, especially the Liberal and Labour parties, do have some identity, some life of their own, particularly when the parties are in opposition and there is some interaction between the ideas of the leadership and the views of the local activists. However, there has been an increasing tendency, more noticeable when a party is in government, for leading politicians to regard the parties as electoral machines and the annual conferences as public relations exercises where the activists are manipulated and the wider electorate impressed by what they see on television.

Thus these intermediary agencies, the Civil Service, Parliament and the parties do execute the policies and have an effect on the method of work and mode of performance of the political leaders, but the primary relationship is between the leaders and the led, between the

Prime Minister with his colleagues and the electorate. If ministers pay attention to pressure groups or to backbench revolts, it is because they suspect that this is evidence of real reactions among voters. The electorate in Britain is fairly steady in its voting habits but new voters come on to the list, former voters die and there is the phenomenon of different rates of abstention on each side. These factors, together with the small percentage of actual switches from one side to another can lead to one party replacing another in power. The electoral system magnifies the effect of such swings and usually produces definite and clear-cut electoral results.

The mass electorate has a short memory, is little interested in foreign affairs and appears to vote more on its overall impression of its own degree of comfort under the government in question. Thus the emphasis in political campaigning has swung from argument over issues to the creation of images, to the capacity of political leaders to gauge and anticipate the mood of the electorate and to deliver the goods in terms of the general standard of living.

Winning and holding power under these circumstances becomes involved with two related problems. The first is that politicians are encouraged to raise unrealistic expectations by which they are later judged. Thus some may advocate increased public expenditure and suggest that it will be painlessly paid for out of 'a higher growth rate' while others argue that taxation can be cut without any diminution in the other benefits enjoyed by the public simply 'by concentrating social aid on those who most need it'. Then there is the second difficulty that the politicians are not in sole control of the process by which the public's expectations are formed. The content of current western industrial civilisation as put across by the press and by commercial television suggests that the greatest good in life is increased material standards, increased consumption, increased relaxation, so that criteria are set by which the performance of the Prime Minister and the government of the day are judged. When there is a period of endemic economic difficulties such as over the balance of payments in the 1960s and over inflation in the early 1970s, there is an atmosphere of failure about both sets of political leaders and the electorate turns in increasing exasperation from one party to the other, with occasional bursts of support for third parties.

The prevailing tone of the current political system is very different from that of the Westminster Model. Then Parliament was a genuine intermediary between the people and the political leaders. While Gladstone and Disraeli, Joseph Chamberlain and Randolph Churchill, did appeal directly to the voters and conducted major election campaigns, they had to carry the House of Commons. Moreover the House could and did until the 1880s enforce certain changes (and the belief that this was possible hung on for a generation). Because the political leaders had learned their business in the era of small electorates and in a House with some independence and authority, they saw their task and their relations with the electors in a different light. The Victorian theory of political leadership, given that there was a popular element in the Constitution, was that the party spokesmen put forward their own views about the needs of the country. It was improper to search for issues, to put up proposals simply to excite support. The object of political leadership was to take up such problems as forced themselves on the country's attention or needed to be considered (such as Irish grievances or near-eastern foreign policy) even if no one really wanted to think about them. It was also assumed that the electorate had their own independently formulated opinions and that they sat in judgment on their political leaders, in part being educated or convinced by the debates in the Commons and in part giving the leadership their reactions as independent, fair-minded voters.

Nowadays the prevailing tone places less emphasis on discussion and on the judgment of the leadership and of the led. Politicians tend to allege that it is the last year or two before an election that matters and that it is not arguments but subjective impressions that count. They seek to take up issues which will appeal to the public, ignoring those which are damaging to them, so that while their propaganda has a relationship to the real problems of the country, they do not dwell on issues whose solution may be painful or where no agreed or clear solution is evident.

While this approach has been successful when Prime Ministers have been able to meet the expectations of the voters—and no Premiers have received more general acclaim than Macmillan ('Supermac', 'Wondermac') in 1957–60 or Wilson after his 1966 victory—it has also led to great troughs of discontent when governments have not been able to deliver the hoped-for goods. Perhaps because the electorate has been led to expect so much more from government, from the political system at a time when Britain has been adjusting to a new role as a second-level, mainly European power and has been adjusting her economy to a more competitive and exposed position in world trade, there has been considerable alienation and apathy. Because government by argument and open decision has been less practised, because politics has been seen as a problem of management rather than of facing the facts, there have been outbursts of resentment, a tendency by some to turn to protests and to demonstrations in order to obtain results and by others to feel a contempt for politics and a sense of alienation from the whole system.

The next seven chapters consider this present pattern of British government and politics in detail and in the last chapter there is an examination of what views the parties take of possible changes in the pattern of government and of what is likely to be the outcome.

5

POLITICAL LEADERSHIP—
PRODUCING A PRIME MINISTER

1. The process of selection within the parties

In Britain, as in most Western industrialised countries, there is a
slightly ambivalent attitude to political leadership. The Prime
Minister is the representative of the country on all critical international occasions and provides a leadership which, besides being of
one political character, has a broader national aspect. Usually the
Prime Minister runs ahead of his party in the opinion polls in that a
larger percentage of people approve of his conduct than say they
would vote for his party at an immediate election. There is a sense in
which the public, though sceptical and difficult to please, want the
Prime Minister to be a man they can admire, a man who will rise
above the small change of political conflict, who will conspicuously
avoid the failings usually attributed to politicians.

This attitude undoubtedly influences the parties in their choice
of a leader but so do other factors. The procedure for selecting a
leader in the Labour and Conservative parties is now carefully set
down. The Labour party in its early years arranged for the annual
election of a chairman, later called the leader of the party, though
it was rapidly assumed that once he was chosen, there would be
automatic re-election unless some section of the party wished to
make a serious challenge. Once the leader became Prime Minister,
even the formality of annual re-election was dropped. Those entitled
to vote are the members of the Parliamentary Labour Party, that is
all Labour MPs at the time of the election. If, after the first ballot,
no candidate has an overall majority, the one with the lowest
number of votes is eliminated and a further ballot held till one
candidate has an absolute majority. In opposition, a week elapses
between ballots but if the party is in office, the necessary number of
votes all take place on the same day.

In the Conservative party, if the leadership became vacant during a period when the party was in opposition it was laid down (since 1937) that the new leader should be chosen by a body consisting of all Conservative MPs and Conservative peers, all prospective Conservative candidates and the Executive Committee of the National Union of Conservative Associations.

When the Conservative party was in office and the leader died or resigned, it was left to the monarch to select a successor. But the monarch clearly had a duty to choose the person with the greatest body of support among Conservative MPs and the Crown's staff arranged for consultations so that this information could be provided. Trouble arose in 1923 over the selection of Baldwin when it was alleged that certain views, particularly those of the dying Bonar Law, the retiring Prime Minister, were misrepresented to the King. In 1957, the Queen was advised to choose Mr Macmillan after a straw poll of the members of the Cabinet had gone to sixteen to one in his favour but there was grumbling that other sections of the party were not adequately represented. This grumbling was much more serious in late 1963 when Mr Macmillan was succeeded by Sir Alec Douglas-Home. In this case there was careful sounding carried out by Lord Dilhorne, the Lord Chancellor, in the Cabinet, by the Chief Whip among MPs, by the Chief Whip in the Lords and by one of the Chairmen of the Party Organisation among constituency activists. The outcome was a recommendation in favour of Sir Alec Douglas-Home but there were considerable misgivings because it was evident that no candidate had had a clear majority and so a process of weighting was adopted. Mr Iain Macleod, one of the minor contenders for the leadership, held that 'the result of the methods used was contradiction and misrepresentation' and he refused to join Sir Alec Douglas-Home's Government.

As a result of this controversy, a new method was adopted in 1965 for use whether the Party is in or out of office whereby a ballot is held of all Conservative MPs. To be elected, a candidate must have an overall majority and 15 per cent more votes than his nearest rival. If this is not achieved, a second ballot is held two to four days later for the same or new candidates and an overall majority is sufficient. If no candidate secures such a majority, a third ballot takes place among the top three, with the MPs indicating their first and second preferences which are redistributed to produce one person with an overall majority.

Curiously enough, Sir Alec Douglas-Home did not submit himself to this process when it was adopted in February 1965, so that it was first applied when he chose to resign (or was ousted—see below p. 95) in July of that year. Mr Heath obtained 150 votes to Mr Maudling's 133 and Mr Powell's 15 so that a second ballot was required, but before this could be held Mr Maudling and Mr Powell retired from the contest, leaving Mr Heath in possession.

Thus in both major parties, it is the MPs who choose the leader. This is, in fact, the moment of maximum power for backbenchers. It is the one time when their votes are equal, when they carry as much weight as those of any frontbencher, though this moment of power occurs on average only every nine years in the Conservative party (calculated since 1884) and every ten years in the Labour party (calculated since 1922). MPs' motives in such an election are mixed, depending in part on the standing of the candidates inside the party in parliament, in part on the preferences of activists outside the House and in part on the MPs' estimation of the candidates' capacity to win a general election for the party. The weighting given to these various qualities varies with the particular circumstances and with the recent experience of the party.

For instance, in the Labour party, the choice of Ramsay Mac-Donald in 1922 was due to some extent to the relatively colourless leadership of J. R. Clynes in the previous Parliament, MacDonald having a great platform presence, a wide reputation and considerable parliamentary skill. But it was also because the new members just elected were left of centre and MacDonald had a left-wing reputation as a result of his lack of support for government policy during the First World War. In the selection of George Lansbury in 1931, the Parliamentary Labour Party, reduced by the landslide of that year to 51 MPs, had little choice, but members turned to Mr (later Earl) Attlee in 1935 and retained him after the general election because of his reliable performances in Parliament. When Mr Attlee resigned in December 1955, there were three candidates, Mr Gaitskell, Mr Bevan and Mr Morrison. The Labour party had been torn by factional strife since Mr Bevan had resigned from the Labour Government in 1951 and the choice in 1955 turned in part on these divisions. But there was, in addition to the question of what side MPs took in these internal feuds, the question of how the electorate would react. Mr Morrison was considered by many to be too old at 68 and few Labour MPs outside the committed left imagined that Mr Bevan could ever win sufficient general support to carry the party through to a majority. For this reason, Mr Gaitskell was able to add to his anti-Bevanite and trade union support (arranged by Arthur Deakin, General Secretary of the Transport and General Workers' Union)

the middle of the road backing which ensured his election. When Mr
Gaitskell died in 1963, there were again three candidates, Mr Brown,
Mr Callaghan and Mr Wilson. This time Mr Wilson was the left-wing
candidate but he had none of Mr Bevan's extremism nor had he
alienated middle-class support and his relations with the press were
excellent. On the other hand, Mr Brown had some of the voter-
frightening qualities of Mr Bevan in his pungency of personality
and tendency to spark off a scene while Mr Callaghan was less well
known and seemed less capable of making an impact on the public.
So Mr Wilson was able to add sufficient votes to his left-wing base,
from those in the centre and from those with an eye on the next
election, to obtain a majority on the second ballot.

Among the Conservatives, Baldwin succeeded Bonar Law because
some of his ablest rivals were disqualified by their adherence to the
Lloyd George coalition and because of the general reaction against
'the Welsh Wizard'. Thus members of the party agreed with Baldwin
that Lloyd George represented the kind of 'dynamic force' which
would destroy the Conservative party and they also felt that the
country wanted a rest after the turmoil of the war and the immediate post-war years. This same sentiment told against activists such
as Mr (later Sir) Winston Churchill and helped Baldwin bequeath
his leadership to Neville Chamberlain, who combined caution with
ability and a cutting anti-Labour edge rare among Conservative
leaders. It was a reaction to the latter's policy and personality as well
as the memory of Churchill's warnings about Nazi Germany and
obvious qualities in a time of military emergency that led the Conservatives to accept Churchill in 1940. However this was a special
case because the decisive push came from the Labour party whose
leaders said they would not serve in a coalition under Chamberlain
and Churchill became leader of the Conservative party only after
he had been appointed as Prime Minister.

In 1955, when Churchill retired, Sir Anthony Eden had been the
heir apparent for over ten years and had a distinguished record as
Foreign Secretary and as an orthodox Conservative leader with wide
public appeal. His premiership collapsed in early 1957 amid the
ruins of his own health and the aftermath of the abortive invasion
of Suez. The press and the public alike were surprised when the
Conservatives turned to Mr Macmillan rather than to Mr Butler
who had been senior in the party hierarchy, was better known and
seemed to have a wider appeal outside the party. But the Conservatives were in a serious state after the Suez débâcle and Mr Butler's
somewhat detached attitude to the invasion had earned him the

bitter resentment of a strong body of Conservative MPs. At the same time, he had served on the Cabinet Committee that had organised the episode so that those opposed to the invasion as well as those who had wanted it to be carried through to a successful conclusion were equally antagonised. On the other hand, Mr Macmillan was the archetype of a Conservative, a man who combined aristocratic connections, business acumen, a military manner and well concealed ability. The most difficult of all the choices occurred when Mr Macmillan decided to resign, fearing that a bout of ill-heath was more serious than it ultimately turned out to be. In this case, the party knew it would have to face the electorate within a year and all the possible candidates were open to objection. Mr Butler suffered from the same reservations as had beset his candidature in 1957, though the lack of internal divisions (other than on the leadership) and the imminence of an election strengthened his case. An alternative, who was strongly fancied at one time by Mr Macmillan himself, Mr Quintin Hogg, seemed a little too flamboyant, a little too much a figure of fun outside Westminster, where he was highly respected. On the other hand, the three other possibilities, Mr Macleod, Mr Heath and Mr Maudling, all carried less weight and had less experience. In this situation of extreme difficulty, the Conservatives preferred to fall back on a compromise candidate whose chief characteristic in the public eye was his embodiment of the traditional Tory outlook and virtues, Sir Alec Douglas-Home. When the party under Sir Alec just failed to win the 1964 election, its members were deeply upset (as the Conservatives always are) by the loss of power and slightly mesmerised by the capacity and popular appeal of Mr Wilson. As a result there were sufficient murmurings to induce Sir Alec to resign and in choosing a successor, Conservative MPs were clearly thinking of the coming election and the need to counteract the modernising technocratic appeal of Mr Wilson. To do this, they had an effective choice of Mr Heath or Mr Maudling (Mr Macleod had excluded himself by his refusal to serve under Sir Alec in 1963). Mr Heath just won, probably because he had handled both the Common Market negotiations of 1961–3 and the opposition in 1965 to the Labour party's Finance Bill with great precision and efficiency while Mr Maudling conveyed a much more easy-going and relaxed style and this seemed possibly a little less effective as an antidote to Mr Wilson.

Thus the nomination of a party leader as Prime Minister or, if the party is out of office, as a potential Prime Minister mainly depends on two factors: the man's position inside the party and his capacity to add to the party's electoral appeal. When a party is in acute internal difficulties as the Conservatives were in 1957 and 1963 or as Labour was in 1931, there is a tendency to place more emphasis on the capacity to comfort the party faithful, to epitomise the values or outlook of the party. When such matters are less important and electoral victory is a primary consideration, MPs think more of the external image that will appeal, a factor which aided both Mr Wilson in 1963 and Mr Heath in 1965. The difficulty is that there is sometimes a conflict between these two considerations. Some of the party stalwarts might prefer an emphasis right of centre in the case of Conservatives and left of centre in the case of Labour when the task of appealing to the public may require someone who either occupies more of the ground between the parties or who, in some sense, seems to rise above the purely party level in his appeal.

For instance, MacDonald, Lansbury and Wilson were all chosen in part because they were or were thought to be left-of-centre in the Labour party while Baldwin, Macmillan and Douglas-Home were all aided by the fact that they were Conservatives' Conservatives. In certain cases where there was an obvious heir apparent or worthy incumbent—Attlee, Chamberlain, Eden—these considerations made no difference, but the ideal situation for a leader or potential leader was when he could combine both appeals, when he could appear in one light to the MPs in his party and in another to the country. Mr Baldwin managed this to some extent but the two clearest examples were Mr Macmillan and Mr Wilson, the former delighting the old guard Tories who inhabit the House of Commons Smoking Room though in fact he was rather radical and forward-looking. Mr Wilson had a secure base in the left of the Labour party though combining this with an outwardly comforting, highly capable but still cautious, home-spun image.

The most unfortunate position for any leader was endured by Mr Heath who was chosen despite the fact that he was by no means a typical Tory because he was thought to be the best electoral counter to Mr Wilson and turned out, at least at first, to be incapable of striking a responsive chord among the public. One other rather curious exception was Mr Gaitskell who, at the time of his selection, neither epitomised socialist or trade union ideals in the Labour party nor had great electoral appeal, but his choice has to be seen in the light of the alternatives available at that time and the internal struggles in the Labour party. In fact, he was provided with a base by the solid support of the right-wing trade union leaders, who then exercised considerable power in the party. He received the necessary extra support by the difficulty of regarding Mr Bevan, for all his moral fervour, and the elderly Mr Morrison, for all his tactical skills, as effective potential Prime Ministers.

2. The role of the Crown

When considering why certain persons are nominated by the parties as their leaders, it is as well to dispose of any doubts about the role of the Crown in this process. Because the Labour party were clearly obliged to meet and elect a leader in the event of any vacancy, no question of royal influence could arise. But during the period when the Conservative party in office preferred an informal system of soundings, the result of which was conveyed to the Crown, it was inevitable that those who disliked the outcome would, at times, suggest that the monarch's own views had played a part. This point was made, for instance, when George V sent for Mr Baldwin rather than Lord Curzon in 1923, though more emphasis was placed on possible misrepresentations of advice by those around the King. George V, himself, may have thought that to have a Prime Minister in the House of Lords would create difficulties, but in fact the advice reaching the King was quite decisively in favour of Baldwin. In rather different circumstances, George V was criticised (by Herbert Morrison and later by Professor Moodie in *Political Studies*, February 1957) for asking Ramsay MacDonald to lead a National Government after he had tendered his resignation as Prime Minister in 1931.

This case arose because, although the Labour party had a machinery for electing a leader, MacDonald was deserting his party without even informing them of the fact. Thus Labour MPs were not in a position to meet and elect someone (presumably Arthur Henderson) as leader as they were unaware of the situation. Faced with the resignation of the Prime Minister who was not asking for a general election, the King quite properly turned to the leaders of the other two parties, Mr Baldwin and Mr Samuel. They both said they were prepared to serve in a national government under Mr MacDonald and advised the King to put the proposition to MacDonald. George V was unaware of MacDonald's standing with his own party and the critics have argued that the King should have summoned other senior Labour Privy Councillors to find out how many of the Labour party were likely to follow MacDonald. But to have done so would have opened the King to the charge of intriguing behind the back of the man who was still the accredited leader of the Labour party. Moreover the King's task was (and still is in such situations) to find the strongest government available in the existing

House of Commons. The Conservative and Liberal leaders in 1931 had a majority between them and the addition of MacDonald, however few his Labour supporters, could only add strength to the combination, so that George V acted perfectly properly on this occasion.

The arguments about royal preferences were made in a few quarters in 1957 after the selection of Macmillan and in 1963 after the choice of Douglas-Home (in the latter case by Mr Paul Johnson in the *New Statesman* of 24 January 1964) on the grounds that if in any sense, the advice given contained an element of doubt, the Queen or her entourage preferred the 'genuine Tory'—Mr Macmillan or Sir Alec Douglas-Home—to Mr Butler. The only difficulty about this point of view is that in each case there is absolutely no supporting evidence. When the advice about the state of feeling in the Conservative party reached the Palace, it was couched in an unequivocal form and the Queen had no choice unless she was prepared to doubt the word of the senior statesman (in the latter case her Prime Minister) who conveyed the advice.

There is, therefore, no scope for royal influence on the choice of Prime Ministers given the normal alternation of parties. Even in the quite exceptional case, such as 1931, where the two-party system has temporarily broken down, the Crown operates on the advice of the existing party leaders who will only recommend something other than the usual recourse to an election if they believe it is in the interest of the country to turn to a coalition. Facing such a request from existing party leaders who are prepared to put their advice into operation, the Crown again is in the situation which is the only safe one for a non-political monarchy, that of having no choice whatever.

Thus the MPs in the parties either put up the candidate whom they hope the voters will choose as Prime Minister (if the party is in opposition) or they nominate him to the vacant post of Prime Minister if the party is in government. In either case, their candidates have in time to submit themselves to the electorate, so that the second stage in producing or endorsing a Prime Minister lies with the voters and until a Prime Minister has won an election, he does not feel entirely established, though naturally this sense of weakness is far more marked in a Leader of the Opposition who has never won power than in a Prime Minister who has yet to guide his party through a successful electoral campaign.

3. The causes and effects of the two-party system
Turning, then, to the role of the electorate in choosing a Prime

Minister from the two candidates placed before them, the choice is made possible by the party system. The public are, in reality, very far removed from politics, many electors having only the slightest knowledge of the issues, machinery or persons involved. The party system performs the dual function of so cutting down the options that electors can actually decide who will form the next government and of offering the electorate a shorthand or easy method of categorising their preferences by bracketing certain attitudes and policies as Labour and others as Conservative. As a result, one thing about which the voters are clear is that they are selecting the country's leadership for the coming four or five years, that they are arbitrating in the power struggle between the parties. It is therefore worth considering, as part of establishing how the leadership is selected in Britain, why a two-party system exists and what effect it has on the process of choosing the Prime Minister.

It is often said in books on the electoral system that the method of electing one Member of Parliament for each constituency by a simple majority—'winner takes all'—is seriously disadvantageous to third parties, such as the Liberals, and that this explains why Britain has a two-party system. In fact, this is not true. The system gives a tremendous advantage to one candidate only, the candidate with a majority of one or more votes over his nearest challenger since that person is elected and none of the other candidates gets any benefit in the sense of being elected to Parliament. If all of Britain was composed of absolutely identical constituencies in terms of social composition and if identical candidates stood in each constituency, then the party of candidate A who has one vote more than his nearest rival in this standard seat, would win all 630 seats. Such a system cannot be said to favour two parties, second, third, and fourth parties all faring equally badly with no MPs elected at all.

But of course both these hypotheses of identical constituencies and identical candidates are purely theoretical and each has to be modified. The hypothesis about candidates has only to be modified to a slight extent because the Labour, Conservative and Liberal candidates do have much in common and this uniformity is possible because Britain is a small, highly united and homogeneous country. Thus it is possible for a party spokesman to make the same speech all over the country and for it to mean much the same in each constituency. The hypothesis about identical constituencies was inaccurate in a special sense before 1922, when one part of the United Kingdom was different in its social composition. While most of England, Scotland, Wales and Northern Ireland had been deeply affected by the industrial revolution, the rest of Ireland remained a rural country of small farmers and large landowners. Thus, though the electoral system still worked in the same way in Ireland and favoured one party, the Liberals and Conservatives whose appeals meant something to English, Scots and Welsh voters, were largely irrelevant to Irish conditions and a separate party, the Irish Nationalists, captured virtually all the southern Irish seats.

But, after the independence of Ireland in 1922, the rest of the United Kingdom was left a highly homogeneous country and, with a single-member constituency system, the most likely electoral result would be for the party which had its nose just in front of its rivals to sweep the board. In practice, this has not happened because parliamentary constituencies are highly mixed in their social composition and it is the social or class composition which has the closest correlation with voting patterns in the UK. Though the class structure is very similar throughout the country, the proportions of the classes in each constituency vary. At one end of the scale there are Welsh valleys where the population is almost entirely working class and at the other, there are seaside resorts where the vast majority describe themselves as middle class with almost every variation of class content occurring in the intervening range of constituencies. Given that social class is an important factor in voting behaviour, this explains two things. First it explains why an electoral system which favours only the winner, favours the Labour (and formerly the Liberal) party in some seats and the Conservatives in others. Secondly it explains why, however opinion swings from one party to another, it never wipes out either major party. The social composition of the 630 constituencies is sufficiently lumpy or uneven to ensure that the system still favours Labour in certain seats when the Conservatives are at their peak of popularity, while a Labour high tide still fails to engulf the seats where the uneven social scatter has heaped up a mass of middle-class people.

This also explains why the modern Liberal party has had such difficulty. From the 1880s, the Liberals drew their support largely from the lower income groups and were saved from extinction in bad years by the factors that have just been explained. Then this position was taken over by the Labour party and since the 1930s Liberalism has become a series of opinions or attitudes drawing much the same level of support from each social class. Thus when the Liberals have 11 per cent of the votes (as they did in 1964), this tends to mean about 11 per cent support in each constituency so that the other parties have no problem in defeating them. But if the 3 million votes (which represent 11 per cent of those cast) had been heaped up in any way, if Liberal support was 'lumpy' like that of the Conservative and Labour parties, the Liberals would have won far more than the 9 seats they gained in 1964. Indeed most of these nine were due to the fact that there is a very slight tendency to concentration of Liberal support in the Celtic fringe areas of the Scottish Highlands, North Wales and the South-West of England.

4. The reasons for changes in voting behaviour

Thus the two-party system in Britain is a product of three factors: the electoral system, the homogeneity of the country and the fact that class-based parties each have a body of seats where their position ranges from very secure to just winnable in a good year. But when voters turn to the two main alternatives before them at a general election, they respond to a wide variety of motives. As Butler and Stokes have pointed out in their superb study *Political Change in Britain,* working-class voters are much more prone to think in class terms and to consider that the task of the Labour party is to protect their interests while Conservative middle-class voters tend to place far less emphasis on this reason for political action and to explain their choice more in terms of what is good for the nation. In addition, as the electorate dies and is replaced, as social mobility has an effect, as real incomes have risen and living patterns have altered, as social tensions have declined and the Labour party's image become less class aligned, there have been cross-currents amounting in all to some slackening in the class aspect of voting behaviour. Religious affiliations in certain areas still have an observable effect on voters' choices. Also in regions of Britain where one class and one political view is dominant, this tends to have a reinforcing effect so that a larger percentage of working men, for instance, vote Conservative in the South-East than in Wales.

In addition, the public takes stands on current issues, though whether this affects their voting depends on the depth of their feeling and the degree to which one party is regarded as being in favour of one solution and the other party as opposed. For instance, Labour has at various times been regarded as the party in favour of nationalisation though it is significant that many Labour voters do not want any extension of nationalisation. This identification of Labour with nationalisation has fluctuated but the idea that Labour is 'soft on the unions' has grown, particularly since Mr Wilson was forced to abandon his Industrial Relations Bill in the summer of 1969 and has, since 1971–2 appeared to defend the unions' opposition to the

Conservatives' anti-inflation policy. Each party works to identify itself with popular and its opponents with unpopular attitudes on major issues. Thus in the run-up to an election during 1970, the Conservatives tried to identify themselves with lower taxation and efficient, tough government and attempted to label Labour as the party which was in favour of permissive social legislation, the party which was not tough enough in repressing demonstrations and disorder, the party which was pro-coloured immigrant and so on, though such efforts are only likely to change votes if the issue bites really deep. With an election due, at latest, by the summer of 1974, and inflation a serious issue, each party has been struggling to identify its opponents with rising prices, Labour by blaming the Conservative Government, and the Conservatives by blaming the trade unions and pointing to their links with the Labour party. The evidence suggests that voters who are attached to one particular party tend to accept the view of specific issues enunciated by that party's leaders rather than take a stand on current problems and then adjust their party loyalties. On the other hand, the attitudes of the parties can have different electoral implications at different times. In 1964, the belief that Labour was most likely to expand the social services helped that party, whereas by 1970 the same view had somewhat different electoral implications when popular opinion was veering towards the idea that no further expansion was needed and that, in fact, the existing level of the social services encouraged idlers to batten on the rest of the taxpaying public.

Despite the strength of such issues as capital punishment and coloured immigration, the most important issues remain the capacity of the parties to produce economic well-being. Thus shifts in voting can be best correlated with graphs showing unemployment, the level of prices and the level of real incomes. These can be drawn together in the question asked by the opinion polls as to whether the public approves of the handling of economic affairs by the government or whether it is thought that the opposition would do better.

In all this, what part does the actual task of selecting an individual as the next Prime Minister of the country play? The answer is that the act of voting is complex in that the elector is choosing both a particular Prime Minister and government by a particular party. (It is interesting that the appeal of frontbench spokesmen other than the party leader plays virtually no part in electors' minds.) It is hard to separate the support for the party from the attraction of the potential Prime Minister and it is clear that in terms of political loyalty, most voters are thinking in the party shorthand they have acquired from childhood. However, the research of Butler and Stokes shows that the images of the two leaders are highly personal, dwelling on such qualities as courage, integrity, ability and likability rather than on political attitudes and that the force of these images—-that is whether the potential Prime Minister is attractive or not—does have a demonstrable effect on voting patterns. If the government is very unpopular, an unappealing Leader of the Opposition can be carried; similarly the hold of a popular Prime Minister can, in time, be eroded if his government is unsuccessful. As with so many aspects of the decision of how to vote, the appeal of the leadership is a definite factor but the key element remains the total impression the voter has formed of the party in question over a long period of time.

There is clearly no reason why the cumulation of class interests, family traditions, reactions to current issues and to the leaders, which together govern voting, should result in national support being divided fairly evenly between the major parties. Indeed in this century Conservative or Conservative-dominated governments have been in power for 47 out of the first 73 years. Nevertheless until the 1930s, politicians and academic commentators did talk of an 'electoral pendulum', a tendency for support to swing from one party to the other. Both the evidence for and explanation of such a phenomenon were never made explicit, but the maxim appears to have been based on the fact that between 1868 and 1914 the Liberals and Conservatives each had a total of 23 years in power and on the theory that the longer one party was in office, the more voters it alienated. Since alienation is often a much stronger feeling than satisfaction, as the years went by the balance was likely to move in favour of the opposition.

This explanation was never established and since the 1940s, politicians and outside observers have come to realise that on the contrary, there are tremendous advantages accruing to the government. In the first place, the government chooses the election date and should be able either to time this or to manage the economy so as to ensure that the country is enjoying an economic boom just before a general election. In addition, the government receives far greater publicity than the opposition and because it is actually governing and introducing policies, it can much more easily alter its image in a direction which fits in with the mood of the electorate, the opposition being stuck with the impression it created in its last period in office. For these reasons, most politicians do not believe in any swing of the electoral pendulum. Indeed many consider that an opposition can do little to win power for itself. It has to create a good impression but the chief question is the record of the government. The way the question arises in the minds of doubtful electors is whether they wish to keep this government or not. But while the government has a built-in advantage in the ways described, in the 1960s the opposition has been aided by the fact that expectations have been encouraged to rise faster than the actual rate of increase in average wealth so that there has been a definite feeling of disappointment with the government of the day. This told against the Conservatives in 1962–3 and against Labour in 1967–9, in each case affecting the subsequent general election. But the old 'swing of the pendulum' theory also has some validity in the sense that a section of voters do believe that an alternation in power is desirable. Thus when any party has held power for some time there is a mixed situation—special advantages and publicity accruing to the party in power as against the problem of satisfying the high expectations of the electorate and combating the conviction among a significant minority that a regular transfer of power is one of the beneficial features of British democracy.

5. The character of British political leadership

With this highly complex and shifting series of motives and with the choice of party leaders narrowed down by the pre-selection of the parties, what kind of leadership has the British public settled for in this century? There has been a total of sixteen Prime Ministers by 1973 and, not surprisingly, only one has been of working-class origin. The preponderant characteristic has been that twelve have come from families with landed or mercantile wealth where the idea of taking part in the government of the country has been normal, while only four—Lloyd George, Ramsay MacDonald, Harold Wilson and Edward Heath—have pushed their way in from outside what is often called 'the establishment'. Moreover, although six were Liberal or Labour as against ten Conservatives, the preponderant outlook of these men has been cautious or conservative. Campbell-Bannerman and Attlee were both committed to and carried radical policies, but in each case the proposals had been prepared over a long period in opposition and were, in a sense, overdue. The only innovators in peace-time, the only ones who by temperament favoured action and change in domestic affairs were Lloyd-George, Harold Macmillan, albeit in a well-concealed and gentlemanly fashion, and Edward Heath.

The MPs who selected these men as party leaders knew them well because the British system involves a long political apprenticeship,

On average, the premiers had served 24 years in Parliament before being chosen as party leader and 26 years before they became Prime Minister. Given this long preparation for what was to be the climax of their careers, several points emerge. The first is the relatively brief period they lasted, the average being under five years. Also, despite the long apprenticeship and exposure both to pressure and to the observation of their fellow MPs, the nature of the premiership imposed such strains that many fell ill and many exhibited qualities, good and bad, which few even of their closer colleagues had expected. Considering their health, in the period since 1945, Mr Attlee developed eczema and attributed the resignations of Bevan and Wilson to his absence in hospital; Mr Churchill stayed on after many of the Cabinet thought his powers had declined to a level which merited resignation; Sir Anthony Eden seemed to acquire a nervous tension which interfered with his judgment even before he was incapacitated by a bile duct obstruction, while Mr Macmillan decided to give up the leadership because of his prostate operation. At the same time, although the pressures of the office emphasised attributes of character which were well known, other less expected aspects also appeared. Few imagined that Mr Attlee would prove as tough or efficient as he did, or that Sir Anthony Eden would be so tense and reluctant to delegate authority. Few likewise anticipated that Mr Macmillan would achieve such a personal ascendancy over the House, that Mr Wilson would so rapidly take a major interest in foreign policy or that Edward Heath would reveal such determination in carrying through both his policies and, when convinced, his reversals of policy.

It is a further feature, not only of the loneliness, exposure and heavy responsibility of the post, but of the acute difficulties of British readjustment to the loss of world-wide power and possessions and to a new and much more competitive economic position, that few of these men have left office after their brief spells of power with their reputations enhanced. Between the wars, Ramsay MacDonald carried the burden of Labour's failure to grapple with the unemployment problem, a failure to show that a socialist party had anything special to offer just when capitalism was at its most bankrupt. The reputations of the Conservative leaders, Baldwin and Chamberlain, will never recover from the fact that they abandoned Britain's traditional balance of power policy in Europe and allowed Nazi Germany to recover from a position of total weakness to a strength which nearly destroyed the fabric of Western civilisation. Mr Churchill paid in 1945 for the pre-war failures of his party at home and in foreign affairs. The Attlee Government did much and had its impressive personalities but again sank into gloom, purposelessness and a death wish by the end of five years. Conservative leaders in the 1950s had an easier time but Britain lost her chance to take a leading part in the construction of a United Europe, a failure which dogged British politics till the 1970s and there was the misconceived and abortive invasion of Suez which revealed a total misunderstanding of Britain's position in the world. Mr Macmillan's successes in office were eclipsed in his last year by the Profumo scandal and by the impression, created when he sacked seven of the twenty-one members of his Cabinet, that he was more interested in his personal survival than anything else. Mr Wilson started in a blaze of glory as an opposion leader who could actually unite the Labour party and then as a Prime Minister who managed for seventeen months on a majority of six or less. But soon after his victory in 1966, his Government was in the toils pushing a most unpopular policy of deflation and wage restraint. On top of this a sterling crisis forced Mr Wilson into a change of course in November 1967, when he had to accept devaluation of the pound and the withdrawal of British troops from East of Suez. Though the economy recovered as a result of these measures in 1969, the popularity of the Government was slow to follow and he lost the election of 1970. Although the record of Mr Heath's Government is incomplete, his one great success in taking Britain into the European Community has to be set against serious economic problems which forced the reversal of many of the economic policies on which the Government was elected.

It is difficult to say whether this record has been due more to the problems of a country which, in Dean Acheson's phrase, 'has lost an Empire and failed to find a role', whether the British public has wanted more than it was prepared to produce or whether the leaders themselves were not sufficiently clear about objectives and therefore unable to mobilise support, but there is a clear contrast between this post-1918 period and the previous half-century of confidence, of respected political leadership and admired institutions, with its sense of achievement and success.

6

POLITICAL LEADERSHIP—

THE STRENGTH OF THE PRIME MINISTER

1. Party loyalty, the Whips and patronage

Once a party leader has either won a general election or has succeeded to the leadership of the party in power and thus becomes Prime Minister, he falls heir to a position of great authority, The degree of this authority varies but it is possible, by looking at the Prime Minister's security in office, the sources of his strength and the limitations which exist at a time of maximum weakness, to get some picture of the normal powers at the disposal of a Premier.

The first and major factor which confirms the Prime Minister's position is the force of party loyalty. The majority party want their leader to be successful. If he does well, if his methods and policies are acclaimed, they also share in the benefits. They have assured the public that their party will govern well and meet the electorate's desires and the more this happens, the better they are pleased. But if a Prime Minister is encountering difficulties and if the government's policies are bringing unpopularity and press criticism, while some MPs may grumble, the normal reaction is to support their leader. After all, if these criticisms are not countered, the whole party will suffer and if disloyalty in the Commons did lead (which it has not since the 1880s) to the collapse of the government, then all the MPs would have to face a general election under the most disadvantageous circumstances. In general, a Prime Minister at his weakest and most exposed can be sure that if he and his Cabinet decide to push on with a policy, party loyalty will see them through, whatever the feelings of MPs or the reactions of the country at large.

Some may wish to modify this emphasis on party loyalty by pointing to the fact that the Conservatives were almost defeated over the Resale Price Maintenance Bill in 1963 and Mr Wilson in 1969 was forced to withdraw both the Parliament (No. 2) Bill—House of Lords reform—and the Industrial Relations Bill. These cases will be examined in greater detail further on in this book but they do not invalidate the point being made here. The amazing fact is that in 1963 the Conservative leadership was able, at a time when defeat was staring them in the face at a general election due in a few months, to force through a measure which so deeply disturbed many of their backbenchers. In 1969 Labour leaders never lost a clause of the Parliament Bill but the Chief Whip did not try to carry a timetable motion (partly because of the weight of opposition which would object to timetabling a Constitutional measure). He then found that the Bill was taking too long and dropped it because time was wanted for other measures. On the Industrial Relations Bill, despite the warnings of the Chief Whip and carefully compiled lists of hostile Labour backbenchers, the Prime Minister was convinced that party loyalty would carry him through once the issue was put to the vote. He abandoned the bill when he encountered opposition amongst the large majority of his Cabinet and the objections on the back benches certainly played a large part in producing this result. Nevertheless it was an extreme case going to the heart of the relations between the Labour party and the trade unions and this case shows just how far party loyalty can be stretched. Mr Heath demonstrated what can be done by a determined Prime Minister when he drove through the Bill to carry Britain into the European Community in 1972 despite sufficient Conservative opposition to put his majority at risk. He was aided by a few Liberal votes and Labour abstentions but it is impossible to say whether all the Conservative rebels would have persisted had they known that to do so would definitely have led to the defeat of the Government.

In considering the nature of party loyalty, it is important to set aside the idea that it depends in any significant way on coercion or rewards or that it is the product of the alleged spinelessness of MPs. Some writers and columnists have argued that there is nothing wrong with Parliament or the machinery of government, all that needs to be done is for backbench MPs to stand up and behave like men, to shake off undue subservience to the Whips.

This attitude totally misunderstands the position, the party and the Whipping system being part of the interlocking pattern of British politics. It shows a lack of comprehension to isolate certain sections of this pattern and attribute their form to the frailty of over five hundred otherwise quite robust and unusually opinionated men. To understand party loyalty, it must be appreciated that most MPs have spent years in their party before election to the House. They have joined it, worked for it and probably stood as candidates once or twice before election. They identify themselves with the party's general approach and any serious failures of high policy are personal calamities for them. They may want to change aspects of policy, they may at times disagree with members of the Cabinet or even the Prime Minister, but despite this they still wish the party to be successful. Because of this they will defend the party in public and this means supporting the Prime Minister's actions in the lobbies and in the constituencies.

The idea that the Whips continually exercise pressure on MPs has some truth but they do so largely in terms of party loyalty. The story of an aristocratic and autocratic Conservative Chief Whip, whose patience deserted him, seizing a doubting Conservative MP by the collar of his coat and seat of his pants and propelling him towards the door to the division lobby saying 'in five minutes you can do what you —— like with your conscience', is just possible, given that Whip's well-known judgment in handling particular cases, but it is worth telling because of its unique character. The Whips do have the sanction that they can 'withdraw the Whip' which means the expulsion of the MP from the party and this in turn means that the MP cannot be readopted by his party at the next election. If such a person then contests the election as an independent, he is likely to lose, as only one MP who has been opposed by his party has held his seat at a general election since 1945, though Mr Dick Taverne did so at a by-election in Lincoln in 1973. On the other hand, no Whip wishes to have to take such action, the press fastens on stories of rebels and splits which are damaging to the party and the effect of having to oppose a former member, even in a safe seat, is extremely unpleasant. The Conservatives very rarely use this weapon (they did it once in 1942) and though the Labour Whips have done so a little more often, they also dislike the process. When it last happened in 1961 (6 MPs were involved), the Whip had to be restored in May 1963 in time for the 1964 general election.

For Whips or leaders to threaten MPs is usually counterproductive. When Mr Wilson in February 1967 told Labour members at an 'upstairs' meeting of the party that 'every dog is allowed one bite, but a different view is taken of a dog that goes on biting all the time. . . . He may not get his licence renewed when it falls due', he did not create any alarm and was soon claiming that it was a joke that had been misunderstood. The forces at work were revealed in the 1968–9 session when, for a time, confidence in the Labour party Whips virtually broke down but though the Government's majorities fell off on occasion and it sometimes could not go on as late at night as the Whips had hoped, no division was lost and the Government's position was never in danger. The force of party loyalty, reduced possibly in some cases to a mere desire for political survival, kept the rebels, the disillusioned and the disappointed attending and voting in the usual way.

It is sometimes assumed that another weapon available to the Prime Minister and the Whips to compel the backbencher into the lobby is the threat of dissolution. This is a weapon which is in its very nature impossible to use. If a party is so divided that it faces a defeat on a crucial issue, it is not in a position to win an election and therefore cannot call one. In May 1969 when the Labour Chief Whip threatened this in the event of a defeat on a motion to send the Industrial Relations Bill to a committee, it was greeted with scepticism. No one could seriously imagine that if the Government was defeated on a procedural issue, Mr Wilson would ask the Queen for a dissolution. It was highly unlikely that a Prime Minister, who also had his feelings of party pride and party loyalty, would destroy his party by calling an election when it was divided, discredited and badly behind in the opinion polls.

Most Labour MPs realised that in this case Mr Mellish was trying in a somewhat confused manner, to indicate the seriousness of the situation and to say that if the Government lost its procedural motion, it would be so publicly and seriously humiliated that it would be hard for it to recover enough authority to go on governing.

The other often quoted method of ensuring support for the Prime Minister is through the rewards and patronage available to him. (It is not without significance that the Chief Whip's official title is that of 'Patronage Secretary'.) Patronage can take several forms, the most important being the 100 or so posts in the gift of the Prime Minister, of which some 85 are in the House of Commons. With this number of offices, about one in four of the government side have a salaried post while a further group of about 25 unsalaried Parliamentary Private Secretaries are appointed, making one in every three of the majority into guaranteed supporters of the leadership. Moreover, for quite different reasons (discussed on pp. 126–7 below), members are very eager to obtain ministerial positions so that the desire for office influences many outside the third who actually hold posts. Under the Conservatives, patronage also included the award of peerages and knighthoods. Of the 340 Conservative MPs elected in 1951, by 1957 104 had received a knighthood or title of some kind.

Finally the Whips have many minor gifts which they can use, ranging from places on committees of special interest to the MP in question, to membership of the Council of Europe or the European Assembly, or to inclusion in delegations on interesting visits abroad.

Yet though the force of these inducements is considerable, it cannot be compared with party loyalty nor can it be argued that loyalty guarantees certain rewards. It is true that titles under the Conservatives were almost always awarded in return for a long period of unvarying support in the lobbies, but the Labour Government in 1966 was able to do without this form of patronage though it has been resumed by the Conservative Government elected in 1970. As to posts in the government, the pathway to such promotion is somewhat obscure. It may be true that with certain Prime Ministers personal criticism will be resented but in some cases this has led to promotion and there is evidence that both personal disagreements and rebelliousness on issues do not exclude a backbencher from office. Indeed some backbenchers are appointed precisely in order to reduce the number of vocal opponents of government policy, others because a left–right or regional balance has to be maintained while a Labour Prime Minister has usually wanted to keep a body of support on the party's National Executive Committee by appointing a number of the MPs on the Executive to his government. Among the Conservatives, family connection still plays a considerable part and, while there is no left–right distribution, social origins and occupations do sometimes matter. Thus no one can advise a new member as to just what degree or form of loyalty will lead to promotion. Mr Crossman once repeated to the author an aphorism of Mr Bevan: 'You can crawl up the ladder of preferment on your belly or you can go out, form a left-wing group and kick your way into office, but do not try a mixture of the two.' It is not as simple as this, but the point is that none of these courses of action and no degree of personal success or failure materially affect the conduct of MPs in terms of party loyalty. Men who, whatever their talents, are clearly on the Prime Minister's blacklist, men who have been dismissed, men whose ministerial careers are at an end and men who have long abandoned hope, all still support the leadership as regularly as the newest, most ambitious aspirant.

The fact is that the party system is the life-blood of the body politic in Britain. The mass electorate is primarily voting for one or other party and its leadership in the hope that those whom they prefer will form the government. MPs know that in the vast majority of cases they were not elected because of their own qualities or views but because they bore a party label and that their chief task in the eyes of the voters is to keep their leadership in power. Besides this little else matters. Men are drawn into a political life through the parties and while there is plenty of scope for individualists and a wide variety of views within the parties, the few who find themselves unhappy about the constraints of party loyalty soon find their discomfort spreading and they come to realise that there is no place for them in the House of Commons. Indeed it could not operate as an institution under any other system. The MP would not know how to vote on the many complicated issues which he has no time to master, he would not be able to choose a leader or maintain a stable executive. The need for a party machine was illustrated in 1967–70 by the bewilderment of the single Scots and Welsh Nationalist MPs who had no party Whip to let them know the next week's business and to guide them each time the division bell rang and who had no overall political terms of reference from which to operate. Thus party loyalty is the main source of the Prime Minister's strength. It is not personal in that while one candidate or other in a battle over the leadership may have his special following, the whole party rallies once a particular man is chosen as leader and is an actual or potential Prime Minister.

2. Support of his colleagues, the Cabinet and the Civil Service

The second great source of strength of the Prime Minister is the whole apparatus of government at his command. This has several facets, the most important being that he is at the top of the chain of command which leads from him down through the senior ministers in the Cabinet, the ministers outside the Cabinet, Ministers of State and Parliamentary Secretaries linking on to the senior civil servants and Departments of State. But there is also the strength derived from the ubiquity of government and its great powers so that many elements in the nation both inside and outside politics look to the Prime Minister or to the Whitehall machine. The sheer difficulty and involved nature of the decisions that have to be taken means that the initiative in proposing solutions lies almost entirely with the government. Besides the Prime Minister's position at the apex of both the ministerial and the official pyramids, he also has the special help of the Cabinet Office (including the Cabinet Secretariat, the Central Statistical Office and the Central Policy Review Staff) and his No. 10 Downing Street staff in preparing proposals, coordinating activity and following up past decisions.

Not only has the Prime Minister these powers and opportunities but the Civil Service Department works closely under his direction and aids him in remodelling the machinery, altering the atmosphere and, if necessary, in rearranging the senior personnel in Whitehall. He also arranges the ministerial hierarchy inside and outside the Cabinet, he can indicate an heir apparent or allocate appointments, putting any challengers into thankless posts, so as to ensure that there is no crown prince. And if he does not wish to move the men, he can alter departmental functions or create Cabinet committees which will circumscribe particular individuals and, in time, alter the power structure both in Whitehall and in his party.

Most Prime Ministers have taken a special interest in foreign affairs and this tendency has strengthened their position within British government and has been itself emphasised by similar developments in other countries. It has, for instance, been the growing practice, especially since the First World War, for national leaders to deal only with other national leaders. Thus it has to be the Prime Minister who receives the American President or the German Chancellor and he may decide at any time that a crucial international negotiation requires his presence. There is no absolute need for a Premier to take charge of all important foreign problems. Mr Attlee left most issues and tasks in this field to Mr Ernest Bevin and, in his later years, Mr Churchill left more to Sir Anthony Eden than either Mr Macmillan or Mr Wilson did to their Foreign Secretaries. In contrast, Mr Wilson took over the exploratory stage of Common Market talks in 1966, the negotiations with Mr Ian Smith over the Rhodesian constitution and all the important East–West talks that included Britain. Mr Heath deliberately tried to avoid this kind of intervention but had to take charge of the crucial talks with President Pompidou in 1971 which paved the way for British entry to the European Community.

The same trend is evident in internal affairs, though in this area of activity it is much easier for the Prime Minister, if he so desires, to insist on the responsibility of his departmental ministers. Thus Lloyd George tended to run the government himself through a series of *ad hoc* committees rather than through the Cabinet, but Bonar Law, reacting against him, insisted that deputations and difficulties should be sent to the appropriate minister. But, as governments have increasingly been held responsible for all events during their period of office, so the reputation of the Prime Minister has come to be at stake in all critical issues. For example, Macmillan, Wilson and Heath have tended to intervene in serious labour disputes, personally taking charge of the final rounds of talks with the unions

C

and the employers. Prime Ministers have often, for a period, taken control of ministries which were either weakly led or in the firing line, Wilson announcing in August 1967 that he would take overall responsibility for the Department of Economic Affairs while in 1969 he handled the culminating negotiations over the Industrial Relations Bill with the Executive of the Trades Union Congress. Earlier, Ramsay MacDonald was his own Foreign Minister in 1924 and Churchill, too, took over the Ministry of Defence in 1940 and again in 1951.

Using the machinery of the Cabinet, the Prime Minister can do much to frame the context within which decisions are taken. Most Premiers have prior discussions with one or two senior ministers and this has led to talk of 'inner Cabinets' or 'partial Cabinets'. Only Mr Wilson has formally announced his arrangements at this level when he set up a 'Parliamentary Committee' in April 1968 to act as a steering committee on acute political issues which he replaced in April 1969 with a slightly smaller inner Cabinet with the same functions. But it appears that despite these bodies, Mr Wilson's conduct altered very little, most of his preliminary discussions being with the relevant ministers or with members of his own staff, though in 1969 he did dismiss Mr Callaghan from the Parliamentary Committee (leaving him in his office and in the Cabinet) for speaking out in public against a collective decision in 1969. In practice, no Prime Minister likes to go into the Cabinet without some idea of how his senior colleagues will react and he will usually consult some more than others. If this becomes frequent and convenient, talk of an inner Cabinet will arise.

In addition, the Prime Minister can decide when and what the Cabinet will consider and he can always propose that a matter should go to an *ad hoc* committee of ministers whom he can nominate. Mr A. H. Brown in an article on Prime Ministerial power (*Public Law*, spring and summer 1968) has denied that the Prime Minister controls the Cabinet agenda but he has been explicitly contradicted by Richard Crossman in his Godkin Lectures (*Inside View*, 1970). Mr Brown quotes ex-Ministers whom he had interviewed as saying they never had any problem getting items on to the agenda. But this is not the point. Normally Premiers and their colleagues are working together towards the same end and no member of the Cabinet is likely to wish to block another member's proposals in this way. The test of relative power only comes up when the Prime Minister has a strong desire to prevent or pre-empt a decision on a point and a departmental minister is equally determined to get the issue before his colleagues, in this sense challenging the Prime Minister. Not surprisingly, when ex-ministers are asked to recall such episodes, many cannot do so as few have ever wanted to challenge the Premier. Others admit that when the Prime Minister counselled delay, more background work, or a committee, they thought it advisable to agree. On such occasions, perhaps the Premier might have given way had the minister insisted but, as one very powerful departmental minister put it to the author, to go as far as this was to take one's life in one's hands. The same ex-minister explained that he used to look across the Cabinet table at Mr Macmillan and reflect that relations were very much like those between Henry VIII and his court—jovial conviviality and comradeship but having the monarch's ear was nine-tenths of the battle, and to guess wrong or go too far could lead to sudden political execution. (This was said not long after Mr Macmillan had sacked seven Cabinet Ministers.)

The best examples in recent times of the Prime Minister's control of the agenda, are that Mr Wilson's Cabinet never discussed the case for devaluation or for a military withdrawal from East of Suez from 1964 until November 1967, although an increasing number both of ministers and senior officials were thinking along these lines. It would have cut across the normal patterns of Cabinet conduct for ministers whose departments were not concerned, such as Mr Jenkins or Mr Crosland, to have sent a memo to the Secretary to the Cabinet asking for these issues to be put on the agenda for the next meeting. Such a proposal could only have come from an economics minister in the one case or the Chancellor of the Exchequer, the Foreign Secretary or the Minister for Defence in the other, or in either case from the Premier. Mr Gordon-Walker in his book, *The Cabinet,* defends the failure to discuss the East of Suez question on the grounds that the Cabinet was subconsciously working round the problem and finally reached the central issue, to stay or withdraw, at the earliest possible moment when action was possible in late 1967.

But there are two other possibilities. One is that these policies, having been inherited from previous governments, were never examined on their own, they were simply accepted and continued. If this was the case, it would be a very serious criticism of the machinery of government and of the persons involved. It is, however, highly unlikely. Mr Wilson was certainly aware of the possibility of devaluation as an alternative economic policy and argued against it with individual ministers who flirted with the idea during the sterling crisis of July 1966. His views were so well known and (apart from these few days in July 1966) so definitely shared by Mr Callaghan, the Chancellor of the Exchequer, that this subject became known in Whitehall and ministerial circles as 'the unmentionable' and it is scarcely surprising that it was never considered by the Cabinet. More understandably, the Cabinet were not consulted when the Chancellor and then the Prime Minister changed their minds in the sterling crisis of November 1967 and proceeded to negotiate the manner and extent of devaluation with the other major financial powers. The same is almost certainly true of the East of Suez question since Mr Wilson was firm in support of this policy up to and through the summer of 1967, as was the Foreign Secretary and the Commonwealth Secretary and it is hard to see what bold spirit would have forced a debate in the Cabinet on such an issue and against this combination.

The control of information can be illustrated by the fate of Mr Douglas Jay's paper, prepared by his Department (the Board of Trade), on the industrial and commercial effects of entering the Common Market. Mr Wilson decided to handle the preparatory work on the British application in a Cabinet Committee chaired by himself. In this committee it was clear that there was a serious conflict between Mr Jay's paper and others which, coming from different ministers and departments, were much more favourable to entry. When the dispute could not be reconciled, the Prime Minister evoked the rule that the Cabinet will consider only opinions and not disagreements on matters of fact and Mr Jay's paper therefore was not circulated, though his continual efforts to reopen the issue finally led to his dismissal in August 1967.

In broader terms, the Prime Minister chairs the key Cabinet Committees on defence and overseas policy and long-term economic strategy. He can set up *ad hoc* committees which he can also chair on critical matters, such as the negotiations with Rhodesia or winter emergency fuel supplies (earlier examples in foreign affairs being the committees which ran the Suez operation in 1956, arranged Indian independence in 1947 or conducted the pre-Munich negotiations in 1938). The Prime Minister chooses the chairman and nominates the members of these committees. Mr Wilson introduced the practice that there was no automatic appeal on disputed issues from a committee to the full Cabinet; the chairman was given powers to refuse an appeal and to settle the matter himself. In addition, committees can be used to hold in check a difficult colleague, or bolster a weak one, Mr Butler having a committee imposed on him when he became Chancellor of the Exchequer in 1951, while Mr Tom Fraser was saddled with a committee, when he was Minister of Transport from 1964 to 1967, in order to push matters along. Mrs Castle, his successor, showed her fire and self-confidence by insisting that the committee be disbanded as soon as she took over the ministry.

Thus in both institutional and personal terms, the relations between Prime Ministers and their senior colleagues are complex but normally emphasise and reflect the former's position of authority. As Sir Anthony Eden has put it:

A Prime Minister is still nominally *primus inter pares*, but in fact his authority is stronger than that. The right to choose his colleagues, to ask for a dissolution of Parliament and, if he is a Conservative, to appoint the chairman of the party organisation, add up to a formidable total of power. (Anthony Eden, *Full Circle*, p. 269)

Lord Butler's comment was that:

I think that on the whole the Prime Minister has tended to stop being an equal among equals. There is a tendency not exactly to dictatorship . . . but to be the leader who does control everything, and things are getting more and more into his own hands. (*The Listener*, 16 September 1965)

Sir Alec Douglas-Home's description of the situation was that:

Every Cabinet Minister is in a sense the Prime Minister's agent—his assistant. There's no question about that. It is the Prime Minister's Cabinet, and he is the one person who is directly responsible to the Queen for what the Cabinet does. If the Cabinet discusses anything it is the Prime Minister who decides what the collective view of the Cabinet is. A Minister's job is to save the Prime Minister all the work he can. But no Minister could make a really important move without consulting the Prime Minister, and if the Prime Minister wanted to take a certain step the Cabinet Minister concerned would either have to agree, argue it out in Cabinet, or resign. (*The Observer*, 23 August 1961)

The chief reasons for the relationship illustrated by these comments are, as has been argued, party loyalty and patronage. The latter has more force with ministers than with backbenchers, because ministers have set their feet on the ladder of promotion and most would prefer to go further. Even if not bent on advancement, being ministers they all have something to lose. There is the additional point that those committed to certain policies wish to have the Prime Minister's confidence because this gives their proposals the best chance of success. Occasionally certain ministers achieve a position where they are virtually indispensable, while it is often the case that to dismiss one or more might not be worth the arguments that would take place over the issue which produced the break. But the old idea that a minister

who resigns or is dismissed can be a serious threat because he may
rally dissident feeling on the back benches has little force nowadays;
the back benches simply do not have that degree of cohesion nor
can such criticisms counter the normal effect of party loyalty. As a
result, men who leave a government soon cease to attract attention;
they revert to the status of backbencher and this explains why there
has been a steady decline in the number of resignations on points of
principle in the last twenty-five years. (See R. K. Alderman and
J. A. Cross, *The Tactics of Resignation*.)

The support the Prime Minister receives from the Civil Service
is what would be expected from a highly loyal and competent profession. His own staff falls into three groups. There is a small personal
office which deals with the Prime Minister's constituency and political correspondence. Then the No. 10 Downing Street staff, consisting of eight people, look after day-to-day requirements and briefing
and the particular task of advising on non-political patronage
(Church appointments and the Honours List). This task is performed
by one secretary while another keeps the diary and a third looks
after the Premier's parliamentary questions and speeches. There is a
press secretary with an assistant and then the Principal Private
Secretary and two assistants (one specialising on foreign affairs)
who provide briefs, collect material from the departments and do any
background work needed for the Prime Minister. Finally there is the
Cabinet Office which numbers about a hundred and serves the entire
Cabinet and its complex of committees. While this office is not
simply at the service of the Prime Minister, the Chief Secretary to the
Cabinet has often acted as a personal adviser and the effect of the
Secretariat is to warn the Prime Minister of the issues and problems
that are coming up from the departments. The Central Policy
Review staff (Lord Rothschild's 'think tank') has also tended to
work to and build up the advice available to the Prime Minister.
The Secretariat insist that the papers put to committees and to the
Cabinet are properly processed, that all departments with an interest
have been consulted, they attend the Cabinet itself and take minutes
and then distribute these instructions among the departments,
following them up to see that action has been taken. Before he
became Prime Minister, Mr Wilson said that he thought Mr Macmillan had not been adequately forewarned of some politically
explosive problems (such as slum landlordism—'Rachmanism'—in
London) and he proposed strengthening the No. 10 staff. But, once
in office, he agreed with his predecessors that the machine provided
the Prime Minister with all the support and information that he

needed or could absorb and his only change was to put up the No. 10 staff from seven to eight. Mr Heath said little about this before assuming office but two years later David Watt, an acute observer, noted that 'Mr Heath has already extended the Prime Minister's grasp over the central levers of Whitehall power . . . [He] . . . has used his control of the central apparatus to great effect. He has imposed his ideas on the Civil Service, he has interfered even more firmly than most Prime Ministers in the central management of the economy . . . and he has used his control of the Cabinet machinery . . . to get his views established' (*Financial Times,* 25.8.72).

3. Influence over the mass media

A final source of strength to the Prime Minister is his opportunities to time and handle his initiatives on public affairs and their reception by the mass media. In fact, he controls, through his press aides, the public relations of the government. As Crossman puts it, the press are 'fed with the Prime Minister's interpretation of government policy and . . . present him as the champion and spokesman of the whole Cabinet' (*Inside View,* p. 67). The press accept this relationship largely because of the value of No. 10 as a source of news so that many newspaper men wish to remain in good favour with the Prime Minister and his staff. Similarly the Prime Minister can arrange his visits abroad, which usually draw considerable press and television coverage as do his receptions for statesmen visiting Britain. Mr Wilson has always been particularly conscious of the techniques of the mass media, so much so that the Conservatives came to suspect him of regularly contriving some exciting release on the opening day of their Party's Annual Conference simply in order to blot it out of the headlines. But these techniques did not originate with Mr Wilson. Mr Macmillan also appreciated the importance of timing and of television coverage. The Prime Minister is his party's chief political strategist and the fact that he can, to a large extent, choose when and how to act, gives him a constant advantage over the Leader of the Opposition who has usually to content himself with reacting. Only a Prime Minister who is caught in a position of acute unpopularity and finds power slipping from him, falls into a situation where he is having to react to the challenges of the opposition.

4. Right to choose the date of the election

Since the First World War, it has been accepted that the Prime Minister, as chief political strategist for the government, has the right to choose the date of the general election. He may consult party officials, cabinet colleagues or his Chief Whip, but the decision is his, as is the responsibility for any misjudgment.

These then are the sources of the Prime Minister's strength—party loyalty, patronage, the support of his colleagues and of the machinery of government and his capacity, under most circumstances, to set the pace, tone and direction of activity, to set the terminal date for the government and, throughout its period of office to command public attention. As Crossman sums it up:

In the battle of Whitehall, this man in the centre, this chairman, this man without a Department, without apparent power, can exert, when he is successful, a dominating personal control. This explains why a British Cabinet is always called a 'Wilson Cabinet' or a 'Macmillan Cabinet'. It is because every Cabinet takes its tone from the Prime Minister. The way the Prime Minister conducts it and administers it will give it its particular tone. Usually it is dominated by his personality. (*op. cit.*, pp. 67–8)

7

POLITICAL LEADERSHIP—THE LIMITATIONS
ON THE PRIME MINISTER'S POWER

1. Limitations of party loyalty and Cabinet control

None of the powers that have been described are without limit, though in some cases the surprising fact is how remote the limits are. For instance, party loyalty is greatest for a successful Prime Minister who looks like winning any forseeable election, but if he begins to slip and to trail behind in the opinion polls, then party loyalty still holds, because no MP on his side wants an election under these conditions. Matters have to be pretty desperate to reach the position when either other loyalties begin to loom larger than party loyalty or MPs begin to wonder whether party loyalty would be better served by disloyalty to this particular Premier. In the case of the Conservatives, this has happened only once in recent history, when many felt that Neville Chamberlain was so directly responsible for leading the country close to disaster in the Second World War that he had to go (though even then he retained his majority, for only 33 out of 417 Conservatives voted with the Opposition and 66 abstained). This has to be balanced against such examples as the way the Conservative leadership was able, despite many warnings, to lead that patriotic and pro-military party into appeasement in the 1930s, to lead it into and out of the Suez expedition in 1956, and into and out of support for the settler-dominated Central African Federation in the same decade. On the Labour side, a prior loyalty can be revealed if the Prime Minister comes too deeply into conflict with the unions or with the fundamentals of socialist faith. Yet Ramsay MacDonald was able to retain the party loyalty of the vast majority of his backbenchers through all the difficulties of the 1929–31 Government with mounting unpopularity and increasing unemployment, until he decided to walk out on his party. Had he stayed as a Labour Prime

Minister and fought it out with his critics, he might well have won
a majority at a party meeting. Similarly, despite severe by-election
setbacks and mounting economic problems, Mr Wilson was able to
carry his party into a wages restraint (Prices and Incomes) policy
and then, in 1969, on the issue of trade union reform into a head-on
conflict with the Trades Union Congress, in defiance of Labour Party
Conference decisions, against the wishes of a substantial body of
MPs and after a period of governmental unpopularity unparalleled
in modern history, before the bonds of party loyalty showed any
signs of snapping. At the last stages of the Industrial Relations Bill a
minority of members did feel that their loyalty to the unions or their
principles might drive them to vote against their party leader, but
Mr Wilson always reckoned that had this been put to the test, party
loyalty would have triumphed. Mr Heath also has driven his party
hard over entry to the European Community, on decisions to
nationalise failing industries, to raise public expenditure and to
apply a statutory incomes policy and all without serious challenge
to his leadership.

A more normal and regular limitation on a Prime Minister than
the very remote possibility of a breakdown of party loyalty lies in
his relationship with his ministerial colleagues inside and outside
the Cabinet. The limitations arise in several situations. When a
Prime Minister is chosen or wins an election, he has great power
conferred upon him, but his immediate desire is to end any old
party feuds, to draw everyone together round his leadership. So
most new Prime Ministers feel constrained to include in their
Cabinets or other ministerial posts, those men whom they have just
beaten in the contest for leadership or their chief lieutenants when
in opposition. Thus it would be unwise to omit certain individuals
and better if places could be found for a whole series of groups whom
the Prime Minister, on purely personal grounds, might have preferred to exclude. For example, it would scarcely have been possible
for Attlee to have left out such men as Ernest Bevin, Stafford Cripps
or Herbert Morrison just as Mr Heath would not have contemplated the omission of Sir Alec Douglas-Home, Mr Maudling or
Mr Quintin Hogg when he was forming his Cabinet. Whether this
should be described as a constraint or not is dubious because Prime
Ministers want the best government they can assemble and in both
the cases mentioned, Mr Attlee and Mr Heath would have certainly
felt great regret if men of such ability and experience had refused to
serve.

But none of this must be taken as evidence that a politician can force himself upon a hostile Prime Minister. Both Baldwin and Neville Chamberlain were able to exclude Mr Churchill in the 1930s and it is clear that so long as Mr Heath is Prime Minister, however strong or weak he is, he will not have Mr Enoch Powell in his Cabinet. While most party leaders, whatever their relationships, wish to pull together when a new government is formed, the longer a ministry lasts the more it reflects what would now be called 'the manpower policy' of the Prime Minister. If he is successful, his strength grows and it becomes easier for him to sack senior ministers or to let them go if there is a dispute. Thus Mr Wilson felt able, in 1968, to accept one of Mr George Brown's regular resignation gestures, when he would not have been so ready to break off relations a little earlier and Mr Macmillan was able to let Mr Thorneycroft, Mr Powell and Mr Birch go in December 1958, saying it was only 'a little local difficulty'. On the other hand, while a Prime Minister whose policies are unpopular can purge his government in order to give it a fresh image or to indicate a new approach in certain fields, there is a limit to what he can do. For instance, Mr Macmillan was able to sack seven of his Cabinet of twenty-one in July 1962 but he could not have repeated the exercise in that Parliament. Similarly, when Mr Wilson's policies ran into difficulties after July 1966 and there was a forced devaluation in November 1967, he took Mr Jenkins as Chancellor of the Exchequer and probably could not then have dismissed him without a catastrophic collapse in confidence. If the political situation deteriorates seriously and there is discontent in the party and a potential challenge to the Prime Minister, much of his position depends on his relations with the senior five or six members of the Cabinet. The backbenchers and junior ministers may complain and cabal but they can achieve nothing (discussed in more detail pp. 78–9 below) if there is no alternative leader and some cooperation from among the senior men in the government. Thus the criticisms of Clement Attlee in 1947 which led some ministers to suggest that he stood down in favour of Ernest Bevin never amounted to a serious challenge because Ernest Bevin refused to countenance any such move. Similarly, the talk of removing Mr Wilson in March and April of 1969 foundered on the fact that while there was an alternative readily available, Mr Callaghan, none of the influential members of the Cabinet were prepared to move. Had two or three of the top seven been prepared to support Callaghan, the whole picture would have changed.

Thus the Prime Minister has to take the state of the party, the government's standing and the position of his leading colleagues into account. At all times, but particularly if serious unpopularity is encountered, these factors may affect his decisions. But if the Prime Minister is successful, he has increasing scope, indeed almost total freedom to select and promote his colleagues.

Within this framework, the more normal limitations arise from the day-to-day operation of the Cabinet system. Here the Prime Minister has the great advantages already listed. He chooses the men, passes the agenda, chairs the main committees, prepares the ground with preliminary talks; he can decide if and when to show his own hand during the discussions and he can allow the argument to continue by postponing a decision or he can halt and sum up the sense of the meeting. Yet, in almost every government, the Prime Minister has found his views on certain issues overturned, though most ministers agree that when this happens, it is a little surprising and a sign of misjudgment in one form or another. Mr Gordon-Walker in his book, *The Cabinet*, gets the emphasis exactly right when he announces in somewhat surprised tones that 'Mr Harold Wilson and his Foreign Secretary were once overruled by the Cabinet on a matter of great importance'. If this happens more than once or twice, confidence in the Prime Minister will wane.

In practice two or three men set the overall direction and tone of a government. Their views are known and are rarely and reluctantly challenged by the less influential members. For instance, Mr Wilson, Mr Callaghan and Mr Brown set the general lines for the Labour Government for some time after the 1964 general election. Mr Churchill had his 'cronies' who talked matters over with him till late in the night, though he also listened to some of the senior departmental ministers who were not on such close personal terms. Different Prime Ministers have set about running their Cabinets in different ways, but with much the same result. Mr Attlee was brisk. He would call on the minister concerned and one or two others and then sum up the sense of the meeting. Mr Churchill tended to indulge in long reminiscences and anecdotes but commanded tremendous respect. Mr Wilson, on controversial issues where he was himself undecided, has tended to go round the table collecting voices. (This is a better description than 'taking votes'. The Lord President beside him would keep the tally and this led to newspaper leaks giving lists of 'fors' and 'againsts' on such issues as the application for entry to the Common Market, the sale of arms to South Africa, and the imposition of prescription charges.)

In meetings of this kind where important business is being rapidly transacted by politicians with an overriding common purpose, it is clearly wrong to talk in simple terms of Prime Ministerial dominance. On the other hand, several experienced ministers have pointed out to the author that a Premier who cannot get what he wants out of the Cabinet does not deserve to hold such an eminent post. At the same time, no leader wishes to give the impression of brow-beating or overruling his colleagues. The purpose of Cabinet meetings is to keep members informed of major policy developments (the Foreign Secretary regularly reports on what he has been doing), to settle inter-departmental conflicts and to test opinion on the larger policy issues that are facing the government. Often, on these questions, the Prime Minister may not have a clear view. He may be waiting to see how a situation is developing and how opinion is forming among the public, in his party and among his colleagues. But once the Prime Minister has formed a view and wants to ensure its acceptance, the odds are heavily in his favour. For instance, if the division of opinion is serious and opposed to him, the Premier can see those who may be likely to disagree with him one by one, as Mr Wilson did in the sterling crisis of July 1966, when he tackled each devaluer in turn until the opposition crumbled, leaving only George Brown to threaten and then to withdraw his resignation.

The seats around the Cabinet table are arranged in order of importance, the most influential posts carrying places opposite to or close beside the Prime Minister. He will invite the senior ministers, especially those with such important or wide-ranging responsibilities as the Treasury, Foreign Affairs or the Leadership of the House, to contribute and it is a brave junior Cabinet Minister (already overburdened by a heavy departmental load) who will challenge these more experienced, senior men. Also the circulation of information is selective, only a few of the Cabinet receiving the bulk of Foreign Office telegrams. Moreover the burden of their own work usually prevents the departmental ministers from reading even those telegrams of major importance which are circulated to the whole Cabinet. The author recalls that when British support for American policy in Vietnam became critical because of certain events in 1967, a departmental minister explained that he had decided for once 'to be a Cabinet Minister'. This meant that over the weekend he deliberately neglected his own work and waded through the mass of paper on Vietnam so that he was in a position to put his own views. Thus, though there is an element of discussion and decision-making in the Cabinet, the Prime Minister and those he has chosen to be his principal lieutenants are in a strong position. To insist on putting a view and to be clearly in a minority damages a Cabinet member and there is always the restraint caused by the knowledge that soon there will be another ministerial reshuffle and some members will move inwards along the table closer to the Prime Minister while others will move out altogether. When Mr Wilson found that he and Mrs Castle had lost the support of almost all the rest of the Cabinet over the Industrial Relations Bill in May 1969, he may have thought he could still, as in July 1966, win them over one by one or face their resignations (see above, pp. 67–70). But after the crisis had passed, it was said that he intended to punish those whose 'disloyalty' had annoyed him. Of the five names mentioned, Mr Marsh was sacked, Mrs Hart was moved out of the Cabinet, Mr Shore lost his ministry (the Department of Economic Affairs was abolished), Mr Crosland found himself taken away from his chief interest in economic affairs and in fact moved to a less important post and only Mr Callaghan remained unscathed, largely because of the increased public reputation he had earned by his handling of the Ulster crisis in the summer months of 1969.

The history of the proposed Industrial Relations Bill of 1969 has been referred to many times in this book because it was a period of such strain for Mr Wilson and the Labour party that it brought out many of the underlying relationships in politics and revealed the points at which the Prime Minister's sources of strength reached their limits. In the early months of 1969 first Mrs Castle, the Secretary of State for Employment and Productivity, and then the Prime Minister, both came to believe that the economy required strong action against unofficial strikes and that to check these strikes would be electorally popular. But to take such action was to confront one of the founding sections of the Labour party and to unite against the leadership the left, the trade union members and many others who doubted the wisdom of such legislation. Various groups mobilised on the back benches to try and defeat the Bill or, if there was no other alternative, to remove the Prime Minister. They found that there was no proper machinery for the latter purpose and the Prime Minister remained convinced that sufficient MPs never would vote with the Conservatives if it meant the defeat of the Government. He was probably correct, but the fate, only a month before, of the Parliament (No. 2) Bill seemed to provide an alternative method of blocking the measure. The procedural motions to send the Bill to a committee or to endorse a guillotine could be defeated (on the assumption that no government would resign on such procedural issues) and then the Bill could be talked out on the floor of the House. Mr Mellish, the Chief Whip, inveighed against this possibility, threatened dire consequences and even an election but, at the end, told the final Cabinet that he could not guarantee the passage of these motions.

Until this point, Mr Wilson had been secure against the backbench muttering because there was no concerted opposition to him in the Cabinet. The Home Secretary, Mr Callaghan, had indicated his opposition to the Bill but was joined by none of the other senior members nor was there any agreement among the backbenchers as to which of these ministers they would prefer as an alternative to Mr Wilson. Then Mr Mellish made his announcement. The Cabinet, with the exception of Mrs Castle, one by one turned against the Bill and urged Mr Wilson to settle with the TUC. Yet he was not prepared to be instructed in this way. He left the last Cabinet to meet the TUC and refused to make any concessions. At this stage the senior ministers who had remained loyal to him until the last meeting began to fear that the Prime Minister would come back to the Cabinet, announce deadlock with the TUC, and then insist either that the Cabinet would agree to legislation or he would have to tender his resignation. To forestall this, Mr Crossman contacted the Prime Minister and pointed out that senior ministers would even prefer a government led by Mr Callaghan to a collapse and a Conservative victory. Mr Jenkins may also have pressed the Prime Minister to settle. When such powerful voices were raised, Mr Wilson probably realised that at last he was in real danger, but, whatever the precise form of the pressures mounted at this stage, he then returned for a second meeting with the TUC, found an acceptable formula which would allow him to jettison the Industrial Relations Bill and reached a settlement on this basis.

The moment this was done a sigh of relief swept the Labour party and all the normal forces of party loyalty rallied again behind Mr Wilson. Moreover, by the summer of 1969 it was getting too close to a general election for arguments about the leadership and there was a dramatic (though short-lived) improvement in the Government's standing in the opinion polls. As a result, Mr Wilson was back on a pinnacle of authority, able to force through measures (such as the amalgamation of the Prices and Incomes Board with the Monopolies Commission) which many of the Cabinet opposed. He was able to make a major reconstruction of the machinery of government in October 1969 without telling even the so-called inner Cabinet and he was able, as has been said, to punish most of those who had recently resisted him.

2. *The party outside Parliament as a constraint*

This episode also reveals the extent to which the Annual Conference of the party can be regarded as a constraint on a Labour Prime Minister. In theory, the Labour Party Annual Conference has an important role in the life of the party. It elects the National Executive, which is the governing body of the party, and the resolutions passed at the Conference are the policy of the party, those which are carried by a two-thirds majority having to be included in the election manifesto. The position of the National Executive has never been a serious difficulty for a Labour Prime Minister because it is accepted that he and the Cabinet must lead and because it has always been possible with a combination of faithful trade union members and the appointment of a number of the MPs as ministers to keep a loyal majority. Until the leadership of Mr Gaitskell, the Conference had not rejected the stand taken by the party leader on a major issue and many in the party assumed that if this happened, there would be the most serious repercussions and that such a division could not persist for long. Mr Gaitskell took this view in that he was deeply shaken when the Conference in 1960 rejected the defence resolution which he had supported in favour of one embodying the policy of the Campaign for Nuclear Disarmament. He said he would 'fight, fight and fight again' to bring the party he loved back on to what he regarded as the correct course and, in 1961, the decision was reversed.

In power, Mr Wilson was able to treat the Conference much less seriously and simply ignored or failed to become excited about defeats. Executive policies were lost twice (on defence expenditure and on unemployment) in 1966, three times in 1967 (Vietnam, Greek despotism, and prices and incomes) and, most blatant of all, the Government's insistence on a statutory prices and incomes policy was rejected in 1968 by a majority of five to one. But this does not mean that a Labour Prime Minister is not concerned about such defeats and that the prospect of rejection does not act as a constraint. Mr Wilson was prepared to delay the closure of certain mines in 1967 in order to win the support of the National Union of Mineworkers for certain resolutions, and he also announced the construction of aluminium smelters in the outlying regions in order to improve his reception at Conference. In the case of the Industrial Relations Bill, the earlier divisions in the Cabinet (the principles of the Bill having been accepted) were between those who wanted a lengthy measure in the autumn of 1969 and those who felt that the party could not face the long-drawn arguments culminating in an overwhelming conference defeat and therefore carried the Cabinet for a short, quick Bill before the summer recess. In opposition, the Labour Party Conference is more formidable just because the Leader of the Party is not Prime Minister and the members of the National Executive are not eclipsed by powerful ministers. A Leader of the Opposition may feel he has to give way to strong currents of feeling in the party and the Conference (as Mr Wilson did in turning against the terms on which Britain joined the European Community) when he could have surmounted such pressure had he been in office.

In fact, the relations between a Labour Prime Minister and the Party Conference are much the same as those of his Conservative counterpart both when the Conservatives are in opposition and in office. The Conservative Conference has none of the constitutional powers and theoretical independence of the Labour Conference but the prospect of a serious defeat produces very much the same reactions. Mr Heath, in opposition, found his position continually under fire at these gatherings and every speech he made to his Party Conference was a test of his capacity as a Conservative leader. While his strength and the respect for him enormously increased after he won the general election of 1970, he would still regard a defeat at a conference on a matter where, for example, Mr Powell's views were opposed to the Government's, as an exceptionally serious blow which should be avoided if at all possible. In this sense, the thesis of Professor R. T. McKenzie in his *British Political Parties* is correct, that the power structure within the parties and the relations between the leader and the rest of his party are much the same in both the Conservative and Labour parties because in each case the relationship is governed by the power the political system confers on the Prime Minister, though the Labour Conference counts for more when that party is in opposition.

Professor McKenzie's argument is less satisfactory if it is extended to suggest that the motives people have for joining the parties, the atmosphere within them and the techniques each leader must apply in order to hold his party together are also similar. Professor Samuel Beer is right to emphasise in his *Modern British Politics* that the approach of the two parties to these problems, their outlook and spirit are radically different though the facts of a nation's position in the world, and the long-term nature of social and economic development does mean that the margin open for political change is small. In the sense that these limitations operate equally on both parties, there is little difference. However each party finds that the reactions to them of the major pressure groups is different and that their approach to problems has a different flavour though no party leader wishes to be at loggerheads with his active followers. In this sense, for the leaders of both parties, open challenges and defeats at the party conference are an ominous sign.

3. Governing through the House of Commons

It is argued or even simply asserted in many books that the chief limitation on the Prime Minister is Parliament and that this is the main task of the House of Commons. This is quite wrong and contrary both to the belief of contemporary politicians and to their practice. For the majority of MPs, as has been argued, the task in the Commons is to support their leaders. They regard the conflict inside the House as an extension of the struggle for power in the constituencies, their duty being to rally their party. For the government the Commons may be a nuisance in that its procedures dominate the timetable of departments and periodic attendance is required from busy ministers. But the Commons is also one of the agencies through which the government operates, enabling it to explain its policies and defend its record. Nothing pleases a Prime Minister more than to hear his cohorts behind him cheering as he scores points off the opposition. For the opposition, the objective is not to alter what the government is doing—that is its responsibility—the task is to explain to the public the opposition's case for taking over the government after the next election. Mr Iain Macleod did, on occasion, attack this view, saying that the opposition both wants and can have some influence. He cited particular government alterations in the Finance Bill which looked like amendments he had moved in previous years. It is impossible to prove whether these changes were prompted by the opposition or by outside bodies or whether they originated in the Treasury but, whatever explanation is correct, the fact that the amendments were incorporated is not a serious constraint on the existing political leadership. It can accept them or not as it feels inclined.

In so far as the House of Commons does constitute a constraint on the Prime Minister, the pressure comes from the government's own backbenchers. The resistance of the opposition is expected and, in this sense, taken for granted. Among government backbenchers, the normal attitude is one of loyal support, but the leadership knows that if it moves in certain specific directions, it will encounter objections, for example from the left in the Labour party or, in the case of the Conservatives, from those in favour of capital punishment or in sympathy with the white Rhodesians. No one reaches the leadership of a party without an excellent sense of just what will and what will not arouse objections. At the same time, the leadership knows that, in the last resort, it can survive such objections (as the Conservatives did over Resale Price Maintenance, over the dissolution of the Central African Federation, over the Restrictive Practices Act or, more recently, over British entry to the European Community and as Mr Wilson did over so many economic issues in 1967–9). But no government wants a conflict if it can be avoided and this desire for harmony does have a marginal effect on a Prime Minister and on his senior colleagues which it is very hard to assess with precision. The reason is that the effect is a matter of influence, not of direct, clear-cut power to accept or reject. Thus it is possible, when searching for examples of such influence, to find cases when one minister concerned will say there was a modification in order to meet backbench pressure, and another minister equally involved with the same measure will deny that this was the reason, attributing the modification to his insistence or to an outside pressure group. When the author put a list of possible cases of backbench influence to Mr Wilson in mid-1967, he went through each carefully to demonstrate that on no occasion was he consciously deflected from his original purpose, even over mode of presentation or timing, by any estimate of what dissident groups on his back benches might say. On the other hand, when he encountered greater political obstacles in late 1967 and in 1968–9, it would seem clear that backbench pressure had at least a marginal effect. Likewise, it seems probable that Mr Heath's changes of policy in 1971 and 1972 were due to external factors such as the level of unemployment and the rate of world inflation rather than to backbench pressure, but this must have had some influence, for example when the Government was surprisingly defeated over immigration regulations in December 1972.

The way in which backbench pressure operates will be analysed in greater detail in Chapter 10 but in considering the position of the Prime Minister, his first and hardest task is that of formulating policies and of securing his ministerial colleagues' support for them. Then putting the policies through Parliament is a process which, if the government is reasonably successful, will add to his strength. The process makes promulgation and execution of the policies easier. Yet all political leaders have a developed sense of the reactions of those around them. The Prime Minister wants both party and public approval and, other things being equal, he will always prefer the method or solution which will raise his standing among his backbenchers—he knows he can rely on party loyalty to see him through under almost all conceivable circumstances but he would rather cement than strain this loyalty.

4. Governing through the Civil Service

Just as Parliament is an agency through which the government operates politically, it operates administratively through the Civil Service and here again there is a reciprocal influence on the Prime Minister and his plans which is hard to locate and estimate with accuracy. Crude suggestions either that politicians who know their own minds ought to be able to do exactly what they like with the governmental machine or that senior civil servants seek to win over or mislead ministers must be discounted. But it is also clear that senior civil servants, really able men who have spent their whole lives in government whose duty is to advise ministers as to the best course of action, are bound to have an influence. Some of this derives simply from the complexity of modern society and the need for long-term policies. Thus public expenditure is planned over a five-year period and each summer 'hard' decisions are taken for three years ahead. So any government will inherit commitments in public expenditure, foreign policy commitments in the shape of external alliances, trade and defence agreements and commitments in the form of fixed expectations on the part of the electorate. It is part of the function of the Civil Service to point out these limitations to new ministers.

But a Prime Minister and his colleagues may feel that the limitations are greater than those arising from the continuous nature of administration. This may occur to them when they find that they have inherited departments with elaborate and positive opinions as to how policy should be operated or when departments argue that to adopt certain policies would create too many administrative difficulties. While civil servants will always try to meet a minister's wishes, if they and their colleagues consider that a policy is mistaken, they are bound to say so and the effort imposed on the minister is much greater when he goes against their views than when he accepts his department's policy. On the other hand, it is equally exhausting for a minister if his department has no policy to recommend, as this means that the politician has to collect the evidence and to think through a problem, something for which he has no time and often lacks the necessary training. One of the most active and successful innovators in Mr Wilson's Cabinet told the author that he signed many papers put to him when he was not sure that they were right and when he had not had time to pursue the detailed background to the proposals, simply because he felt he had to reserve his energies for one or two issues each month where he knew he would have an uphill battle with his officials. Neville Chamberlain was able to carry through his policy of appeasing Hitler in the late 1930s but he clearly felt the weight of Foreign Office disapproval and remarked that the cultivation of better relations with Germany 'will carry us safely through the danger period, if only the FO will play up'. The other type of burden mentioned was encountered by Mr Tom Fraser when he became Minister of Transport in 1964. At that time his Department had no fixed ideas about the best method of coordinating road and rail transport and of covering the costs so that nothing could be announced until the preparatory investigations had been carried out. Mr Fraser found it difficult to look busy and creative in this period and, as a result, there was public criticism. Mr Wilson, who had never had any close political links with Mr Fraser, reacted to this criticism by suggesting a move but Mr Fraser preferred to leave the Government. His successor, Mrs Castle, was not only more dynamic and publicity conscious, but received a plethora of proposals she could adopt from the study groups set up under Mr Fraser. While in this case the original weakness of the Ministry of Transport affected a particular minister, it can touch the whole government and the Prime Minister himself if a situation arises where public expectations have been aroused on a specific issue and the officials cannot suggest or have not ready a suitable response.

The position is complex, because the Civil Service likes a decisive minister who will take decisions and stick to them, who can state and win his case in the Cabinet and who launches policies with panache. For all his excess of temperament and his tendency to browbeat officials, Mr George Brown exhibited most of these virtues at the Department of Economic Affairs in its early days and there is no doubt that it was an exciting place to work, the minister having the enthusiastic support of his officials. But where ministers are weak or inactive, much falls to the civil servants. For instance, most Cabinet Committees have an equivalent official committee which meets first and goes over the briefs so that each department knows what the other is going to say and tentative conclusions may be reached. In one case in 1965, the Minister of Housing and Local Government found that at a Cabinet Committee he had a brief making a plea that government supervision of sport should come under his ministry. Half-way through, he exploded, saying this was rubbish and that sport should go to the Department of Education and Science. The other ministers agreed but when the Minister of Housing happened to glance through the minutes of the meeting a day or two later, he found that the recorded decision was to give sport to the Ministry of Housing. He called in his senior adviser, to be told that the prior official committee had reached this conclusion after carefully considering the interests of all departments and they had not realised the minister wished seriously to abide by his momentary departure from his brief. In this case he did, but the episode illustrates the independence of mind and vigilance required of ministers who wish to go against the settled views of their officials. These most able men are in their departments for most of their lives while ministers are two or three year birds of passage. An unwelcome new idea, if slowly worked out and subjected to long inter-departmental consultations, may well still be 'under consideration' when the next minister takes over and he may have other interests so that it can quietly be allowed to die.

The enthusiasms and doubts of officials are naturally particularly influential on matters of internal Civil Service organisation. They have been known to make flat statements that the Inland Revenue is so overworked that major tax reforms cannot be contemplated by any Chancellor of the Exchequer for several years ahead. More tentatively, officials may say that they are not opposed to parliamentary reform but that it is impossible to meet all the minister's requests for information because parliamentary reforms have led to the establishment of a Select Committee of the House of Commons and it has called for so many documents. Usually the Prime Minister recognises the special claims of officials to advise on these points and when Mr Wilson was reorganising the structure of the economic and industrial departments in October 1969, he consulted the permanent secretaries, but the ministers to be affected by the changes were not informed of the decisions taken until the last moment. Similarly the men who have worked most closely with Mr Heath on these questions are the Secretary to the Cabinet and the Permanent Secretaries to the Civil Service Department and the Treasury.

The total effect is like that of a ship with its existing course and momentum and a crew with established practices which can easily tire out a new or unconventional officer at the helm. And while the effort involved is clearly greater for junior officers, the same thing can happen, in a rather different way, to the Captain. When Mr Wilson, through the Queen, commissioned Lord Fulton to investigate the service and then endorsed a Report (in 1968), many of whose recommendations were regarded by senior officials with some scepticism, the service became 'Fulton-minded'. It spoke the jargon of the new business studies used in the Report. But in practice, those concepts that were acceptable (the staff college and a uniform grading structure) were put into practice while others were quietly buried below hatches and the ship sailed on much as before.

5. Relations with the pressure groups

Probably the greatest limitation on a Prime Minister and his government comes from the various power blocks in the community, their power being largely negative; to refuse to cooperate, to strike, to fail to participate or to follow new rules. In some cases, this non-cooperation or failure to respond may come from the public at large rather than from specific pressure groups. For example, over the years it has been established that no amount of exhortation will end absenteeism at work or, in times of balance of payments problems, persuade Britons to holiday at home. The relations with industrial, professional, regional or religious pressure groups can vary from one party to another and from one Prime Minister to another. For example, Neville Chamberlain sacked Lord Swinton (then Sir Philip Cunliffe-Lister) in 1938 because he had offended certain industrialists who were close to the Conservative leadership when post-war Labour governments would have shown no such sensitivity to business reactions. Pre-war Conservative administrations viewed the trade union movement with some suspicion but Mr Attlee, on the other hand, expected to retain, above all, the confidence of the leaders of the larger trade unions. When the Conservatives came to power in 1951, they went to great lengths to convince the TUC that the latter's close association with government built up between 1945 and 1951 was not at an end. There was steady consultation and cooperation throughout the 1950s while the Labour Government, elected in 1964, tried to maintain similar relations with the Confederation of British Industries and with its members. When the Conservatives returned to office in 1970, there was a short period when this pattern was broken as the trade unions strongly objected to the new Industrial Relations Bill while the Government tried to control inflation by defeating selected, pace-setting strikes. After two years in which both sides suffered some bruising setbacks, this approach was modified. By 1973 it was accepted that the unions could not defeat a government backed by public opinion and Mr Heath and his colleagues accepted that any industrial and incomes policy was operated more satisfactorily when there was a degree of communication and understanding between the two sides.

The lessons of the past twenty years in this field are complex. On the one hand, it is clear that pressure groups which act in a manner contrary to the public interest or to the interests of their members can be challenged and defeated by the government. For example in 1911 and in 1948 the British Medical Association refused to accept major health proposals made by the government and found that in the end they were abandoned by the doctors. In the winter of 1972–3 some elements in the trade unions wanted to defeat Mr Heath's anti-inflation policy and were, in effect, abandoned by the workers.

But, on the other hand, no government can take such victories for granted in the way in which a Cabinet can be sure that 99 per cent of its legislation will pass through the House of Commons. These outside bodies, even if like the British Broadcasting Corporation, British Petroleum or British Rail under a degree of government control, have a life and will of their own. In conflicts with them as well as with totally independent bodies, the government has to be careful to choose its ground and to have public opinion on its side. The public does not seem to take the view that there is an entire category difference between decisions on prices made by ICI, by a nationalised industry, by local government (in housing, for example) and by a government in its prices and incomes policy. The government cannot simply say 'we make laws and they must always be obeyed'. The laws, like the decisions of the rest of the established agencies affecting the lives of the citizens, must be seen to be fair and reasonable. There is a special problem for the Labour party if it is in conflict with the unions, since they are built into the power structure of the party and can challenge a Labour government not merely by external confrontations but internally through the Party Conference and by enlisting the support of trade union sponsored MPs in the House of Commons.

Thus the Labour Government of 1964–70 faced great problems in putting its wage policies into effect and was left in 1969 with an effective choice between continuing a statutory prices and incomes policy and introducing a new Industrial Relations Bill. It chose the latter but, in the end, lost both. The Conservatives after 1970 found, to their dismay, that they did not have the easy and automatic backing of the community for all aspects of their policy in this field. When public opinion, at least in part, accepted that the National Union of Mineworkers had a case during its strike in

1972, this helped the miners inflict a humiliating defeat on the Government. Even when a government can, by taking tough action, force such groups into line, the results may be damaging; there may be a short-run flight from the pound or a long-run decline in the morale of an industry or a government department. At the same time, too many concessions can also be harmful, delaying the closure of uneconomic industries or preventing the building of new airports if and when they are needed.

The conclusion is that this is the key area of political action in internal affairs. The Prime Minister receives his mandate from the people; they expect him to govern but there are sub-leaders and representatives for sub-sections of the community whom he has to convince, appease, cajole or, if necessary, isolate and defeat. It is in this area that much of the real opposition to a government comes between elections, though the penalty of failure is not to hand power to these groups or sub-leaders. They cannot govern. The result, if the public accept the criticisms of its current political leadership, is to hand power over to the Leader of the Opposition at the next general election and he becomes Prime Minister to see if he can handle these relationships in a manner which will produce better results and be more acceptable to the country.

As a result, there is a constant temptation for political leaders to encourage conflict or at least to back outside groups which might make life difficult for the government. Mr Wilson often attacked external forces on the right in high finance for example, or on the extreme left pointing to 'closely-knit groups of politically moti-vated men' who, he alleged, were behind certain critical strikes. In opposition after 1970, the Labour party contemplated how far to support trade union strikes against Mr Heath's anti-inflation policy. The arbiter, in these cases, remains the electorate. To behave too selfishly, to be damaging the nation in the interests of a sub-section brings retribution at the polls. The electorate expect the Prime Minister and his team to do better than the groups, to be fair and to preside over increasing prosperity, but he must convince and carry them, realising that there is no simple or single loyalty to the State and that, on each case, he must show that the govern-ment is pursuing the correct policy.

8

POLITICAL LEADERSHIP—CAN THE
PRIME MINISTER BE SACKED?

The broader limitations on the Prime Minister which come from the outlook and practices of the electorate at large will be considered in the next chapter. The other aspect that remains to be examined in order to assess the strength of the political leadership in Britain is whether a Prime Minister can be dismissed. The direct relationship between the leadership and the led comes out again at this point because the one type of dismissal that is clear and definite is by the voters at a general election. Though in this sense the voters also appoint a Prime Minister, the last chapter explained how the parties operate to reduce the choice to workable dimensions and thus a potential Prime Minister has two hurdles (or one in the case of a party in office) to clear, the preliminary selection and then the election.

So the question arises, can a Prime Minister be dismissed by the preliminary selectors, the MPs in his party, changing their minds and —a rather different issue—can a party leader who is not yet a Prime Minister but merely Leader of the Opposition be removed and replaced? There is a difference of emphasis both between the parties and between the strengths of Leaders of the Opposition and of Prime Ministers.

1. Strength of a Labour leader

The Labour party has never dismissed a leader in either capacity since 1922, though George Lansbury did decide to resign after the attacks made on him at the 1935 Labour Party Conference. Ramsay MacDonald never faced a serious challenge and in 1931 he left the Labour party of his own volition. Since 1945 there have been attempts to remove all three of the leaders, Mr Attlee in 1947, Mr Wilson in 1969, and Mr Gaitskell in 1960 while he was Leader of the Opposition.

The last episode was somewhat different because the Leader of the Opposition does not have the power and patronage that are available to the Prime Minister. Both the strength of party loyalty and the support for the leader as a potential Prime Minister will depend on the estimate, particularly among his fellow MPs, as to whether he looks like being able to win the next general election. As a party draws close to an election or if the party and its leader are ahead in the opinion polls, MPs' support naturally becomes more and more positive. On the other hand, in opposition, there is machinery through which a challenge can be mounted since in the Labour party there is a formal annual re-election of the leader and all that is needed is a rival candidate. Moreover, the opponents of the existing leader will not come forward unless they have a candidate ready to accept nomination so that such challenges have a proper method of proceeding. In 1960 Mr Wilson was the challenger and scored 81 to Mr Gaitskell's 166 votes. Mr Wilson and his backers stood on two issues. The major source of his strength was the Left who regarded Mr Wilson as a genuine socialist and as either opposed to or more flexible about defence policy where Mr Gaitskell was emphasising membership of NATO and the need for a nuclear deterrent. The other point, accepted by some who were not of the Left, was that Mr Gaitskell could never unite the Labour party because of his tendency to decide what was best, to say so, push the matter to a vote and then insist on observance of the policy laid down in this way by the Parliamentary Committee (the Shadow Cabinet). It was argued that a federal party of diverse views simply could not be led in this way in opposition and while the members would gather round and show adequate loyalty to a Labour Cabinet when in power, this type of unity and single-mindedness was not necessary, not feasible and therefore not to be sought after in opposition. There was something in this point both in terms of the correct tactics in opposition and of the suggestion that the Labour party is easiest to lead if the lines of division between left- and right-wing policies can be blurred rather than sharpened. Probably because he could provide this more flexible approach, Mr Wilson obtained more votes than those of the left wing alone, but not enough to defeat Mr Gaitskell. The latter had the backing of party loyalty, much trade union support and strong support from the more right-wing members of the party who may have agreed with him on defence, or who had always been anti-left (anti-Bevanite), who liked his style of facing the issues and deciding on the principles involved, or who wanted to move the Labour party towards a more modern form of Social Democracy. Although this contest excited tremendous bitterness, the machinery available meant that it was 'above-board' and it was about a crucial issue—the content of policy and style of leadership that was suitable for the Labour party.

Attempts to remove a sitting Prime Minister are different in that there is no machinery readily available. Labour backbenchers could ask the Liaison Committee (which organises Parliamentary Labour Party meetings) to accept a motion of no confidence in the leader which would have to be debated and voted on by open show of hands on the following Wednesday. The Prime Minister has effective ways of combating such a move, by holding a snap meeting, by rallying the hundred ministers who must vote for him (meaning that his opponents must get at least seven-tenths of the remaining members to vote against) and by raising all the forces of party loyalty and fears of an electoral débâcle which would return the Conservatives to power. Thus this method, by itself, is almost impossible. For it to work, some senior Cabinet Ministers must agree on an alternative candidate and join in the move to oust the Prime Minister. All this is described as 'plotting' and, though in theory the quality of the leadership is the most legitimate concern of all for backbenchers, there is a sense in which such activity is subversive in form. It has to be conducted largely in secret to avoid counter moves, it is an attempt to deprive a man of his office, it could be interpreted (and is so interpreted by the Prime Minister's entourage) as an 'anti-party' move, it has to combat the normal inclinations of the party loyalists and lastly the Prime Minister has considerable powers of retribution against those who try and fail.

An attempt was made to unseat Mr Attlee in September 1947, when the Labour Government's popularity had slumped and there had been administrative errors, including a fuel shortage. Sir Stafford Cripps sought to persuade the Prime Minister to stand down in favour of Ernest Bevin but the move was halted by Ernest Bevin who dismissed the idea with scorn. During the lifetime of the 1966 Labour Government, Mr Wilson suspected a number of plots to remove him, starting at the time of the sterling crisis of July 1966, reviving when Mr Ray Gunter resigned in mid-1968 and reaching a climax in March and April of 1969. The course of this last (the only serious attempt) to remove Mr Wilson has already been described, but the problems facing his critics on the back benches merit a little further examination. In the first place, no such effort would have been made in 1969 had Mr Wilson not created a situation which produced a temporary alliance of forces against him. By deciding to support

Mrs Castle, the Minister of Employment and Productivity, in producing and carrying an Industrial Relations Bill which imposed sanctions on unofficial strikers, he antagonised his former associates on the left of the Labour party and at the same time upset the traditional loyalists in the trade union group. These defections left him exposed to the longer-term critics in the centre and right wing of the party who disliked his style of leadership and who blamed him for refusing to devalue and for holding on east of Suez until the 1967 sterling crisis forced his hand on both points. But the problems faced by those who wanted a change were almost insuperable. It was extremely difficult to raise the issue at a meeting of the Parliamentary Labour Party since only a limited number of MPs were prepared to sign a critical motion, while Mr Douglas Houghton, the Chairman of the Parliamentary Labour Party, said he would not put such a motion to a meeting of the party unless it had 120 signatures—that is unless the outcome of the vote was a foregone conclusion. Mr Houghton was far more interested in stopping the Industrial Relations Bill and he felt that the leadership issue could be considered afterwards. In any case, he was not prepared to act until enough backbenchers were ready to stand up and be counted. (And an open show of hands would have been necessary, as the provision for a secret ballot only applies when the party is choosing a new leader.) Mr Houghton also knew that the Prime Minister would cling to his office and use every resource open to him.

Part of the problem for Mr Wilson's critics was that there was no agreed alternative candidate. Some trade unionists and older members preferred Mr Callaghan, but he was unacceptable both to the left and the 'radical right' of the party. Mr Jenkins had a considerable body of support among this latter group but was suspect among the left and among the older, more working-class members, while Mrs Castle had excluded herself by her sponsorship of the Industrial Relations Bill. Nor was this situation fortuitous, for Mr Wilson had so arranged his reshuffles of senior ministers as to ensure that there was no 'crown prince'. He had wanted to keep Mr Jenkins out of the Treasury in November 1967 (preferring Mr Crosland) precisely because Mr Jenkins was a potential threat, but this proved to be the only change that was feasible since Mr Callaghan, who had to be moved from the Treasury, would only accept the Home Office (the post held by Mr Jenkins). Mr Wilson had appointed Mr Stewart to the Foreign Office because he was no challenge to the Prime Minister and kept the more charismatic Mr Denis Healey permanently at Defence since this office never endears its holder to

Labour MPs. At the time of the Industrial Relations Bill crisis, the attitudes of the leading ministers were that Mrs Castle was identified with the much-hated Bill, Mr Jenkins gave her his usual support (in return for her steady backing of his economic policy), Mr Healey agreed with the Bill and while Mr Crossman had his doubts, he preferred a short, quick Bill to a long drawn-out contest lasting until the autumn. And all, at this stage, were agreed that Mr Callaghan, who was the only senior minister who both opposed the Bill and had let his views be known, was less desirable than Mr Wilson.

The backbench discussions about changing the leadership certainly worried the Prime Minister but he realised that the revolt was not serious so long as there was no acceptable alternative candidate for his position and no move among his Cabinet colleagues. Also the Prime Minister knew that the moment he could escape from the impasse in which he was caught, he would be free from danger. But before realising the depth of the crisis, and attracted by his conviction that trade union reform was both desirable and desired by the electorate, he had made statements of purpose which made it hard to go back. At the same time, to go forward would mean riding rough-shod over the TUC, straining the forces of party loyalty to the utmost, and thus creating the situation in which attempts to remove him had some faint chance of success. At the last moment. Mr Wilson realised that this was the more dangerous alternative and when senior Cabinet ministers came round to the views of the back-bench critics (see above pp. 78–9), he reached a face-saving settlement with the TUC, the critics collapsing immediately as a wave of relief swept the party. The entire crisis supports the view that a Labour Prime Minister who is physically fit and wants to retain office disposes of sufficient power to prevent any effective challenge to his position.

2. Strength of a Conservative leader

In the case of the Conservative party, the position of the leader is almost identical, although a Conservative Prime Minister is in an even stronger position than his Labour counterpart, while a Conservative Leader of the Opposition is slightly weaker. The reason for the difference is that the Conservatives are accustomed to being in power and regard it as only natural and proper. They therefore tend to be more severe on leaders who have lost power or who do not look like winning back power than the rank and file of Labour MPs, many of whom have no basic objection to being in opposition. Thus the Conservatives have sacked A. J. Balfour in 1911, Austen Chamberlain in 1922, some of them nearly succeeded in removing Baldwin in 1930 and Sir Alec Douglas-Home was part-persuaded, part-urged out of his post in 1965. All these occurred when the Conservatives were in opposition. A further factor is that most Conservative leaders have had both a high sense of loyalty to the party and other sources of activity and satisfaction on which they can fall back. As a result, they have been less tenacious of power once their leadership was widely questioned. The only one who fought for his position was Baldwin and he managed to fend off his critics, aided by the rapid decline of the Labour Government which made his elevation to the Prime Ministership seem fairly imminent. This difference of degree between Labour and Conservative leaders of the opposition may have ended with Mr Heath because he is the first of a newer type of Tory leader whose chief interest, as with Labour leaders, is in politics and he showed no signs of standing down when he was subjected to severe pressure in 1967 and 1968. Also Mr Heath was the first elected leader and the Conservative party, like the Labour party, adopted a procedure for this purpose but did not adopt machinery for removing a leader. This manoeuvre has therefore probably become as difficult for the Conservatives as it is for the Labour party.

Once in office, Conservative Prime Ministers show the full degree of power and security that has been described in the case of Labour Prime Ministers. There were no attempts to remove Baldwin or Neville Chamberlain before the last crisis. Mr Churchill was criticised for staying on when his health and strength seemed to be declining in early 1955 but very few of his colleagues were prepared even to mention the matter to him. Sir Anthony Eden, on the other hand, was widely and openly criticised soon after he became Premier, particularly in the columns of the *Daily Telegraph*. Before this challenge became serious, there were the disastrous events of the invasion and withdrawal from Suez. Eden was widely criticised for his general nervousness and interference in departments, for his serious misjudgments and lack of candour, and for both going into Suez and for calling a cease-fire. He returned from sick leave in December 1956 and resigned in January 1957. However, there is no evidence that his colleagues or his party wanted him to leave at that moment. The Conservative party had suffered a terrible blow to its morale and wanted to hang together. Any immediate repudiation either of the Prime Minister or of the Foreign Secretary, Mr Selwyn Lloyd, would have seemed like a confession of error. Sir Anthony actually resigned because his doctors told him he could not carry on.

The other case in which it has been suggested that a Conservative Prime Minister was edged out was that of Mr Macmillan in 1963. In the second edition of his *British Political Parties*, Professor Robert McKenzie has said that this 'is perhaps a marginal case, but [Mr Macmillan] is nonetheless a serious candidate for the list of Conservative leaders who have, in effect, been forced out of office'. The facts are that the Government's and the Prime Minister's credit had both declined seriously in 1962 and in early 1963 Mr Macmillan had to repudiate suggestions that he was going to retire. Some Conservatives felt he had handled the Profumo scandal badly, others that he was too old and that he was by then associated with an old-fashioned approach and a certain lack of success. In October 1963, hit by a prostatic obstruction which required an operation, he resigned. But before his illness, he had offered to go if this was thought to be in the best interests of the party and he actually left the Cabinet Room so that his colleagues could discuss the situation more freely. When he had left, no one moved against him and all the members departed assuming that he would remain as leader, though one saw illness in his face and doubted if his health would last. What drove Mr Macmillan to announce his resignation was the view, later proved wrong, that his prostate trouble was malignant and that he would be weakened and incapacitated either for a very long time or permanently.

Thus the only Conservative Prime Minister to be rejected by his party while in office in this century has been Neville Chamberlain in May 1940. This was at a time of national disaster, in a war, with defeat staring the country in the face when Neville Chamberlain's cautious, doctrinaire and almost half-hearted leadership seemed to epitomise the nation's inadequate response to the German challenge. Yet even then, the Government's majority was still 81 (33 Conservatives voting against and some 60 abstaining) and both Mr Chamberlain and Mr Churchill thought at first that Chamberlain could carry on but as the leader of a national or coalition government. It was the Labour party's refusal to serve under Chamberlain which killed this idea and, once it was realised that there would have to be a new Prime Minister, Churchill soon emerged as the only possible candidate. (Chamberlain for a moment toyed with the idea of Halifax as Prime Minister but he was not the man for the occasion, he was in the House of Lords and himself refused to contemplate the idea.) The Conservative party elected Churchill as their leader but only after he had been appointed as Prime Minister.

So it can be seen that the Prime Minister has a very strong position and while this can become even stronger when he is successful and looks like remaining in office for a long time, much of his power and invulnerability remains even during periods of political adversity. The forces of party loyalty, control of patronage and the support of the governmental machine remain intact except in the most unusual situations and even then, a Prime Minister has great resources with which to alter, evade or surmount these unusual dangers. It is true that the office is a lonely one, that few speak to the Premier with complete candour and that holders of the office have tended to worry, to overwork and to tire themselves out. Under these circumstances, and particularly with certain types of personality, Premiers may suspect plots and fear cabals but the objective powers of the office remain. By the time a politician reaches the premiership, he is usually well aware of how to use them.

D

9

THE LEADERSHIP AND ITS RELATIONS WITH THE ELECTORATE; THE STATE AND THE CITIZEN

1. Politicians and the public

The assumptions which underlay the Westminster Model were that the politicians had beliefs and known methods of handling problems, perhaps even a list of policies, and that the electorate had its views, the voters picking those leaders whom they regarded as being most appropriate for the time. The rejected party might change its mind or the situation might alter, the government might fail or the voters might decide on another approach by the time of the next general election. But the democratic process was an interaction between the leadership and the led in which Parliament played the vital roles of explaining the issues to the people and of reflecting the electorate's views on government policies with the constant possibility that Parliament could go on to intervene and alter these policies or remove the government.

Now Parliament plays a much diminished part (discussed in Chapter 10) and since the government knows it will remain in office till the Prime Minister chooses to call the next election, the relationship is a much more direct, if rather muddled one, between the leadership and the voters. Also the old view of two relatively independent sets of opinions reacting on each other is over-simplified. Now the politicians in part tackle the problems on their merits and in part try to pick up the prevailing mood of the electorate. At the same time, the advocacy of the party leaders helps create the climate of opinion and the standards by which the politicians are themselves judged. Thus the Labour leadership, and Mr Wilson in particular, spotted the public's impatience with the rate of improvement in living standards and with many of the discomforts and old-fashioned methods prevalent in Britain in the early 1960s. The Labour party's appeal was adjusted as far as possible, given the long-term nature of political attitudes, to this mood, but the achievement of rapid growth then became the yardstick against which Mr Wilson's administration was measured. In the run-up to the election which took place in June 1970, it was clear that the public's frame of mind was different. There was disappointment that the expectations raised by the Labour party had not been fulfilled. In part, this led to scepticism about the possibility of sustained and rapid growth and in part it encouraged concentration on rather different issues. There was irritation about the rate of inflation, about high taxation, alleged spongers on the social services and worries about the increased level of crimes of violence. The Conservatives reacted to this mood, which suited them, by framing and stressing policies on these issues while the Labour party and, in particular, Mr Wilson responded by fighting a totally negative campaign. When the election due in 1974 or 1975 comes, the Conservatives will be judged by the expectations they raised of slower but reasonable progress against a background of greater economic and social stability. It is dangerous for a political system if the parties in turn fail to achieve the targets they have set for themselves.

It is clear that some of the targets parties set are very hard to achieve, especially in a single five-year term, yet it might be thought that if a party promises to cut taxation, it should be able to redeem this promise. But it is quite possible for politicians to encourage attitudes and expectations which are mutually incompatible. Thus the public have come to expect a certain standard of comfort in hospitals or a certain level of support if they are unemployed and parents expect that children who achieve a certain scholastic standard will be able to enter a university. Yet these standards require public expenditure and party propaganda may create a situation in which the voters expect both improved services and tax reductions. The unfortunate aspect is that if one side of the equation has to be sacrificed, the disappointment is far greater or of more political significance than the pleasure felt at the achievement of the other side. A further unrealistic attitude which both political leaders and the public encourage with equal enthusiasm is an exaggerated notion of what any government can achieve. Thus if anything unfortunate happens, the public will blame the government and the politicians are usually ready to assume responsibility or at least to allow the opposition to blame the government. This is bad for public confidence in the system since there are, in fact, many things about which a government can do nothing. One reason for the confidence felt in the late Victorian system was that voters had been carefully indoctrinated with the view that large parts of the nation's life were outside the competence of the government. It was accepted that booms and slumps, public mores, prices and so on were settled by forces outside the political arena. Thus when politicians said they would or would not give Ireland Home Rule, provide free elementary education, or end church rates, they could do as they had promised. It is possible, with the present relations between government and the governed, not merely that the former tries to do too much and that the latter expect too much but that because of these exaggerated expectations, faith in the system is being undermined. This may explain why, at a time when the tasks of government are set so wide, the public's enthusiasm for democracy is less positive.

2. Contact through the parties

The connections between the leadership and the electors are multiple and by no means clear. In practical terms, the political views of the voters are channelled into forms which permit the choice of a Prime Minister by the party system and the parties do provide a steady means of contact. They constantly explain the policies of the two front benches to the public. All the time, the parties are spreading news and propaganda about the nation's affairs and the attitudes of their leaders among the electorate. Because the parties also select local political officials (constituency chairmen, secretaries, agents), find and run candidates in local government elections and have a certain amount of patronage on local administrative agencies at their disposal, they create a field force which projects the party in the constituencies, though most of this reaches only the party faithful. The broader public contacts political leaders and receives its information through less committed channels.

The counter-flow up from the party activists is harder to assess but it is clearly more significant when a party is in opposition. Then the politicians have no official sources and advisers and the pressure groups, though interested in potential leaders, clearly spend most of their time on those in power. The party contacts are partly through MPs, partly through full-time officials and partly through the range of activist meetings of which the chief is the annual conference. The most important connection is the series of consultations by which an opposition tests the mood of its rank and file and accepts some of this in framing its programme for the coming election. Thus before 1970 the Conservatives conducted elaborate polls, set up working parties and brought in sympathisers from all walks of life to help them prepare their various policies. In general, party leaders respond to the tone and specific complaints put to them by their main supporters and by MPs and they get a strong impression of the mood of these supporters at regional conferences, women's conferences, youth meetings and, in particular, at the annual conference. Though specific points or instructions are not usually made or accepted, all this serves to show where the shoe is pinching and has its effect.

3. Contacts through officials and pressure groups

When a party is in power, its own machine diminishes rapidly in importance as the Prime Minister at once acquires a much larger and more expert body of advisers, that is the Civil Service. By far the best-documented stream of information reaching ministers about public reactions comes from their field force, the officials handling the application of policies to actual situations. For example, it is the large and highly skilled group of officials engaged in research, advisory and administrative services which tells the Minister of Agriculture just how the farmers are faring, while similar groups warn the Minister of Education of impending staff shortages and of the response to new projects in further education and alert the Minister of Trade and Industry about impending mergers, closures or developments in industry. This method of contact has tended to be overlooked by commentators because it is compartmentalised and specialised by function but it is the main way in which a government finds out whether its policies are working and decides what needs to be done next.

One difficulty is that the Civil Service, understandably, like to be certain about public reactions to the policies they are applying or intend to introduce and for this they turn to the representatives chosen by the various interests. The most extreme case is in agriculture where the 1947 Act obliges the government to consult each year with the leaders of the producers' organisations, that is the farmers' unions. It is easy to appreciate that if such bodies exist (and they cover most producer but few consumer interests), it is much easier for civil servants to deal with them than attempt to form an opinion about how all the doctors, farmers, companies making paper or local authorities will react. The element of difficulty or obscurity comes from the fact that it is not always clear that the leaders of these pressure groups do accurately represent their members' views. If these leaders have to be re-elected at intervals, they may also have a political game to play within their organisations and they may have to appear more moderate or extremist than the average of the people they represent. The pressure group leaders may simply not know what their members feel or they may wish to use their position to press their own views. Extreme examples are the way the larger trade unions move from the right to the left of the Labour party, or vice versa, depending not on swings of opinion among their members but on the views of the general secretary of the day. At times there are clear indications that a gap exists as when the farmers took to demonstrations in 1970 in part because they considered the leadership of the National Farmers' Union was too moderate or too much in cahoots with the Government. The author recalls a minister defending a policy on the grounds that all the members of the major pressure group concerned wanted it and when, meeting the secretary of the pressure group on a later occasion this was mentioned, the official said, 'My members want it! I have never asked them and I would have an awful job putting this policy across if I did' but it was true that he felt that the Government was on the right lines and had said so.

Such divisions inside pressure groups cannot be carried too far. Ministries are successful in as much as their policies yield the desired results and if the pressure groups are wrong in their estimates of reactions and if the result is that policies misfire, the pressure groups or their leaders will soon be discredited. There has to be a certain relationship between the minister, his department, what it wishes to achieve, the outside bodies that have to be dealt with and the general public, because if any one of them gets too far out of line, the actual operation of the policy or the service begins to falter and this soon becomes evident. But the effect of relying on this institutionalised method of gauging public reactions, is that it places too much emphasis on those groups or sectors of opinion that can readily be organised. The author once obtained permission to study the preparation and passage of a piece of minor legislation, a Bill dealing with the fishing industry. In order to find out the reactions of those involved, to estimate what would be the best solution to the problems of the industry, the officials had carefully consulted all the interests involved. It had taken a period of nearly two years to meet the owners of the trawlers (through their Federation), to talk to the fishermen's representatives, the port authorities, the marketing and transport concerns, the retailers and some large firms involved in canning and processing the fish. As a subsidy was called for, the Treasury were involved and when they insisted on a lower rate than the Ministry had indicated, there had to be a second round of consultations. The officials were a little taken aback when it was pointed out that two key groups had not been consulted—the public in the form of consumers and in the form of the subsidy-providers or tax-payers. Yet the civil servants could scarcely be blamed for there is no fish-eaters' union or anti-fish subsidy league to talk to. In traditional political theory, this is the task of Parliament, but the House of Commons was, as with most legislation, presented with the final negotiated product so that these general interests were never specifically considered. Normally this is not necessary, as it can be assumed that the public want plenty of cheap fish, but as the government expands its activities and plays a larger part in people's lives, the sense that they are not being considered has spread among the public. Moreover, this can lead to administrative errors which at best cause irritation and at worst explosions of anger. An example of the kind of reaction which an elected representative of the public might detect or foresee which would possibly escape a civil servant occurred in the last war. Then, at the worst stage of the submarine war, the most critical shortage was of shipping space. A division of the Board of Trade calculated that the total consumption of toilet paper required two shiploads of wood pulp per year, that more than one newspaper per family was sold and that if the Government announced that for the duration of the war no more toilet paper was to be made but people could use old newspapers, two ships would be released to take supplies to the army in the Western Desert. Such a proposal reached the Cabinet and was torn up by Mr Churchill who said the shipping space saved would not be worth the blow to morale that would be caused.

4. Opinion polls

These generalised or unorganised responses of the public which ought to be channelled through Parliament, now reach the leadership in a variety of ways, the chief ones being public opinion polls, by-election results, the mass media and politicians' hunches formed as a result of their own experiences and contact, while the atmosphere in the House of Commons plays a relatively small part. (It is curious how the House tends to make MPs Westminster-oriented and cuts them off, to some extent, from the moods and reactions of the mass of the non-political public.) Probably the most influential of these sources of opinion is the regular polls provided by such organisations as Gallup and National Opinion Polls, though there was some scepticism after all the polls except one predicted a Labour victory in 1970. Nevertheless, politicians have become fairly sophisticated in their interpretation of this material. They look chiefly at the overall party ratings, but also at the response to individual proposals. It is appreciated that the standing of a party is not necessarily affected by its attitude on single issues and that some issues have much more effect in forming or altering party support than others. A party can be associated with an unpopular policy much more easily if the other party is in agreement or if the issue does not link up with existing patterns of political belief. However, it is possible to observe political leaders following public opinion on specific issues. For instance, in 1970 in the lead up to the general election, both parties were committed to seek entry to the Common Market but found that this was an unpopular policy, so that each tried to suggest that it would take a tougher line in seeking 'adequate safeguards' for Britain. Similarly, when law and order became an issue, though several leading Conservatives, including Mr Heath, voted for the abolition of capital punishment, every effort was made to try and identify Labour as the abolitionist party, the Conservatives attacking the timing of the decision to end hanging and alleged 'softness' on other aspects of punishment for this purpose. In 1972–3 it seemed clear that a main issue in the next election would be inflation and both parties were working hard to blame the other for the rapid rise in the cost of living. Labour blamed the Conservatives because they were the government, because they had put up rents and some other charges and they tried to establish a connection between price rises and membership of the Common Market. The Conservatives blamed wage increases, pointed to the trade unions and their share in determining Labour policy and argued that price rises would be worse under Labour.

Broadly politicians have sensed that, as Butler and Stokes have demonstrated (op. cit. p. 53 above), certain reactions among the public are central to changes in party allegiance, the chief ones being the overall impression as to whether the government is or is not competent in running the economy and the reactions revealed by replies to the question 'Are you better off than you were this time last year?'. The politicians also appreciate the 'salience' (to use Butler and Stokes' word) of certain issues; the deep dislike of trade union methods, hostility to layabouts, dislike of high taxation, desire to repress hippy or student agitators, worries about coloured immigration and so on. The effect is not to produce a subservience to gusts of public feeling (the extremes of racial feeling in 1964 and 1967–8 were resisted and tended to dampen down in time) but to force the Prime Minister to think continually about the degree of economic success his government is achieving and about how far it can afford to alienate voters, leading to some changes of electoral behaviour at the margin, for example by avoiding emphasis on matters where his view and that of his party is unpopular on a 'salient' issue.

5. By-elections

By-election results similarly require discriminating interpretation but this is well understood by any Prime Minister. While by-elections appear to be simply a reaction to the overall record of the government, they can become attached to one particular issue and can have a definite influence in this way. It was the shock Mr Baldwin received when a 7000 Conservative majority was overturned at East Fulham in late 1933 that led him to fear any public association of the Conservative party and rearmament. Referring to this in November 1936, he said:

Supposing I had gone to the country and said that Germany was rearming, and that we must rearm, does anybody think that this pacific democracy would have rallied to that cry at that moment? I cannot think of anything that would have made the loss of the election from my point of view more certain.

More recently, it was successes of Welsh and Scottish National candidates at by-elections in 1966 and 1967 that forced this issue into prominence and led the Conservatives to appoint a Commission under Sir Alec Douglas-Home to examine the case for a Scottish Assembly and the Labour Government to appoint a Royal Commission under Lord Crowther (when he died, under Lord Kilbrandon) to consider devolution for the whole country. More usually, by-elections are taken as indicators of public reaction to the overall record of the government though it is realised that the results tend to be less favourable to the government than is likely at the subsequent general election. But, for this reason, a governing party that improves its position at a by-election is riding high and it was just such a success in January 1966 at North Hull that led Mr Wilson to decide to hold a general election two months later. Because of the effect on party morale and on public estimation of the government, party managers try to time the holding of by-elections for periods when they hope the political situation will be favourable. As a result, when the 1966–70 Labour Government faced considerable unpopularity, by-elections tended to come in batches as a number accumulated while the Whips (responsible for the timing) waited in the hope that the political situation would improve. But when a batch of vacancies could not be held up any longer and four or five by-elections were held on the same day, the impact became even greater as such a spread of elections provides a much better picture of opinion throughout the country.

6. *The press and television*

The impact of the mass media, of newspapers and television, is not so clear cut but none the less is important. Politicians often become familiar with the press and with journalists and become accustomed to their methods. They know that it is the unusual that is news and that there are fashions in journalism, that journalists are not necessarily more closely in touch with the public than politicians and that too much importance and influence need not be attributed to editorial opinion. Yet Prime Ministers know that if they are doing well, part of this will be reflected and intensified by a favourable press and that when they are doing badly, the position will be made worse by generally hostile treatment. Thus the press cannot, of itself, create a mood in the country but it acts as an accelerator and intensifier of feelings that are spreading for more objective reasons. When Mr Macmillan's policies were succeeding he was dubbed 'Wondermac' and 'Supermac' by the cartoonist Vicky and this tone permeated the press. When Mr Wilson had held the fort for eighteen months on an unbelievably slender majority, *The Economist* called him 'Britain's clever little man' and said that the 1966 election was a simple issue, 'Were you, or were you not for Mr Wilson?'. Equally both leaders received severe treatment when their leadership encountered difficulties. Mr Heath has always had a more neutral treatment by the press largely because they (and the public) cannot easily grasp or characterise his personality and they are left to concentrate on his policies. Over-emphasis on the qualities of a Prime Minister by the media is, perhaps, understandable though moves from excessive praise to serious condemnation may puzzle the public when the man has changed very little but the policies of his government have run into a bad patch.

For a leader, attacks by some of the press are more indicative of public feeling or at least sound a greater note of danger than others. For the traditionally conservative *Daily Telegraph* to attack a

Labour leader does him little or no harm but for the *Daily Mirror* to do so is most serious. It indicates that a paper which prides itself on being close to the people, and to pro-Labour people at that, detects a groundswell so strong that it feels it must register a protest. On the Conservative side it is similarly criticism from papers that normally aim to express conservative views that indicates something is wrong. It was the Northcliffe Press that turned on Baldwin in 1930 and made his life so difficult, while attacks on Sir Anthony Eden in the *Daily Telegraph* in early 1956 came from such a pillar of the Conservative establishment that the Prime Minister felt it necessary to issue a statement saying he did not intend to resign. Suggestions that a Conservative leader should resign would have little effect in Liberal or anti-Conservative papers such as the *Guardian* and the *Observer* but when a former Conservative candidate, Mr William Rees-Mogg (later the Editor of *The Times*), wrote a feature in the pro-Conservative *Sunday Times*, 'Why Home Must Go', this appears to have been a major factor in making Sir Alec Douglas-Home decide to resign.

Television is less opinionated and a better medium simply for conveying information back and forth between the leadership and the public. The BBC and the ITV companies are by law obliged to give each party a fair share of political time and overall fairness can be enforced by the fact that the Prime Minister appoints the Chairmen and controlling boards in each case. This does not prevent disputes. Mr Wilson became convinced, during the 1966 election and in 1967–9, that the BBC was hostile to him, feeling that he was not treated with proper respect and that the questioning in interview programmes he took part in was too hostile. Some of his staff went so far as to attribute the Labour defeat in 1970 to the BBC but this showed an element of obsession and a gross over-estimate of the effect of television. On the other side, at certain periods in 1963 nad 1964, both Mr Macmillan and Sir Alec-Douglas Home were mercilessly pilloried in satire and current affairs programmes and Mr Heath was often hard pressed by questioners during his difficult period as a leader who had not won an election and was trailing behind his party in the popularity ratings. Prime Ministers can retaliate in these cases. For many newspaper men, the report that they are out of favour in No. 10 Downing Street, the source of so many good stories, may cause serious alarm. A phone call to an editor from No. 10 complaining about an article or a news story tends to produce a reprimand for the journalist rather than a rude rejoinder. A Prime Minister or Cabinet Minister who storms out of a BBC or ITV programme or who writes to say he will never be interviewed by Mr X again causes consternation among the television authorities. Yet all in all, television is a medium which has greatly reduced the effect of politically biased journalism because the BBC and the ITV are bound to give both sides fair coverage. The constant exposure of politicians to viewers who support another party or no party, does show the public that these men are not unreasonable, that they have a case that can be stated and such evidence does make denunciations of political opponents as total blackguards much less plausible. It is interesting that in this process of direct communication between the politicians and the public, between the leaders and the led, Parliament could have acted as a medium and played a major part by having its proceedings televised, but for reasons which will be discussed in the next chapter, it refused to do so.

7. Personal contacts

The final line of communication between the Prime Minister, his colleagues on the front bench and the public is personal contacts and impressions. By the time most political leaders have been in public life for twenty years, they believe they have some idea of what is acceptable to the electorate. This may be a hunch, or simply a reliance on the views of specific persons. Asked why he had George Tomlinson in his Cabinet, Mr Attlee said that if he was puzzled about a problem, he used to turn to George. And if Mr Tomlinson said 'it sounds all right as you put it, but I have tried it on my wife and she won't wear it', he always concluded that the vast majority in Lancashire would not wear it. Some political leaders rely on their agents, others sniff the atmosphere at meetings or in their constituencies. Few fail to form some impression of how a policy is being received and such perceptions do play a part in their attitudes to proposals put before them. And there is usually a fairly rapid check on the accuracy of their perceptions in the form of by-elections and opinion polls, all of which serve to remind politicians that a general election is never more than four and a half years off.

Put together, all these contacts give a picture of how political leaders and the public react to each other. It is a remote kind of contact because the leaders are obsessed with politics and power while the public are only remotely interested. Most citizens would rather not have to concern themselves with any political issues and if they have to react in any very positive way, this is usually a sign of failure on the part of the politicians.

8. The public's reactions to politics

The reasons for changes in the public's attitudes are complex and hard to analyse but it is evident that after a period of time, the public's mood alters. Only rarely in Britain does the public demand radical reforms. At the time of the 1959 general election, there was a mood of gratitude, of relief that living standards were rising. Coinciding with the 1964 and 1966 elections, the atmosphere was one of moderate restiveness, of disappointment that living stand-ards had not risen faster and a feeling that Britain had missed several boats and needed to be brought up to date. By 1970 the prevailing sentiments had moved to the right, against the concept of widespread provision of welfare, against high taxation for the good of others and in favour of a tougher application of the law in all forms. The party leaders in part form and in part react to these moods. By their previous campaigns, they create expectations. By their successes and failures they fulfil or disappoint these hopes and by their propaganda they try to convince the public that the other party is responsible for whatever is unsatisfactory in the current situation. As the public's mood shifts, so both parties adjust and move in the same direction, though usually the traditional view of a particular party makes it easier or less easy for it to fall in with certain changes of mood. Thus in 1963–6, the Conservatives be-came regional planners and talked about growth and modernisation of industry but these arguments came more naturally to the Labour party and it benefited most from this trend in thinking. In the late 1960s, the Labour party was pushed into emphasising the restrictions it had imposed on coloured immigration, its efforts to clamp down on 'scrounging', and its interest in reducing direct taxation, but all these arguments seemed more appropriate in the mouths of Conservatives and they gained most support from the emphasis on these issues.

As Henry Fairlie has put it in his book, *The Life of Politics*, the parties are like buses which move along and if they miss the public at one stop, if everyone has boarded the other bus, they drive on with new paint and advertisements hoping in time to arrive at a stop where the public are still waiting and find the rival bus a less attractive conveyance.

In this interaction, it may appear as if the public are largely passive, acted upon by the political leaders. While there is some truth in this, the electorate can retaliate and alter the context in which decisions are taken and the reaction of the rank and file, either spontaneously or through their organisations, can have a great effect on the success or failure of government policies. In some cases the possible reactions are obvious—voting for the other party, registering a protest by voting for third-party candidates or not voting at all. But it is also possible collectively to refuse to accept a government policy. For instance, the experience of the Labour Government's Prices and Incomes Policy between 1966 and 1969 was that unless there is a total statutory prohibition on all increases, attempts to hold down wage increases cannot do more than damp down rises by about 1 per cent a year on average. It was slowly appreciated that attempts to hold back personal consumption as severely as the 1968 Budget intended, are simply defeated by wage demands and inflation. There are some situations which are widely regarded as unacceptable or as signs of governmental failure. For instance, in 1972, the unemployment level reached one million and this was widely held to be intolerable and led to almost panic reversals of government policy on public expenditure and subsidies for industry in order to create more employment.

There are a number of dilemmas along these lines faced by every government. Perhaps the best example is that the public want faster growth and this means more investment which, with a growth rate of 3–5 per cent, usually involves certain restraints on consumption and yet the public can also refuse this restriction on consumption. In this sense the country could become ungovernable with the political leadership increasingly discredited because it cannot, to put it crudely, provide the university places, new hospitals and houses which the voters want as well as the tax cuts or wage increases which are demanded at the same time.

9. Direct action

A more specific form of spontaneous reaction is the strike, sit-in, demonstration or non-cooperation which began to be used increasingly in the late 1960s. Strikes, even with political motives, are an accepted feature of industrial society, but with the growth of interlocking industries, elaborate transport systems and an intensely competitive situation in foreign trade, strikes can rapidly draw in the government and can be used to break its wages and industrial policies or simply to step outside the normal bargaining procedures. New groups entering upon these procedures, such as nurses and teachers, have served to indicate declining confidence in the normal machinery for adjusting disputes. Farmers followed suit in early 1970, trying to get a better price review by disrupting traffic and pelting ministers while students had, for several years, been seeking to indicate their desire for more democracy within the universities by occupying university buildings and by protests and demonstrations. While the tough line taken by the Labour Government in its early years showed that the powers of pressure groups and representative bodies such as the FBI, the NFU and the NUT could be resisted, with the decline in the support for and authority of the Government and the approach of the 1970 general election, there was evidence of a capacity to get action by disruption of a spontaneous or rank-and-file kind. One explanation for this conduct was that it did appear to yield results which endless democratic discussion through 'the normal channels' had failed to produce. Another was that these demonstrations, being good visual material, received far greater attention on television and in the press than orderly representations and therefore brought the case of the protester before a far larger audience.

The Conservatives thought, after 1970, that the reaction against strikes and inflation was strong enough to permit them to challenge and defeat a series of trade unions. They succeeded in 1971 but lost to the miners in 1972 who won by preventing movement of fuel and essential supplies in and out of the power stations. There was some public support for the miners and the government learnt that it must pick its battlegrounds and carefully cultivate public opinion. There is little evidence of a general public hostility to the idea of a strike or a sit-in (one was undertaken by 6 MPs in a House of Commons Committee in 1972)—it depends on who is taking such action and for what purpose.

10. Why do people obey the government?

These activities have given some point to a question that in the past has seemed somewhat unrealistic or abstract in Britain, namely why do people obey the government? In the jargon of political science this put in the form of 'what gives a political system its legitimacy?' Clearly if all citizens actively or passively resisted or refused to obey a government its authority would collapse. Since earliest times, systems of authority have put forward reasons why their subjects should respect and obey them. Perhaps the government was that of the father of the tribe or the clan to be obeyed because of filial duty, perhaps power lay with a king to be supported because he was God's anointed vicar on earth or perhaps the system rested simply on long-established custom and awe. When he wrote in the 1860s, Walter Bagehot (in *The English Constitution*) argued that the reason why people accepted the decisions of the government was that they thought it was all the work of Queen Victoria. The monarchy had tremendous traditional respect and reverence from the aristocracy, the middle classes and the illiterate masses. It was a symbolic or dignified government they could all understand. Behind this dignified monarchical front, the real (or 'efficient' in Bagehot's terms) government was free to operate through the Cabinet and the House of Commons.

The implications of Bagehot's thesis was not necessarily that if the people ever did realise how and by whom they were ruled, they would at once treat their political leaders and the institutions of government with scorn. He might have retorted that once education was as widespread among the masses as it was in the ruling 'ten thousand' in 1865, all would be well. The unique virtues of a system of government by open discussion with a delicate balance between executive and legislature would then be appreciated by everyone. But several aspects have changed in the ensuing century. In the first place, the monarchy clearly cannot lend legitimacy to the rest of the machinery of government. It has respect and affection but this is needed to maintain the monarch's own position as a ceremonial head of state. Nowadays certain standards, stricter than those the community expects of its own members, are imposed on the monarchy and while the Crown is generally cheered, when Edward VIII wished to marry a divorcee he had to abdicate, and when the Duke of Edinburgh expresses the mildest of opinions on current affairs the press descends upon him. The monarchy is no longer an institution whose acceptance can cloak or cover all the controversial actions of the government. Indeed the slightest sign of a controversial action on the part of any member of the royal family causes immediate trouble and is hastily disavowed.

Nowadays any legitimacy British government is going to get has to come from its own powers and virtues. The general public today is probably as well educated as the political classes were in Bagehot's period but they lack the same feeling that the government is 'theirs', that it is run by them for a homeland and an Empire which they are privileged to guide and lead. The identification of a small élite with a system which confers great prestige and power upon them as individuals is necessarily different from the attachment of 40 million adults even if they, a hundred years later, are relatively well educated and informed on political matters. This mass electorate has taken the place of the illiterate and awestruck citizenry of Bagehot's day and while the mystique of monarchy has gone, there is the same feeling of being on the receiving end of government, the same feeling that 'they' do things to 'us'. If anything, this is intensified since modern governments tax, regulate, aid and supervise the average citizen so much more than the governments of a hundred years ago. At the same time, the special virtues remarked on by Bagehot have gone. Government by discussion, where a good case wins the day, where strong feelings penetrate Parliament, alter the balance of forces and produce a different result, is no longer in operation. When the electorate now pause and survey the government, they see a massive complex of authorities with no clear sign of public control, with no clear channels by which pressure can be exercised and results achieved. To put one party in power and then, four or five years later, to replace it with another seems to make little difference. Much that affects the individual can be traced to no specific persons or institutions; decisions seem simply to emerge from the machine and local or individual complaints apparently have little effect.

In this situation, the public tend to judge the system by the material results of government. In this they are encouraged by several aspects of modern culture. On the one hand, the entire weight of advertising emphasises that the good life depends on the volume of new consumer goods the individual or the family can purchase. On the other, the politicians encourage people in the belief that they, the governors of the country, are responsible for everything that happens and therefore ought to be able to solve all problems. Very, very seldom does one hear a minister in Parliament in answer to the question 'What have you done about X?' say 'X is none of my business' or 'X is quite outside the area of governmental activity'. If, after this, the results are not as people want, there is no special legitimacy on which the government can fall back. It is obeyed because it is there, because it is backed by the police and the courts and there is little evidence of a special reverence for our democratic system. It is not easy for observant members of the public to point to any facts that demonstrate that the British system is markedly better than those of other more or less democratic countries in other parts of the world though there is still in certain circles a pride in the degree of freedom and tolerance. But there is no special reverence for Parliament and politicians are viewed with a mixture of feelings, a mixture of hope that they can live up to the omnicompetence they claim, of hope that they will provide the leadership any country needs and of contempt if they fall below the targets they have set themselves.

If, then, the question is repeated—'What gives the British system its legitimacy?', the answer is a mixture of satisfaction, tradition and inertia. It is accepted because nothing better offers, because of the residual national pride which fails to see any advantage in foreign methods, because there is no positive motive for change and because the system has provided a fairly steady rise in living standards. The theory that the voters did choose the government and therefore ought to obey it until they have time to choose another has some force, and respect for the institutions does go beyond a willingness to support or put up with the government of the day. There cannot be any denying the truth that if people are not satisfied with what they have got, they can at least participate in throwing the government out at the following election. For those who do not wish the party in question to be out of power, it is comforting to reflect that the amount of past practice which is open to change by a new administration is relatively small. At one time, before the populace were enfranchised, democracy was seen as a method of making sweeping, indeed revolutionary changes in the structure of society. While this was likely, those with property and power resisted an extension of the right to vote. But as Victorian Britain became a little more prosperous and working men had something to lose, they came to accept and, in Bagehot's time, almost to revere the system of government. Then they could be safely admitted 'within the pale of the Constitution'. The parties accepted that commitments by past governments had, by and large, to be honoured and one Cabinet did not try to undo all the work of the last. By the 1970s it is even more true than before that the decisions that can be taken in any five-year period alter only the margins of public policy, though the cumulative effect on the political atmosphere can be considerable. But the result is that the frustration felt by the supporters of a defeated party is quite tolerable.

But it is precisely this position that causes much of the apathy. While few wish to see sweeping changes which would carry the country back into a *laissez-faire* era of the pre-1930s or would impose rigid Marxist patterns of the kind being applied in Eastern Europe, much of the criticism of British politics and politicians springs from disillusionment about the system's capacity to push through any changes, to achieve anything. In the 1960s, each party in turn promised rapid growth in the economy, each party sought to get Britain into the European Common Market, each party attempted to control wages in the interests of safeguarding the balance of payments and of social justice, yet by and large each party failed in these objectives. These failures were serious not only in themselves but because they undermined confidence in the capacity of British

democracy to produce satisfactory results and now it is precisely
by its capacity to produce results that the system is judged.

11. Personal freedom

This may be a little unfair and many Britons who have travelled
abroad have a vague perception that in Britain, personal freedoms
are more secure and individual liberty is more respected than in
many comparable countries. In the United States, a Bill of Rights
was embodied as a group of amendments in the Constitution and
citizens who feel these rights have been violated can seek a remedy
in the courts, even if the threat comes from the United States
Government itself. This method has been followed in many countries
some of which have incorporated a list of freedoms based on the
United Nations Charter of Human Rights in their Constitutions. In
Britain, the opposite method has always been applied. Apart from
principles built upon ancient charters and the restrictions on the
power of the Crown imposed in the years just after 1688, there are no
formal guarantees of liberty, the assumption being that citizens are
free until they encounter limitations placed on them by the need to
avoid damaging the freedoms of other citizens. For instance, freedom
of speech means that an individual can say what he likes provided
he does not defame others. Freedom to enjoy one's property again is
only bounded by the condition that it cannot be used in a manner that
will injure one's neighbour, though public authorities can acquire
an individual's property compulsorily if this can be shown to be
in the public interest. No one can be arrested or detained except
upon a criminal charge and after conviction or for debt or contempt of court or, in certain special circumstances, if the person is a
lunatic, mental defective or infant.

At the same time, this area of freedom depends on the support
of an active public opinion and of a Parliament which is eager to
protect it. Recently there have been restrictions imposed which
have led some observers to argue that British citizens would now be
better off with a written series of rights which could be defended
in court. For instance, the 1968 Commonwealth Immigration Act
denied British passport-holders of Asian descent their right of access
to Britain on the same terms as other British passport-holders. In
introducing this legislation the Government probably had the support
of a majority in the country, though such legislation would almost
certainly have been struck down as contrary to any normal Bill of
Rights by a court with powers of review. The Northern Ireland
Special Powers Act of 1922 gave the Home Secretary of Northern

Ireland authority to detain without trial upon suspicion only which is reminiscent of Section 18b of the Wartime Emergency Powers Acts in Britain, but again this departure from the normal principle of no detention without trial in peacetime would also be contrary to any charter of human rights. A further example was the War Damage Act of 1965 which retrospectively reversed the decision of the House of Lords in the Burmah Oil case. As a last example, there are many local Acts of Parliament which unduly restrict freedom of assembly and speech, one being the Edinburgh Corporation Act which has the force of statute law and makes it illegal to distribute leaflets and pamphlets in the streets of the city. Nor has the public shown any alarm about these developments.

12. The place of the courts

If the courts in Britain were given powers to suspend or invalidate such legislation, it would give them a quite new quasi-political role which they have never exercised, at least since the seventeenth century. In Canada, the courts have acquired some powers of review by the application of the Bill of Rights of 1960 to new legislation and they have been drawn into a confrontation with the executive when they declared legislation which discriminated against Red Indians null and void. But for a British Court to have rejected or invalidated the Commonwealth Immigrants Act of 1968 (the Kenyan Asians Act) would have produced an outcry in a country where the tradition that all power lies with the political leaders who are in control of Parliament has very deep roots. The way parliamentary sovereignty has operated in these cases has led to some questioning of the political system but only by the small minority who are interested in the machinery of government, the quality of public life and the area of freedom open to minorities or special groups.

The courts, it is accepted, deal with criminals and the judges, while sometimes criticised for leniency, have more often tended to fall in line with the popular press's attitudes towards criminals and punishment. In the civil sphere, the vast bulk of the courts' work has been on two themes—divorce and industrial reparation—so that issues between the citizens and the State and the broader issues of personal freedom have not been prominent (in sharp contrast to the era when the judges had to establish their own independence from the Crown). This also explains why the courts and the legal profession have largely been exempt from the calls for change or modernisation and from the accusations of irrelevance or partiality which have been levied at so many of the other aspects of the political system in the 1960s.

13. Public inquiries and administrative tribunals

One area where the courts might have become more involved in critical problems of the relations of the State and the individual is the vast group of cases arising from the development of economic and land-use planning where land has to be acquired and planning permission granted (or withheld). If a dispute arises in such cases, the aggrieved citizen appeals to the minister, but instead of turning to the courts, the latter sets up a public inquiry. The reason for this procedure is that English (and Scots) law has tended to regard the task of the court as determining matters of fact, leaving the judge then to apply the law. But in arguments over what would be the best line for a motorway, where a factory would best be sited and so on, there is not the same clear division between fact and law. The motorway could be built on one of several routes, and there is no law or legal principle which could guide a judge in saying that X route was fairer, would make a better motorway or do less damage to private interests than route Y. For these reasons, it was decided to use the form of a public inquiry but the decision whether to accept the outcome of the inquiry lies with the minister whose department was often a party to the original dispute. The extent of the problem can be measured by the fact that the annual number of planning appeals is about 7000.

There have been objections to this form of proceeding which reached a peak after the Crichel Down case in 1954 when it was revealed not only that officials of the Ministry of Agriculture had behaved inefficiently and unfairly in handling a dispute over the sale of a piece of land, but that the system for handling such disputes had failed to cover this type of case. As a result a Committee on Administrative Tribunals and Enquiries was appointed under Sir Oliver Franks and its Report (Cmd 218) in 1957 set the pattern for the future development of these bodies. It accepted the system but urged more uniformity, careful application of the principles of 'openness, fairness and impartiality', with the right to legal representation, reasoned decisions, a system of appeals and, in the case of inquiries, the publication of the inspector's reports to the minister. The total effect was to make the Civil Service 'Franks-minded' and these principles were, broadly speaking, applied in subsequent years. There have been occasional problems since, such as 'the Chalk pit case', but in 1962, the Government accepted that if new evidence appeared, the minister must give the parties concerned an opportunity to comment on this before he accepts or rejects his inspector's report.

There are many different kinds of administrative decisions in which the public has an interest but where other considerations of cost to taxpayers or side implications on other parts of the community have to be taken into account. It is hard to devise procedures suitable for all the different types of case. One example is the procedure set up by the government for the closure of a railway line under the 1962 Transport Act. This procedure has often caused great heart-burning. It required British Rail to announce an intention to close a line and then evidence could be led to a Transport Users Consultative Committee on the question of hardship and on the planning aspects to the regional planning council. The exasperation was caused by the fact that British Rail was not obliged to explain the economic and financial problems it was facing in running the line, it was not required to try economies or improvements before announcing an intention to close and the minister could still decide to close even if it was agreed that there would be both planning problems and hardship caused.

Simpler considerations of equity apply when the State has either conferred a right or imposed obligations on citizens (for example by granting social security payments or levying a tax) as in these cases it is only fair that the legislature's intention is carried out and that the rules are applied equally and impartially. But here again, these issues have not been left to the courts but have usually been entrusted to special administrative tribunals, boards or hearings. The impact of these bodies on the public is considerable; Rent Tribunals have dealt with as many as 15 000 cases a year and Industrial Injuries and National Insurance Tribunals with 50 000 to 60 000 a year.

But though aimed at a mixture of informality and the rules of fairness that normally apply in a court, when most citizens encounter such bodies and find as their opponents a well-briefed property company lawyer, an employers' representative or a tax inspector, they often feel overawed, puzzled or outsmarted.

So considering the entire system of determining disputes between the individual and the State, it cannot be said that the situation is satisfactory. In part this is because there are great gaps where no body exists to listen to complaints about harsh or unfair decisions (the Crichel Down case could not have been taken up in this way). In part it is because of the complexity which means that citizens, even if they are of considerable professional status, have little idea of how to proceed in cases of dispute. As a result, a confused suspicion spreads that everything is managed by a vast complex of bureaucratic organisations far away from the individual concerned (for many Scots and Welsh, they suspect literally far away in London, for Londoners far away in a psychological sense), a suspicion that remote, not very well informed officials apply rules without much thought about the particular case and the persons affected.

There have been suggestions as to how this problem could be remedied. A number of experts on constitutional matters have argued the case for a general administrative appeal tribunal which would be the final authority on all such issues. This exists in France in the form of the *Conseil d'État* but the Franks Committee (though not empowered to examine situations where no tribunal existed) reported against such a council to hear appeals from tribunals and appeals against a minister's decisions after an enquiry. The Government accepted the Committee's arguments that the existing variety of tribunals were all supposed to be expert in the particular field of administration in which they were working, that these proposals would mean an appeal from an expert to an inexpert body and that the effect of a *Conseil d'État* or administrative court being the final court of appeal would be the creation of a body of administrative law. British lawyers had, since the middle ages, tried to establish the principle that the State had no special privileges before the law and that to create a body of administrative law might be interpreted as a move away from that principle. Under the Franks Committee's recommendations, appeals on points of law lay to the ordinary courts so that the old common law principles would still, as far as possible, be applied in these administrative cases. Secondly, and probably more important in the Government's eyes, was the very British conviction that a minister's decisions were political, they should be final and the only resort against them should be political criticism. It is entirely against the British tradition of an almost unfettered executive to create situations where a court could veto decisions or pass on the justice or administrative good sense of a minister's actions.

14. The Ombudsman

Another method of attempting to bridge the gap between the citizen and the State, or at least of removing the frustrations and sense of impotence felt by some citizens, was to appoint an Ombudsman. This was proposed in 1961 by a committee under Sir John Whyatt (set up by the British Section of the International Commission of Jurists) which also made other recommendations about a general tribunal to hear appeals on discretionary matters not covered by other tribunals. The Ombudsman was to consider cases of mal-administration or unusually harsh or unreasonable decisions. Public interest was aroused by the proposal but the Macmillan Government turned it down in 1962 on the grounds that it was incompatible with the final authority of the minister in question and that a citizen with a grievance could get at the minister through his Member of Parlia-ment. The Labour Party included the proposal for an Ombudsman in its 1964 election manifesto and, after coming to power, produced a White Paper in 1965 and passed the necessary legislation in 1967.

The Act provided that complaints to the Ombudsman, or Parlia-mentary Commissioner as he is called in the Act, can only be present-ed through a Member of Parliament and the subjects which he can investigate did not include local authority matters, the nationalised industries, personnel questions in the armed forces or Civil Service, the police, government contracts or the health service. Also the Ombudsman cannot examine the wisdom of ministerial decisions, he can only consider cases of maladministration given the existing policies determined by the government. In so doing, all depart-mental files have to be made available, though a minister may forbid the publication of information in the Ombudsman's report.

Between 1967 and the end of 1970, the Parliamentary Com-missioner fully investigated 1515 cases and decided that in 164 there were elements of maladministration leading to injustice. But the instances were relatively trivial (the biggest group was in the Inland Revenue), they received little publicity as the report simply goes back to the MP raising the question and there is no easy method of ensuring that the source of the maladministration is removed. (There is a Select Committee of the House to which the Ombudsman reports and it can ask officials what remedies they propose to take but this happens rarely and may produce little or nothing.)

Yet there was evidence that with proper scope and publicity, this could be a useful method of airing grievances. Half the cases put up by MPs were outside the terms of reference and the public sent in as many complaints as MPs without realising that this was not the correct approach. As a result, there has been steady pressure to expand the system and in July 1969 Mr Wilson accepted in principle that there should be Ombudsmen for local government,

But, even by April 1972, the Conservative Government could only report that it was examining ideas for a Commission to receive complaints about local authorities. Northern Ireland was ahead in that the Commissioner for Complaints was established in 1969 as part of the reform programme brought in at that time to try and alleviate the grievances of the minority community. This Commissioner can be approached by the public directly and can hear complaints against both local government and certain public bodies and organise a reconciliation. In September 1973, Health Service Commissioners for England, Scotland and Wales were introduced, patients getting access only after a preliminary complaint to the reponsible Health Services authorities had been made with an unsatisfactory result.

Thus the experience of the past five years has been that the work of an Ombudsman is useful but it is not well understood, direct access is limited (except in Northern Ireland), the concept of maladministration is restricted, too many areas are still excluded (police and nationalised industries) and the results receive little publicity. Nevertheless, the use that has been made of the system and its gradual extension has shown how many of the public at one time or another feel that some authority has not dealt with them fairly and that if only they could explain their case to some omnipotent and entirely just person, all would be well.

15. Enforcing the law: the army and the police

When laws have been enacted and have to be applied in particular cases, they are, in the last resort, enforced by the courts (which, as has been said, have contracted out of most of the difficult and upsetting areas) and then by the police. The military have been used in Northern Ireland in the 1920s and again since 1969. Either in time of emergency or in time of war, special powers can be taken by the government. These methods of enforcement play little part in the normal political life of the country. The forces themselves are governed by military law set out in the Army Act and there is no such thing as martial law. The powers and duties of soldiers in a situation such as the 1969 riots in Londonderry and Belfast are different in degree and not in kind from those of the ordinary citizen. All alike are under an obligation to try and stop riots, though soldiers clearly have a greater responsibility in that they are equipped and brought there for that purpose. Officers and men must exercise their own judgment whether to use force and, if so, how much. The normal courts continue to operate (unless there is an actual invasion or loss of control of a wide area including the place where the local court sits) and all alleged offences committed during the riots, including any accusation of excessive use of force by the military, can be tried in these courts.

Of much more consequence to most citizens is the position of the police as they are the coercive aspect of the State with which people are regularly in contact. Here also, the vast expansion in the activities of the State and in the complexity of society have led to many more people being involved in such contacts. The police have not merely the old, central task of the detection and prevention of crime but, because they are an available force, they have been used for many aspects of social welfare work, investigating cases and keeping contact with those under some kind of supervision. Also the growth of private car ownership and of traffic has involved them with many who, in former days, would never have had any dealings with the police. The public's attitude to the police is somewhat ambivalent as there is a strong desire for firm enforcement of law, a strong desire to support the police in their efforts to cope with law breakers and yet inevitably a percentage of those who have had dealings with the police have also had complaints or have resented the way they have been treated. Thus in this aspect, as so many other of the State's relations with the citizens, the awe has gone, there is no automatic respect and the police are judged very much by results, results which are complex in that they involve the ability to crack down on certain categories of offenders while dealing fairly and impartially with the public as a whole.

Worries about the relations between the police and the public led to the appointment of a Royal Commission under Sir Henry Willink in 1959. It considered two major issues, the most suitable size of force—local, regional or national—and the question of public accountability. The problem was that until then Chief Constables in charge of a police force had been responsible for their administrative efficiency to the local Watch Committee (or Police Committee in Scotland) from which they drew a half of their funds. Also the actions of the police had to be justified in that the propriety of their proceedings had to be accepted by the courts. But in the enforcement of the law fairly, impartially and efficiently, the Chief Constables were not under any external control, though the Home Secretary has, in some sense, a responsibility for law and order throughout the country. (In the Metropolitan area, he is the police authority.) The Report of the Commission was followed by the Police Act, 1964. It provided that the local police authority would still be the source of pay and equipment and could discuss the efficiency with which these were utilised by the police force. The Home Secretary (and Secretary of State for Scotland) was given general powers of supervision and inquiry, for which he was responsible to the House of Commons, but still fought shy of claiming responsibility for the efficient operation of individual forces in particular situations. This was still the exclusive task of the Chief Constable. At the same time efforts were made to increase the efficiency of the police by cutting down the number of separate forces which by 1973 were reduced from 125 in England and Wales and 33 in Scotland to 47 and 20 respectively.

Yet the chief sources of complaint, the conduct of individual officers in particular situations and the overall handling of certain episodes such as student protests, strike pickets or demonstrations, have continued. In Sheffield in 1963 two detectives were found guilty of 'brutal and sustained assaults with weapons of the nature of a truncheon and a short flexible piece of gut-like material . . . for the purpose of inducing confessions of crime'. In 1964 a detective sergeant in the Metropolitan Police had a mental breakdown and an inquiry found him guilty of the fabrication of evidence, while in the same year there was an inquiry into allegations of corruption in Wolverhampton. While there is considerable public support for the police and for the enforcement of law and order, the respect for the police has been undermined by a number of factors. There is the general tendency among the younger generation to question author-ity; there is the increasing involvement of normally law-abiding members of the public through traffic offences with the police and there are the doubts created by episodes such as those described above. These have continued in the late 1960s with charges of running crime rings being made against some members of the Metropolitan Police while the brutal murder of two policemen in Glasgow led to charges being made against men who had themselves recently left the police force.

At the committee stage of the Police Bill, the Government rejected a plea for an independent body to investigate complaints against the police on much the same grounds as the arguments made against an effective Ombudsman or against scrutiny of the administration by parliamentary committees. It was argued that outsiders would not understand the pressures on the force and that the process would demoralise officers and prevent them getting on with their work. On the other hand, an obviously fair and independent procedure would be a protection for the vast majority of industrious and honest officers and it is clearly important to do everything to maintain public confidence.

16. The politicians and the public—conclusion

The main task for the political leaders of the country is to achieve the rising standards of living which are desired by most of the electorate and to win the approval of the voters and particularly of those who are normally their supporters together with the relevant local spokesmen, opinion leaders and pressure groups. For the public, there is a distinction between the Prime Minister, the MPs of his party and the whole apparatus of the State, the men who collect the income tax and rents, the boards who provide electricity and run the railway or bus service to work, and the police who are to be avoided when driving at speed or after a few drinks, but there is also the linkage that such persons and organisations are all 'them' who do things to 'us'. And while at times much is hoped for from 'them' and certain enthusiasts appear to have a steady confidence that a certain brand of political leadership will do markedly better than the alternatives, for most of the voters there are only marginal differences, no party recently has been markedly more successful than the others and for many members of the public, the less they have to turn to the politicians for solutions, the better they are pleased. In this situation the State has legitimacy in that things could be a lot worse, no one wants fundamental changes and there is resentment against any minorities who appear to be exploiting the rest of the community. But this is legitimacy in the sense that there is an acceptance of existing structures, an acceptance springing more perhaps from realism than from respect or loyalty.

GOVERNING THROUGH PARLIAMENT

1. The role of Parliament

The old nineteenth-century role of Parliament as a body which chose the government, maintained it and could reject it, which operated as an intermediary between the electorate and the executive, has gone. In a political system dominated by the direct relations between the leadership of the country and the voters, the major function of Parliament has altered. Now Parliament is one of the agencies through which the government operates and it is the place where the struggle for power continues in a restricted form between elections. Those who were brought up on the older theories of the Westminster Model in which, despite party loyalties, there was a balance between the executive and the legislature as a whole, expect that the House of Commons will still regard its main functions as being to consider and amend legislative proposals from the government (and from private members), to scrutinise public expenditure and to expose government policies to continual questioning and debate. In practice, there are shadows of the first two functions remaining and the third has been incorporated into the power struggle aspect of the Commons. But for ministers, shadow ministers and most MPs on both sides of the House, the division that comes to mind is not between the executive and the House but between the government and the opposition. The main function of MPs is to support their leaders, to attack the other side and to score the maximum points with the electorate in preparation for the next general election. In 1964 and 1966 a number of Labour backbenchers who believed in the older, more historical functions of the House were elected. They wanted to restore, to some small extent, the House's powers to scrutinise and, on occasion, to resist the executive over

items of legislation, finance and general policy but their attitude
was greeted with genuine surprise by many older members and by
others in their own 'intake'. For these more orthodox members,
the machinery of the House had to be used to protect Labour
ministers and to project their achievements. They thought that it
might be excusable to exploit situations to promote the individual
MP's career within his own party or to look after constituency
interests but it was quite inexcusable to open up opportunities for
Conservatives to criticise the Government.

For the Prime Minister and his colleagues, the House can be
useful in providing a forum in which they can explain their policies
and it is, in any case, necessary to legalise government actions and
to vote money. But many ministers regard the House as a drag.
Question Time has become increasingly taken up with party claims
and counter claims or with constituency points (see below pp.
144–5) while debates often strike ministers as largely a waste of
time. The ministers who like the House either do so because, in
their opposition days, they enjoyed its fellowship and had few other
contacts in London, or they feel so confident of their capacity to
score off the opposition that they like revealing their talents. They
are conscious that their strength with the Prime Minister and chances
of promotion bear some relation to their performance in the House
and to their popularity in the parliamentary party. But the House
may well seem a curious, wayward, ill-informed, trying body to
ministers with busy departments to run and managing the House
may constitute a distraction from their chief and more interesting
task of governing the country.

Turning from ministers to backbenchers, for the younger, more
ambitious members the task is to defend their party and to make a
reputation for themselves so that they will, in due course, be promoted to a junior office or, on the other side, to a shadow post.
The object in this case is not money or prestige. A junior minister
in one of the less important departments has no very glamorous
task. He cannot speak in or out of the House on subjects outside
his department. He cannot write for the papers or take part in
television programmes and his sole opportunities in public are
sharing the replies at Question Time and answering for the government in adjournment and sometimes in wider debates which concern his ministry. The motives for seeking office are partly that the
life of a backbench MP soon becomes unsatisfactory and offers
so little scope for achievement, for registering even the smallest
impact on a restricted area of public life, that the average MP

looks with envy on any minister who has a positive job to perform, however limited the field. One quality of backbench life which is distracting for those with a professional or commercial training is that it lacks coherence, there is an aimlessness which is debilitating. Constituency work takes some time and leads to a multiplicity of minor preoccupations but it by no means occupies the entire day. Then the questions arise; should the MP speak in a debate?— he may not be called. Should he sit on a Select Committee or will the work go unnoticed? Should he try to write a newspaper column? An article is more likely to be accepted if it says something new but this might annoy some of his party leaders. All the time he is encouraged to dabble in this or that to no lasting effect and the relief that such an MP feels when given an actual job, a place to go from 9 a.m. onwards with a definite task to perform, something to do which stretches his capacity more than drinking tea, gossiping and writing letters, is enormous.

For the man who enters the House at a later age who does not expect to get and perhaps does not want office, there is no point in continual exertions to catch the limelight and this is the kind of member who is particularly prone to regard his function as support-ing his leaders. On the Labour side, there is a solid body of such members who inhabit the Tearoom. On the Conservative side this element is based in the Smoking Room and is composed of the men with estates or directorships who do not see the House as their primary source of prestige or income. They, likewise, would find it most unusual and uncongenial if they were expected to devote them-selves to constraining and criticising a Conservative Government.

There are groups who take a different view, but they are a minority. The left in the Labour party use the House to register their protests against right-wing men and measures, whatever party is in power, though many of them feel that once this is done on the floor of the House, once the outside public has been informed of their dissent, they will support their leaders in committee and in the division lobbies. Only a few, largely of the younger members, consider that at least for the first few years after an election, the House as a whole should keep a wary eye on the government and seek to support or influence its policy irrespective of the line taken by the official opposition. These members are interested in the issues, in extracting information from the government, in finding out precisely what is being planned, how policies are to be applied and whether the machinery of government is working well but, as has been said, this is the approach of a minority and, if well done, simply suggests to the more orthodox MPs that the person concerned ought not to be a backbencher but is either seeking office in a rather unusual way or ought to be in some other occupation.

This analysis of the House of Commons is put forward and supported in rather different ways by two very able contemporary commentators, Mr Henry Fairlie in his book *The Life of Politics* and Mr Ronald Butt in *The Power of Parliament*. Fairlie argues, in the same fashion as that employed above, that Britain has an executive-dominated legislature, that the House of Commons can do little to stop a government and that its traditional functions are largely meaningless. But he adds the value judgment that this is desirable because it exists and cannot be undone. Fairlie emphasises that the House has no corporate feeling, it cannot stand apart from the government and the parliamentary reformers' idea that the House can recover some of its former powers is both impracticable and, in his judgment, undesirable. It will not happen because the House cannot reform itself; it can only act with the permission of the executive. In other words, the executive has to propose to the House that reforms should be instituted and why should any executive wish to make rods for its own back? Does it make sense, Fairlie asks, to expect the government to set up committees to scrutinise its work and to expose it to criticism when the government itself would have to table the motion setting up the committees, fix their terms of reference, select the members and appoint the chairmen? For Fairlie, the task of the House is as it is, to keep the party battle going. The accountability of the government arises simply from the ministers' desire to win the next election and, as individuals, to have the minimum of embarrassment and the maximum of political credit. These motives can be exploited to good effect by skilful MPs who understand the system and work with it rather than try to change it.

Ronald Butt arrives at much the same conclusions and he adds certain extra points. His political position is conservative and though some of the ultra left share his views, they are typical of the older Conservative members. Such members are often landowners or men of wealth who have little ambition for office and no concept of the House as a countervailing power to watch over the executive. In their eyes, to seek to strengthen the critical functions of the House is pointless since they tend to trust the (normally Conservative) government. In strong personal positions and moved by loyalty, they back their Prime Minister. But if these men do rouse themselves to tell the Premier that something is going wrong, he takes notice. The Labour party equivalent is a serious rebellion by the trade union loyalists. Such actions are quite exceptional on both sides, taking place only a handful of times during each political generation, but then with definite effects. Conservative members dismissed Chamberlain (in their eyes), vetoed Mr R. A. Butler for the leadership and nearly stopped the Resale Price Maintenance Bill. Labour members slowly killed an incomes policy and undermined Wilson's Industrial Relations Bill. With this evidence of cases where the House of Commons has had some influence and reading all the journalistic and academic comment about the ineffectiveness of Parliament, Mr Butt felt he had to argue that these comments showed a misunderstanding of the situation. He cited the various occasions when Premiers had been influenced to prove his point. Moreover all this influence was exercised without any reforms, Select Committees or other institutional changes proposed by the more theoretically minded parliamentary reformers. (The author interviewed an archetypal example of the older kind of Conservative. This was Mr J. G. Stuart, later Viscount Stuart of Findhorn, who was asked if, after all his years in the House, there were any reforms he would like to see carried out, any changes at all? 'Yes,' replied Mr Stuart, 'there is one thing I have always thought ought to go. We ought to abolish the special allowance paid to the Leader of the Opposition. It is quite ridiculous to pay taxpayers' money to encourage someone to oppose the Queen's Government.')

Yet, part of the argument that the Commons' powers, whatever their value now, have declined as compared with a century ago, is an historical one about the relationships between the executive and the legislature in Victorian Britain. Butt also attacked the accepted view in this case, quoting statements by politicians who thought that in the 1850s and '60s Parliament was so strong it was becoming hard to maintain an effective executive. These views could be quoted to suggest that though Parliament was more powerful in these years, some Victorian politicians regarded this as an undesirable departure from the British tradition of a strong executive capable of controlling and commanding Parliament except on a few special occasions. Even on its own terms, this is a selective view, as only the 1846–60 period was one of unusual instability (Peel's 1841–6 Government was strong enough as was the Palmerston Government after 1860) and the estimate of executive-legislative relations inherent in the Westminster Model is based on a broader period from 1832 to the 1890s when most commentators accepted that a reasonable balance had been achieved.

E

2. How the executive gained control of Parliament

Before joining battle on the value judgments in the theses of Fairlie
and Butt, both of which agree basically with the assessment given
here of the powers and role of the House of Commons today, it is
worth establishing the facts, both historical and contemporary.
In the period from 1832 to the 1880s, the number of party issues (in
the sense of nine-tenths of one party voting together) fell to 25
per cent of all divisions for the Liberals in 1860 and 31 per cent for
the Conservatives, this low level of party cohesion being much the
same from the 1830s to the early 1880s. The House could and did
sack governments (such as Russell's first Cabinet in 1852, Aberdeen's
ministry in 1855, Lord Palmerston in 1858, Russell again in 1866
and Gladstone in 1885) without having to face a general election.
It could and did reject, revise and remake legislation on the floor
of the House (such as the 1858 India Act or the 1867 Reform
Act). Individual ministers were censured and driven from office
by the House, examples being Russell in 1855 and Ellenborough
in 1858. The House controlled a large part of its own timetable,
it had a corporate spirit and it could force information out of the
government, the best example being the stream of diplomatic
Blue Books in which the Foreign Office had to reveal the course
of its negotiations with foreign powers almost as soon as the events
had occurred. Select Committees were set up by the House with
full powers of investigation. Sometimes they did more than just
report, and drafted legislation which could be adopted and introduced either by the government or by a private member. There
can be no doubt, then, that the loose nature of party discipline, the
small electorates, the relative security of the private MP against the
executive, all gave the House not merely much greater power than
it enjoys nowadays but powers which altered its entire role and
position in the system of government. Under these circumstances
the House had an independence and authority which would be
utterly alien and unfamiliar to MPs accustomed to contemporary
conditions.

During the Victorian period, in order to exercise these functions of
controlling, scrutinising, appointing and removing the executive, the
procedure of the House was adapted to suit these tasks. It is, of
course, true that in order to watch over an executive, the system of
supervision has to be constructed in parallel so that information
about the salient issues is extracted at the right time and the process
of scrutiny is based on this information and takes place when the

decision is still open. In the nineteenth century, the first step in legislation was a motion asking leave to introduce a Bill. At this stage the Bill was not printed but the sponsors explained why they felt legislation was necessary and the lines on which they were planning to draft the measure. This gave warning to the outside interests and to members and gave them time to gather their thoughts and explain their views before the First Reading, which was purely formal but provided for the printing of the Bill.

The Second Reading debate then dealt with the principle of the measure and could go on as long as members wished to speak, the government soon sensing whether it could proceed or whether modifications were needed. Once past this hurdle, there came the committee stage taken on the floor of the House, when detailed amendments could be moved clause by clause, and again all amendments had to be taken and this stage went on until each had been dealt with. Finally there was the Third Reading debate when the House had a look at what it had done to the draft Bill during the committee stage and decided whether to pass the measure.

A similar stage by stage supervision obtained in financial matters. Since the 1790s, administrative reforms had gathered together the raising and spending of money into an annual exercise in the hands of the Treasury, the process being completed by the Exchequer and Audit Departments Act in 1866. To permit proper supervision, Gladstone devised a 'circle of control' which followed the same annual cycle. In the spring of each year, the House considered the civil and military estimates and could and did move and carry reductions in individual items in Committee of the whole House called the Committee of Supply. Then in early April, at the end of the financial year, the new taxation was set out in the Bugdet and listed in the Finance Bill which was discussed in Committee of the whole House, the Committee of Ways and Means. The money for expenditure, as set out in the Estimates and finally authorised for expenditure in the Appropriation Act, was passed to the Treasury which in turn handed it out in a carefully controlled flow to the spending departments. At the end of the year, the accounts from all these departments went to the Comptroller and Auditor General, an official of the House of Commons, who put the audited accounts before the Public Accounts Committee of the House to ensure that every penny was spent in the way set out in the Appropriation Act. So the House watched over estimates, money raising, money allocation, its actual expenditure and the legality of what had been done.

So long as the House was not bound by strict party ties and so long as it had control of the major part of its own timetable, the general task of commenting on and questioning government policy was relatively simple. There was no need for a Question Time, since a member could intervene in business by moving a motion on a number of pretexts and raise any subject in an immediate debate. If the House was worried, the government could not refuse a full explanation nor could it return to its other business till members were satisfied. The House might decide to act on its own by appointing a committee to inquire into the matter or a private member might move resolutions or introduce his own measure.

This pattern of parliamentary activity was rapidly altered (though much of the descriptive language remained the same) in the twenty-five years before the First World War. The electorate increased, party battles became much more intense and for the government, over 90 per cent, indeed up to 97 per cent, of divisions in the House became party divisions in that over nine-tenths of the party voted as the Whips indicated. With these changes went a different attitude to legislation. For radicals such as Randolph Churchill (Conservative) and Joseph Chamberlain (Liberal), the task of the House was not to talk over and often talk out measures. If a party had been elected on a given programme, this was an indication that the public wanted these measures passed. This was an early sign of the leadership reaching over the heads of the House to the electorate. The voters had pronounced and the newer, more radical leaders considered that the House should then give up its extensive powers; the measures endorsed by a majority at the polls should be passed with reasonable rapidity. This view, the increasing tempo of legislation and the use of the procedures of the House to obstruct measures (by Conservative backbenchers, called 'the Fourth Party', by 'the colonels' opposed to the abolition of purchase of commissions and then by the Irish) led to the first restrictions on private members' capacity to interrupt or hold up business whenever they liked—or whenever they could get the House to listen to them, for there was always considerable self-discipline. The new Standing Orders adopted in 1882, after Speaker Brand had intervened in 1881 to stop a forty-one-hour sitting, allowed the closure of debate by a simple majority. Further changes were made between 1887 and 1891, the process being largely completed by A. J. Balfour between 1895 and 1902. In 1902 Balfour brought in his 'reforms' called Balfour's Railway Timetable because under them, the government took control of virtually all the time of the House. It decided what was to be debated, for how long and when the final vote was to be taken, so that the government could plan its legislative programme and could forecast accurately when each legislative train would reach the various stages on the journey to enactment.

These parliamentary procedures rest upon the government's command of a majority. If this does not exist then both the government and its control of the timetable collapse but while the one lasts, the other is intact. The government now announces each Thursday the next week's business. Private MPs rise and ask for time for this or that motion or debate which they particularly want, but normally the only concessions the Leader of the House will make is through 'the usual channels', that is in private discussions with the opposition Chief Whip. This is because both front benches accept that it is the function of the House to permit the two sides to state their cases and each party in power has respected the right of the opposition to determine the subjects of debate for about one-third of the total time of the House.

The methods used for controlling debate are the power to apply the closure by a simple majority, though normally the majority must consist of a hundred members; the power to send bills upstairs for their committee stage to a Standing Committee and the power, when bills are taken on the floor of the House or in committee to impose a guillotine. This is a preliminary timetable resolution which requires the vote to be put on certain clauses at a certain time irrespective of whether all the amendments to that clause or to previous clauses have been discussed. Whether a guillotine has been imposed or not, the Speaker has the power to select and group amendments in order to cut down the number and to confine debate to the salient points, but even with this power of Speaker's selection, a guillotine may mean that blocks of amendments are never reached.

This control by the government of the life and work of the House is pervasive and for most purposes has ended any corporate sense of 'the House' as a body which could oppose the government of the day. It is safely assumed that a government can obtain the passage of virtually all the Bills it introduces. This is true also of amendments. Professor Griffiths, in a recent study for PEP, found that in the committee stages of all Bills in three recent sessions, 907 amendments were moved by ministers, of which 906 were carried. Backbenchers moved 3510 amendments and 171 were carried and most of these were not opposed by the government.

Besides this control of measures, the government also controls the processes and personnel of the House. Acting through the

Leader of the House and the Chief Whip (aided by the opposition Chief Whip), the government appoints the members of Select Committees, nominates the chairmen, and can guide the Committees by suggesting suitable subjects. The Whips agree to give a certain amount of time for private members' Bills and private members' motions but they then encourage all their own back-benchers to ballot for these opportunities. They also circulate among their backbenchers suitable motions and advise about appropriate and acceptable Bills for those who come out high up on the list of names which emerge from the ballot. Of course members can disregard this advice. Once on a committee, a backbencher is relatively safe and Select Committees have been known to reject government suggestions as to suitable subjects and go their own way. But most members realise that if they do so, the government may refuse to implement their recommendations and may, as in the case of the Select Committee on Agriculture, simply refuse to set up such a Committee in the next session.

The way this government control has come to be accepted as normal and proper can be seen by the irritated reactions of ministers and Whips on the odd occasions when something goes wrong. For instance, after the day's business is over which is normally at 10 p.m. the government can put through unopposed items (such as the nomination of committees) but if an MP shouts 'object' the matter is postponed. If this is repeated on several occasions, the government can either give up the proposal or take government time, have a short debate and then push the matter through. But though the only effect of this kind of obstruction is a minor rearrangement of government business and a slight delay, the reaction of the Whips and the Leader of the House can be intense. The culprit is sent for and denounced, for this is regarded as a very serious crime. The most spectacular case where the government lost control of the timetable was in the spring of 1969 over the Parliament (No. 2)—House of Lords Reform—Bill. The situation was abnormal in that the substance of the Bill had been agreed between the two front benches, but when the inter-party talks broke down (over a Rhodesian order), the Shadow Cabinet gave their members a free vote and a group of them resisted the measure. The normal forces of party loyalty did not help the Government precisely because there was no official opposition. So the ministers in charge of the measure felt they could not bring in a guillotine or send the Bill to a committee upstairs because most of the Conservatives would have voted against and, not being an issue of confidence between the parties, sufficient Labour dissidents might also have voted against the government to leave it in a minority. So the Bill had to be taken on the floor of the House and all selected amendments had to be debated and voted on. As a result, though the government won every division, after nine days only 5 out of 20 clauses had been passed. This would have been counted a great success and a reasonable rate of progress in the 1850s or 1860s but was so unprecedented and so humiliating, given the contemporary assumptions about government control, that the Bill was dropped.

The effects of the timetable and work of the House passing under the control of the government have been widespread. One sign of the degree of power and independence of a legislature is its capacity to extract information from the government. In the nineteenth century, the House of Commons forced successive ministries to publish collections of despatches dealing with Britain's relations with foreign powers shortly after the events had taken place, simply so that the House could judge whether the policies had been appropriate. As party discipline tightened and governments could rely on regular majorities, motions 'that papers be laid' on given subjects were increasingly resisted. Thus the flow of this information began to decline in the 1890s reaching a trickle, mainly on peripheral issues, by 1914 and ceasing totally after 1918. The contrast can be seen by comparing the information available when the Commons in 1856 forced the publication of all despatches dealing with the origins of the Crimean War before hostilities were over and the capacity of successive governments to keep the House and the public in total and persistent ignorance of what led up to the invasion of Suez in 1956. In the latter case, no information, other than private memoirs, has been published and though Labour leaders talked about revealing all the secrets when they won power, once in office in 1964, they also refused publication. The other great method of investigation and discovery of information was by the appointment of Select Committees, governments often feeling that they could not oppose motions seeking to elicit the facts on any situation. Again party loyalty has stopped this and apart from the Select Committee experiment instituted by the Labour Government after 1966 (see pp. 147–51 below), this has come to a halt. Now all inquiries are set up by governments which prefer to rely on Royal Commissions, ministerial committees or investigations by outside nominated bodies, though occasionally one or two MPs are appointed as members.

3. The legislative process

The most important effect of this degree of government control has been to render the House of Commons incapable of adapting its procedure to keep pace with altered administrative practices. It is generally accepted that control systems have to be organised in parallel to the activities that they are intended to monitor and the procedures for legislation and the scrutiny of expenditure and for raising taxation have been described to show how this worked in the Victorian period. By the 1960s, the legislative process had altered enormously but the only changes in House of Commons procedure had been to make it less capable of controlling even the old pattern of legislation. Now legislation arises either from major political commitments made by the Cabinet (or earlier by the Shadow Cabinet while the party was in opposition) or it is of a more routine nature and comes from within the departments when they find their existing powers insufficient or inappropriate for the conduct of administration along accepted lines. Once it is agreed that legislation should be prepared, the civil servants consult with the outside pressure groups, they clear their ideas with other interested departments and negotiate any financial aspects with the Treasury. Sometimes, if a matter is difficult, a committee may be set up to gather facts and produce a report. The whole process will take months or even years if special problems are encountered.

When a Bill has been negotiated in this way and drafted, it is then presented to the House for the first time. The old stage of asking the House for 'leave to introduce' a Bill when the possibilities can be debated before any negotiations or drafting have been started has been abandoned. (The last remnant of this procedure allows MPs to have one short speech a day to introduce a 'Ten Minute Rule' Bill.) Occasionally the 1966–70 Labour Government opened up a discussion at this stage by publishing a 'Green Paper' which set out alternative possibilities, but this was rare. Thus the House receives what is, to all intents and purposes, a finished product. The opposition state their view of the Bill during the second reading debate. Then it is usually sent to a committee. During this stage, the government may accept amendments or amend its own Bill if deficiencies in drafting come to light. Pressure groups that have narrowly lost points or who feel strongly opposed may brief members in the hope that with extra publicity and a show of support from friendly MPs, the government may relent during the passage of the Bill. But on controversial Bills, many of the amendments at the committee stage and the debates at the end of each clause on the motion 'that clause X stand part of the Bill' merely give the opposition a chance to reiterate its objections. This ground can be traversed again three times, at the Report, Lords' Amendments and Third Reading stages all on the floor of the House. So the procedure is admirably adapted to permit the opposition to make its case several times over and for the government to explain the virtues of the measure an equal number of times. What the procedure does not permit is an exploration of alternative approaches, an understanding of the views of outside groups (unless they think it worth briefing MPs) and there is no scope for public opinion to form and react before the government has committed itself to a definite approach to the problem. With this process of legislation, any changes the ministers may want to make look like concessions to the opposition. Government backbenchers are expected to be present at all stages and though they are entitled to speak for half the time available on the floor of the House, in committee they are expected neither to speak nor to move amendments but simply to keep voting for the government's proposals.

4. *Authorising public expenditure and taxation*

In financial matters, much the same reduction in the capacity to scrutinise has taken place. As early as the 1880s, it was found that the Commons could not adequately examine and comment on the estimates. They were too complex for treatment on the floor of the House. Also the opposition did not want to waste time on such minutiae preferring to tackle the government on wider issues arising from the conduct of foreign or domestic policy. As a result, the scrutiny of the estimates in the Committee of Supply became a formal vote to reduce the money for this or that department by a nominal figure so as to permit a general attack on the government's policy in that field. Instead of these days being taken together in the spring when the estimates were published, 'supply days' (now numbering 29) were scattered throughout the session so that the opposition, which is allowed to choose the subjects, could always have some time available should it wish to raise some immediate aspect of government policy. To meet this gap in the old 'circle of control', an Estimates Committee was appointed in 1912 and re-appointed in every session, except during the two world wars, until 1960 when Standing Order No. 80 made the sessional appointment of the Committee mandatory. At first, the Committee was not very successful as it had no staff and a body of 24 to 28 members is not very effective for cross-examining witnesses. After 1945, the Committee was allowed to divide itself into sub-committees, it gave up scrutinising the estimates in detail and began to look at the way money was being spent in selected fields and how far government policy was being achieved. While this was useful and did hold the attention of members interested in the specific subjects being examined, the sub-committees moved from one area of expenditure to another each session so that they developed no expertise and could not follow up previous work.

Thus House of Commons scrutiny of the estimates virtually ceased. Meanwhile, within the executive, the Treasury in 1961 accepted the Plowden Committee's proposals and began to plan public expenditure on the framework of a five-year rolling programme. Under this procedure, each summer a committee of officials called the Public Expenditure Survey Committee (PESC) prepares a Report forecasting public expenditure over the following five years. The figures for the first two years are easy as these decisions have already been taken, years four and five are merely projections on current assumptions while the hard decisions have at this stage to be taken for year three. At the same time a Medium Term Economic Assessment is prepared by the Treasury to show the anticipated resources available in the five years ahead. With the PESC Report and the Economic Assessment before them, a Cabinet Committee of ministers with the same name (PESC) then decides the levels and share out of expenditure for year three. Only the conclusions or any outstanding disputes go to the full Cabinet.

But while Whitehall changed from organising public expenditure on an annual basis to a five-year rolling programme, the House of Commons was still authorising expenditure on the old twelve-month pattern. To complicate matters even further, the House only authorised annual 'supply services'. Charges on the Consolidated Fund (such as interest on the National Debt, the Civil List and certain salaries) do not require annual authorisation and were not included. Neither was the expenditure by the nationalised industries nor that of local authorities. The PESC Report, on the other hand, covered the whole of public expenditure. Thus there was no House of Commons scrutiny of public expenditure and virtually no understanding of how the decisions had been reached. All that happened was a series of complaints when the results of the overall programme began to affect spending in a particular field. Occasionally, when there had to be a drastic reassessment of public expenditure, it became evident from the leaks and rumours of resignations that something important was going on in Whitehall, as occurred in the summer of 1966, but neither Labour backbenchers nor the House in general were able to find out what was happening or to discuss the issues.

Labour members of the Select Committee on Procedure obtained permission from the Chancellor of the Exchequer and the Chief Labour Whip to look at this topic in the 1968–9 session. A curious combination of factors made it possible to propose a reform. The key was the willingness of the Treasury—ministers and officials—to contemplate a slight change. The reason was that the Chancellor had promised the International Monetary Fund that public expenditure was to be kept to a level no higher than the estimated growth in the Gross National Product, that is 3–3½ per cent. With great difficulty this target had been achieved but the largest cuts were in areas of expenditure which did not require annual authorisation. When the House of Commons annual Vote on Account was tabled, it therefore showed an increase well above the 3½ per cent level. This caused great embarrassment to the Treasury and a flutter in confidence in the City. It was this experience that convinced the Treasury 'hard-liners' (for there were numbers of officials who wanted reform for other, more democratic reasons) that a system of authorising public expenditure which caused widespread misunderstanding was undesirable. If a substantially reduced programme of public expenditure had been achieved after great trial and tribulation, why not let people know? And there was the further point that if MPs or outsiders still demanded more money, they could reasonably be asked what other items of expenditure they would cut, thus winning immediate allies for the Treasury or forcing those wanting more expenditure to admit the need for higher taxation. At this propitious moment it was fortunate that the Chancellor of the Exchequer was open to reformist arguments and that the Select Committee on Procedure was in a most progressive mood and under an able, eager chairman. Finally the Conservatives were so committed to cuts in public expenditure that they could not oppose proposals that would make it easier for the House to understand and control this monster.

In July 1969, the Select Committee reported in favour of the publication both of the five-year rolling programme in the form of an annual White Paper with a full explanation of what changes had been made that year and of the Medium Term Economic Assessment. The Report called for a major debate each year on this White Paper and recommended the creation of a new Public Expenditure

Select Committee to take the place of the former Estimates Committee. This was to be a body of 72 members divided into 8 sub-committees each specialising in a particular field of expenditure and backed by adequate staff. The previous November, the Government had assented to the idea of an annual white paper on expenditure and a debate, the paper being published and the debate being held for the first time in the winter of 1969–70. It is interesting that the Treasury was only willing to publish the white paper in the autumn of each year after rather than before the hard decisions for the third year ahead had been taken and made no commitment to publish the Medium Term Economic Assessment, actually refusing to do so in 1971.

The new Conservative Government after 1970 decided to accept the Select Committee on Procedure's recommendations and a Select Committee on Expenditure of 49 members (6 sub-committees) was created in 1971. It had the right to examine policy and to question ministers and was organised into a General Sub-Committee which examined the whole PESC system and a series of specific sub-committees, each specialising in an area of expenditure. Once the General Sub-Committee had done its survey of the system, it turned to inform Parliament of the issues embodied (or concealed) in the annual expenditure white paper, the first of these reports being the Fifth Report of the 1972–3 session. Meanwhile the various sub-committees reported on public expenditure in their fields.

The result has appeared unimpressive to some in that the issues embedded in the Public Expenditure White Paper remained obscure to most MPs and the annual debate did not become a major parliamentary occasion. On the other hand, more information did become available, some scrutiny did take place and Treasury officials did change some of their methods under pressure from MPs on the Committee. Viewed in the long term, the formation of the Expenditure Committee was a major step towards bringing House of Commons procedure back into line with current administrative procedures without which any attempt at scrutiny would be impossible.

On the other side of financial procedure, that of authorising taxation, the House is bound by a Standing Order of 1713 which prevents anyone, other than a minister, proposing a new or increased or varied form of taxation. Since 1966, debate has been founded on resolutions moved immediately after the Chancellor of the Exchequer's Budget Speech. These are far-ranging debates on the state of the economy, though for some third of the time members have actually talked about taxation. The second reading of the Finance Bill follows and from 1969, the Bill has then been divided, clauses and schedules which involve issues of principle being taken on the floor of the House while the more detailed clauses are sent upstairs to a Standing Committee. Here again the Standing Orders, which prohibit proposals to raise taxation or to provide relief if this would mean that other taxes would have to be raised, limit debate to general proposals about overall rates of VAT, supertax and corporation tax. The Speaker has to use his power of selection drastically, choosing about a quarter of the amendments put down but the discussions are extensive, the committee stage usually allowing some twenty hours of debate followed by a Report Stage and Third Reading. (There are other taxing Bills involving health service contributions, road-bridge tolls and so on, but these occur in the normal way at intervals during the session.)

It is probably in this area that the House of Commons has had most effect in persuading governments to modify their original proposals. The most noteworthy example was in 1937 when Neville Chamberlain reacted to the hostility with which his National Defence Contribution was received by withdrawing it and substituting a new and simpler tax. There were special reasons in that Neville Chamberlain was peculiarly sensitive to business opinion and between the introduction of the Budget and the withdrawal of the tax, he had moved from being Chancellor of the Exchequer to the post of Prime Minister and naturally wished to start in a congenial atmosphere. But more recently, between 1960 and 1969, there are a series of cases in which the government has brought in tax changes at Report Stage following on earlier pressure either from members on its own side or from the opposition. Concessions were granted to horticulture in 1961, tax relief for the blind was extended in 1962, there were three detailed concessions in 1964, many alterations in the capital gains and corporation taxes in 1965 and so on, perhaps the most well-known example being the abolition of income tax on owner occupiers under Schedule A. It was to this field of tax changes that those such as the late Iain Macleod pointed when he wished to emphasise the continuing power of Parliament and the efficacy of opposition.

The reasons for this flexibility are that little party capital is made out of these alterations and since tax changes have to be kept secret to avoid forestalling, there can therefore be no prior negotiations with outside interests. Therefore these negotiations take place during the committee stage of the Finance Bill so that besides their direct representations to the government, the various pressure groups often brief MPs individually and the opposition as a whole. The issues are extremely complex and little understood by the public so no great attention is fastened on these debates and concessions can be made without apparent loss of face. The ministers involved recognise that MPs are being well briefed and though they will not necessarily concede directly they encounter a good case, they will usually move the amendment themselves at a later stage.

The chief weakness of the House of Commons in matters of taxation: the way in which it has not been able to keep pace with administrative developments is that it has no method of collecting information (other than the briefing from outside pressure groups already mentioned) on the social and other side-effects of a tax or of examining possible future departures in taxation policy. If this work is being done by the government or by outside agencies, it is arguable that the Commons should know what information has been collected and, if no work is being done, Members should be in a position to insist that this be remedied. The Select Committee on Procedure took this view and in 1971 recommended that sufficient members should be added to the Expenditure Committee to enable it to set up a sub-committee on taxation and finance. The whole body could be renamed 'the Expenditure and Finance Committee' though, the Select Committee on Procedure added, this taxation sub-committee might in time develop into a separate Select Committee on Taxation and Economic Affairs.

The government appointed a Select Committee on the Corporation Tax but refused a permanent sub-committee on taxation so that outside interests are, as before, consulted when new taxes are being considered but there is no mechanism by which the House of Commons can know about or participate in such investigations.

5. *Pressing the government from the floor of the House*

Turning from the functions of legislating and authorising both expenditure and taxation to the other traditional function of pressing the government, the procedures involved have also undergone change but there has been a greater effort made to keep this weapon sharpened and up to the armour it has to pierce. This is because, without some capacity to criticise, Parliament would be quite meaningless and because this capacity is of use to the opposition, a point which ministers who may one day return to opposition, appreciate. Formerly, the methods of control or influence were all

concentrated on the floor of the House. Measures could be defeated
or amended. Powerful speeches which had an almost visible effect
on the House could lead to concessions without any vote being
taken. So the great methods of exercising pressure were votes,
speeches, the use of procedure to delay a measure and the demand
for the relevant documents to be published or for the appointment
of a Select Committee.

With the growth of party voting and the government's virtual
monopoly of the timetable, the floor of the House has become much
less important. However, attempts have been made to make up for
this by the development of other devices such as Question Time,
Ten Minute Rule Bills and the practice of asking wide-ranging
questions each Thursday when the business for the following week is
announced. Also, since party loyalty is the first consideration when
there are party battles and divisions on the floor of the House, the
preliminary or supplementary debates within the parties have
acquired a slightly greater measure of influence. In addition, there
have been attempts to increase the influence of the House in a
manner which escapes party divisions, particularly by the creation of
more select or 'specialist' committees.

The methods by which MPs attempt to influence ministers from
the floor of the House are by their speeches in major debates on
government business, by calling for emergency debates under
Standing Order No. 9, by the use of Ten Minute Rule Bills, Private
Members' Bills and motions, adjournment debates, Question Time
and abstention or cross-voting in divisions. It is hard to say whether
speeches have any effect nowadays. A brilliant attack or defence
(such as Iain Macleod's assault in 1950 on the then invincible
Aneurin Bevan) can affect the career of an MP. A persistent and
well-argued case has to be answered and this may eventually have
some influence on a minister. But, on the whole, members either
support their leaders or make constituency points or obtain some
publicity for their rebellious views. But as the vote is a foregone
conclusion (in outcome, if not in numbers), debates tend to be
formalised occasions and, apart from the opening and the winding-
up speeches, are attended only by the handful of MPs who wish
to speak. Members who are invited to appear on television or who
write newspaper columns can have a far wider public audience
and a far greater impact, even on ministers who are fellow members,
than those MPs who merely speak in debates.

With the tight government control of the timetable, it is barely
possible for the House to switch to debate some urgent topic which

is filling the press and current affairs programmes and thus occupying the attention of the public unless the opposition choose this subject for one of their supply days. The procedure designed to permit backbenchers to call for such a change has been the request for an emergency debate 'on a definite matter of urgent public importance'. But while there were, on average, five such debates per annum between 1900 and 1920, restrictive rulings by successive speakers cut the average to under one a year after 1945 and by 1966 no such request had been granted for three years. The Select Committee on Procedure recommended in 1966 that all past restrictive rulings should be abrogated and the Speaker instructed not to give explanations (which might in time become restrictive) in future. The government accepted this recommendation and despite pressure on MPs not to make full use of the Standing Order, after the new rule was adopted, this once again became a fairly regular method of debating urgent topics on the floor of the House, there being an average of four such debates each session.

Ten Minute Rule Bills, Private Members' Bills and motions and adjournment debates have very little effect. Many are simply propagandist and are the result of prompting by the Whips while half-hour adjournment debates, divided equally between the backbencher who raised the issue and the minister, are normally used to press constituency points. In the past, Question Time has been regarded as an effective method of pressing ministers. It developed simply because the old freedom to raise any issue in a short debate at virtually any time had disappeared. A fixed part of the Order Paper and a fixed time was first set aside for questions in 1869. As the numbers of questions asked grew, the procedures had to be tightened up, the number of oral questions rationed and Members were in practice allowed only one supplementary question. In the 1930s and 1940s, Question Time was largely dominated by backbenchers and those concerned with the point at issue were left to press their interrogation or were supported by others with a similar grievance. However, at all times questions have been asked for all sorts of reasons ranging from the sheer desire for information to an attempt to trip up the Prime Minister on a major policy issue. By the late 1960s, Members were putting down up to 300 questions a day and the Speaker attempted to reach more oral questions by speeding up the exchanges so as to cover forty to fifty questions in fifty or fifty-five minutes. As a result, it became very much easier for a minister to brush aside any interrogation since not only was the original purpose of the question soon left behind but also the front benches have tended to intervene to try and score broader party points to which the minister in turn makes the usual party retort.

The other and most publicised method of registering opinion is by abstention or cross-voting. The practice has to be reconciled with the point already explained that no government has been put out of office in this way in peacetime since 1895. This method reached its peak under the 1966–70 Labour Government and the form it took was that, for practical purposes, no Labour MPs cross-voted in the sense of joining the Conservatives in voting against the Labour Government. However Labour MPs were prepared to abstain and with the Government majority hovering at around 90 in the years 1967–70, on 26 occasions in these two sessions an average of 27 mostly left-wing critics abstained. It is significant that when Mr Macmillan was under heavy fire over his handling of the Profumo case in 1963, with much the same majority as the subsequent Labour Government, he also faced 27 abstentions in the critical debate. On the Labour side a number of the regular post-1966 abstainers were present between 1964 and 1966 but with a majority varying between 6 and 3, they did not avail themselves of this luxury. Thus it is clear that abstention is not done in order to defeat a government nor is it carried far enough to create serious problems, so that the purpose is partly a game of bluff with the government, partly to allow the critics to signal to those in their parties outside Westminster. This method of indicating disagreement may have some effect on ministers as it does heighten tension and produces considerable adverse publicity. Though it is impossible to point to actual policy changes because of abstentions (or the threat of abstentions), there could be a general wearing-down effect on ministers who may seek for other methods or other language if such modifications would help them to get by in the House without one of these carefully staged scenes.

6. Pressing the government: upstairs and informal methods

Some writers have argued that since the parties became so strong, it was inevitable that the influence formerly exercised on the floor of the House should decline but that much the same influence is still exercised by the meetings of the Parliamentary Parties. On the Labour side, there is the Parliamentary Labour Party (PLP) which includes all ministers and Labour peers. It elects a chairman and a Liaison Committee. When the party is in opposition it also elects the Parliamentary Committee or Shadow Cabinet. The PLP normally has a meeting every Wednesday morning to discuss general issues and a meeting at 6 p.m. every Thursday to consider the next week's business. In addition it is divided into regional and subject groups which organise meetings on a wide variety of topics. Among the Conservatives, the equivalent is the 1922 Committee (since it was founded in that year) but it has its weekly meetings without ministers or shadow ministers present, dealing with the party leaders through an elected chairman. The Conservatives also have area and subject committees.

After the 1966 election there was an attempt to push the Government into certain policy changes, particularly the abandonment of the East of Suez defence commitment, by means of debates and votes at PLP meetings. The Prime Minister reacted hotly saying that votes were not customary but his presence and that of his senior colleagues on important occasions showed that importance was attached to these gatherings. The Labour Government also took the precaution of sending a special, private 'whip' or request to attend to all the hundred and eleven Labour ministers in both Houses. If most of what was sometimes called 'the payroll vote' attended, the critics would have to carry seven-tenths of the backbenchers and if this had ever happened, the press would have treated it as a total collapse of confidence in the government. This illustrates one of the difficulties in pressing a government at such meetings. The proceedings and the vote would inevitably reach the press, thus putting the prestige of the government at stake. Once this seems likely, the Prime Minister can evoke the sentiment of party loyalty with much the same effect as when he faces opposition on the floor of the House.

In the 1922 Committee, there are no votes and less divisiveness but the opinions, as conveyed by the Chairman to the Party Leader, may have more influence than the PLP has with a Labour Prime Minister. This is certainly true of the subject groups. In the Conservative party, these groups each have a secretary and a fairly regular membership, the leading members play a prominent part in debates on that subject and briefs are provided by the secretary. The leadership, for its part, will often consult the relevant group. Churchill was reluctant to evacuate the Sudan in 1954 but he told Eden, who was in favour, that if the policy was acceptable to the foreign and colonial groups of the party Eden could go ahead. Similarly some important amendments to the 1957 Rent Act came from the housing committee. This is not the case in the Labour party, the subject groups having no fixed membership. (The meetings are listed on the Whip and any MP can attend.) There is no secretariat and normally no programme of meetings or work, the group

being large if an important visitor is speaking (or, when in government, the minister attends) but small on other occasions.

Besides these formal structures, each party has extensive methods
of contacting its own leaders including deputations to the Prime
Minister, casual conversation, the impression conveyed by the 'sense
of the House' and messages relayed by Parliamentary Private
Secretaries and by the Whips. There is no doubt that the reactions of
the parties do have some effect on the leaders, though probably this
is a little more true in the case of the Conservative party. One
reason for the difference is that the Conservatives are less committed
to pre-determined lines of action and are therefore more open to any
positive case put by their backbenchers. Also Labour Members have
established positions on a left-to-right spectrum of opinion and more
often put their own view rather than transmit the reactions of voters.
As has been said above, the Prime Minister seldom worries if the
opposition is opposing—his fear is of losing those voters who usually
support his party. If Labour MPs are known to have views which are
not necessarily a reflection of the opinions of Labour voters, less
attention can be paid to them. But Conservative MPs are much less
easy to classify, they have fewer dogmatic positions to maintain and
their criticisms of their own party's policies are therefore much less
easy to dismiss in this way. If a Conservative MP X or Y, who has
not been known to take ideological stands, approaches a minister
or a Whip and expresses grave doubts, this is viewed with considerable worry and it is assumed that these objections have been put
forward by the MP only after the points have been put to him with
equal or greater force in his constituency. For these reasons, the
Conservatives are a little more responsive to widespread expressions
of serious doubt on their own back benches.

7. *Standing and Select Committees*
In addition to the activities of members on the floor of the House
or in the parties, there has been an attempt to restore or increase the
influence of the Commons by adopting new procedures, most of
which involve the development of a new committee system. The
reformers, until 1964 mainly outside the House, argued that since the
public wished to vote governments in or out of power and since
every serious vote had become an issue of confidence, it was no
longer possible to restore freer voting in order to improve the
independence and power of the House. But this did not mean that
it was impossible for the House of Commons to exercise some
influence. Here the problem was not so much party loyalty as the

fact that parliamentary procedures no longer fitted into the time-scale or permitted an understanding of current administration. The reformers argued that since departments built up their philosophies over a period of time and since new measures took a considerable period to negotiate, these processes should be opened up so that the informed public could make its reactions clear while principles were still being settled. For this purpose, they advised the creation of permanent or Standing Select (specialist) Committees with powers of interrogation and investigation to watch over each area of government action. These Select Committees were not intended to be tied to producing particular reports but were to collect information and let the House and the public know what disputes were going on and what agreements were being reached within ministries, between them and between Whitehall and the outside pressure groups. If this was done, the reformers argued, it would give the sections of the public concerned with these areas of policy a chance to react and it would once again be worth the pressure groups' while to explain their points to the Commons before the precise details of forthcoming legislation were settled.

It is important to be clear about the distinction between these committees and the Standing Committees of the House (which includes the Scottish and Welsh Grand Committees). The latter are legislative committees set up to take the committee stage of a Bill and they have to reflect the division of party strength that exists on the floor of the House. With a chairman, two front benches and Whips, these committees are microcosms of the Commons with no special facilities for finding out the facts or for doing anything other than what would normally be done if the Bill had kept on the floor of the House. As far as government backbenchers are concerned, their instructions are to be present at these committees but it is hoped that they will be silent as each speech only adds that much longer to the proceedings. Opposition backbenchers, as in the House, make their general case against the Bill. The Select Committees, in contrast, were to be investigating bodies where policy issues were not of first importance, the principal task being to find out what was happening inside the various government departments, to inform the House and the public, thus bringing public opinion to bear at an earlier stage while policy was still relatively fluid.

This type of committee was modelled on the Select Committee on Nationalised Industries which had been set up in 1956 because it was felt that Parliament could not adequately control the range of corporations it had created. The experiment, which had caused some worry, particularly on the Labour benches, was entirely successful. All shades of political opinion on the Committee worked well together elucidating the policies of the industries. The latter, in turn, clearly benefited from an intelligent and penetrating questioning of their assumptions. In 1966, after widespread external discussion of the need for parliamentary reform, Mr Wilson announced his intention to set up one or two similar committees to examine specific areas of policy-making and administration. Mr R. H. S. Crossman, as Leader of the House, began with two Select Committees, one on Science and Technology and the other on the work of the Department of Agriculture, Fisheries and Food. Later, he created a further Select Committee on Education and Science, the Agriculture Committee being closed down in early 1969. The Education Committee was told that it also could not expect to last beyond two sessions and two new Committees were set up, one on Scottish Affairs and one on Overseas Aid. Two other, rather different Select Committees were also created, one to watch over the work of the Ombudsman and the other to watch over the use made of the 1968 Race Relations Act.

These committees had a chequered history between 1966 and 1970. Mr Crossman had originally told the backbench parliamentary reform group of Labour MPs that the committees were to be permanent (so that they could indeed be 'specialist' committees) and two more would be added each session till all the main areas of governmental activity were covered. But he had only been able to get the proposal through the Cabinet on an experimental basis with the life of each committee to be reviewed at the end of each session. Very soon after the first two started work, civil servants and ministers found them troublesome and contemplated closing down the Agriculture Committee at the end of the 1966–7 session. After some argument, it was allowed to continue for a second session which ended with a major report not quite finished. In the new session, the committee was told it would have six weeks to complete its report though, after many protests, the Government granted an extension until February 1969. A distinction was drawn between committees on Agriculture, Education and Scottish Affairs which were held to be 'departmental' and Science and Technology which was held to be a 'subject' Committee and was allowed to continue session by session. By 1970, many ministers regarded the committees as a nuisance, some senior civil servants found that they imposed too much work on the departments and constantly threatened to cut across the officials' direct responsibility to the ministers, while the Whips complained that MPs regarded service on these committees as a good reason for not attending the much less popular legislative committees. Towards the end of the Labour Government, the entire future of the experiment was being reviewed and in October 1970 the incoming Conservative Government announced that it had decided to create an Expenditure Committee of 45 leaving Science and Technology, Race Relations and Scottish Affairs as the only three of the new Select Committees to continue on a permanent basis.

On the positive side, the Select Committees did provide a body of MPs with fascinating work, they forced the executive to provide a mass of valuable information which would otherwise have remained entirely secret and they led to far better informed debates in the House on the subjects being investigated and also to more searching questions. They were hampered by the reluctance of officials to discuss anything connected with policy or to give opinions other than those of the department and the minister. There were clashes between the Agriculture and Parliamentary Commissioner's Committees and the Foreign Office, a serious battle between the Treasury and the Nationalised Industries Committee (over the latter's desire to investigate the Bank of England), a good deal of tension between the Agriculture Committee and the Ministry of Agriculture and a number of other instances of conflict. It might be thought that some conflict and the resultant irritation simply showed that the committees were doing their job properly, but, as Henry Fairlie has argued, few governments are inclined to create rods for their own backs. Some ministers complained about the burden imposed on their officials, others about the debating points which the opposition could extract from the evidence, while the heads of certain nationalised industries asked who was their master, the minister or the Commons Select Committee?

As a result, opinion in the senior ranks of the Labour Government hardened against the experiment. The Conservatives after 1970 were less hostile, though the general tide of opinion had shifted away from the parliamentary reforms. It was understandable that when the new Government came to a conclusion, it preferred to concentrate on a new Expenditure Committee rather than a series of departmental Select Committees. It is, however, possible that the Select Committee experiment may be revived if it is accepted that this is the only way of monitoring regulations and directives made by the European Community. Also, the atmosphere in Whitehall is a little less opposed as many senior civil servants are

becoming disturbed by the state of ignorance the opposition gets
into (and therefore the unrealistic commitments it makes) after a
few years out of office lacking any adequate method of following the
details of policy over wide areas of governmental activity.

8. Televising the House of Commons

One reform or change in Parliament's relations with the public
has been put to the House on a free vote. This was the proposal,
coming originally from the First Report from the Select Committee
on Broadcasting under Mr T. Driberg, that the entire proceedings
of the House should be televised and the tape made available to the
various television networks. The proposal for an experimental
period was debated on 24 November 1966, and rejected by one vote,
to the surprise of most observers. It was raised again on 19 October
1972 and lost by 191 to 165 with both less interest in and surprise
at the result than in 1966. The reason for the rejection was the
belief among a considerable number of members that this innovation would alter the character of debate, elevate the stature of the
frontbench performers and, for the less frequent participants, lead
to the 'I have never seen you' type of comment in the constituencies.

Some reformers have attached considerable importance to this
proposal and were depressed by its defeat. But in fact the degree of
public attention paid to Parliament over the past century has varied
directly with the institution's powers. If debates and votes in the
Commons can be seen to affect British life, they will once again be
the subject of great interest. While television programmes picking
out the highlights in the House would fascinate the minority among
the public who are deeply concerned about politics, it is unlikely
to alter the general standing of the House of Commons with a public
whose interest is not in how the machine works but in what actual
effect it has on their lives.

9. The House of Lords

This point on publicity concludes the examination of the present
state of the House of Commons' nominal powers to play a part in
legislation, to give its consent to the raising and expenditure of
money and to question the general conduct of the government. To
broaden the picture to include the House of Lords is relatively
simple. For practical purposes, the Lords have not used their powers
to insist, for a period of twelve months, on amendments or a total
rejection of non-financial legislation since the argument over a
possible steel nationalisation Bill in 1948–9 and the Parliament

Act of 1949 (which cut the three sessions or two years' delay under the 1911 Parliament Act to one year). The 1964–70 Labour Governments did have some minor quarrels with the Lords, an example being the rejection of the Southern Rhodesian (Sanctions) Order in 1968. Some observers thought the Lords might have delayed the Commonwealth Immigrants Bill or the Order ending capital punishment, but on these major issues nothing happened. Reinforced by a steady stream of life peers since their appointment was made possible in the 1958 Life Peerages Act, the hundred to a hundred and fifty peers who do the work of the House (out of a possible total of just over 1000 qualified to take their seats) help the government by tidying up legislation and by doing the main work on non-controversial Bills and on private Bills. The Lords also provide seats in Parliament for certain ministers who do not wish to enter the House of Commons and a place to which MPs can be promoted, thus creating a vacancy in the Commons.

In 1967 there was an all-party conference on the future of the Lords, the objectives being to retain these useful minor complimentary functions while ending the hereditary basis of membership, the built-in Conservative majority and the delaying powers of the Lords. The solution proposed in a White Paper published in November 1968, was a two-tier system by which only government-appointed peers would have the right to vote, hereditary peers being allowed to speak but not vote while the delaying powers on legislation would be cut to six months. Though agreed between the parties, when these proposals were introduced in the Commons (the Parliament No. 2 Bill) in early 1969, they were bitterly attacked by some Conservatives as destroying the traditional upper House and by a few Labour members as creating a large new area of patronage through which the Prime Minister's capacity to influence MPs, particular the elderly and weary ones, would be greatly increased. As a result, the measure was abandoned and the unreformed Lords continues its quiet supporting role as before.

10. The influence of Parliament

It is hard to give a precise estimate of the effect of Parliament on the other sectors of British government though its role is best understood by regarding it not primarily as a check on the executive but as one of the institutions through which the government operates. Broadly speaking, the support of Parliament for any government with more than a nominal majority can be taken for granted and ministers come to the House to explain their policies, put through their Bills, counter opposition propaganda and keep their supporters happy. For most members, supporting their front bench is normal and the occasions when they rebel are rare and cause them some heart-searching.

If, from this, there is an attempt to abstract those occasions when the House of Commons, and principally the government's own supporters, have caused the Prime Minister or his colleagues to alter their plans in any way, it is very hard to be precise. Since the House no longer actually rejects or alters measures or forces ministers out of office but operates almost entirely by influence, the extent and degree of the influence can only be estimated by examining a series of possible cases. When this is done, however, there is less divergence than might be imagined. Mr Butt, who believes in the power of Parliament, only produces a small list of instances, but he regards them as adequate to establish his case given the role he considers desirable for the House of Commons. Mr Fairlie likewise regards Parliament as capable of achieving next to nothing on its own but finds its function as an ante-room to the centre of authority fascinating and considers that the House offers enough opportunities for Members to edge themselves into the executive, to gain publicity and to be a nuisance, to make the institution worth while.

But to try and provide an actual answer to the problem, the author compiled a list of occasions in the two sessions 1966–8 when there might possibly have been some influence exerted by the House. These were shown to the ministers concerned and to Mr Wilson, most of the former adducing other reasons for the changes that were noted while the Prime Minister denied deviating one iota on any occasion because of backbench pressure. Yet there clearly were such instances, if not in the 1966–8 sessions, at least in the 1968–9 session when backbench pressure played a large part in the abandonment of both the Parliament (No. 2) Bill and the projected Industrial Relations Bill.

The question of whether this or a greater or lesser degree of influence is desirable is a value judgment and depends on the individual's concept of democracy, but certain points should be noted here. At the time of writing (1973), the situation is not static. Mr Butt's view depends, in part, on the existence of a fair number of relatively independent MPs; the kind of Conservatives who served notice on Neville Chamberlain in 1940 and whose mutterings in the smoke room could affect Conservative Premiers, just as Labour leaders are worried if the stalwarts of the trade union group show an unaccustomed restiveness. But this kind of MP is becoming relatively rare. The Conservative local associations are turning increasingly to young men of professional or business backgrounds for whom Parliament is a career, while the trade union element in the Labour Party is losing ground to teachers, lawyers and others with much the same outlook on politics as a profession as the younger Conservatives. For these men there is both more restiveness over the aimlessness of life on the back benches and a stronger motive for not annoying the leader on whose patronage a ministerial career depends. In addition to these changes within the Commons, the public are now beginning to appreciate the small extent of Parliament's influence and its prestige is falling. The alienation of a small section of younger voters has perhaps received too much publicity but it is an attitude which is shared to some degree by other sections of the community. This attitude, together with the frustrations experienced by the abler and younger men coming into politics, may in time lead to a decline in the quality of political leadership available, at least in comparison with the capacity of those setting the pace in other sectors of British life.

When it is argued that because the British Parliament is now under the control of the executive, nothing should or can be done to alter the situation, this denies the capacity of politicians and the public to remedy defects in their own institutions. In fact, the chief restriction on British politicians is imposed by their own and the community's view of what is proper and desirable and if the former, supported by some public opinion, are convinced that changes are needed, there is every reason to think that effective reforms can be carried through. Nothing stops a British government removing or reducing the opposition's freedom to attack the government for roughly a third of the parliamentary session except the belief that this would be undesirable and would hamper both parties in the long run. Similarly no party today would, without some adequate and agreed substitute, abolish the Public Accounts Committee and the right of the opposition to nominate its chairman. If there was a widespread desire to alter the degree of influence exercised by Parliament and to make the life of a backbench MP an attractive prospect in its own right for public-spirited men and if this could only be done by the acceptance of some new countervailing powers, this would be no harder for successive governments than, for example, accepting the limitations involved in joining the Common Market. But it could only be done if there was this general agreement about the direction in which democracy in Britain should develop and about the role which Parliament should play.

GOVERNING THROUGH THE
WHITEHALL DEPARTMENTS

1. A highly centralised country

In addition to Parliament, the other principal agency or institution through which the political leadership operates is the administrative machine. Though local government is important in Britain and there is some decentralised administration, the chief impetus and the major decisions all come from the central departments of State based in Whitehall. Britain has always been a highly centralised country. Wales was conquered and subjected in the middle ages, Scotland's parliament and administration were absorbed in 1707, Ireland lost all but local administration in 1801 and the British upper classes reacted in horror at the prospect not of Irish independence but of an element of internal self-government when it was proposed by Gladstone in 1886. The intensity of their feeling was due not just to fear that the landed interest might suffer but to the affront caused to a governing class centred on London and the Home Counties by the notion that those living in the provinces might prefer a degree of local autonomy. It has remained the accepted practice that all important governmental decisions emanate from the central departments in Whitehall, a practice which is of great help to the political leadership as it collects all the levers of policy-making and administrative control into one, compact, signal box.

2. The convention of ministerial responsibility

The structure and methods of the Whitehall departments, the system of organisation and the practices and outlook of the civil servants are determined by a number of historic decisions and constitutional conventions governing the relations between the administration and the other institutions. Of these, by far the most important is the convention of ministerial responsibility. Whitehall departments are pyramids whose apex is the minister and the whole governmental machine is a larger, all-inclusive pyramid with the Prime Minister at the top. Everything focuses on this control from above. An instruction from the minister is the final word within a department, an excerpt from the Cabinet minutes conveying the decision of a committee of the Cabinet or of the full Cabinet outranks all other orders and is the source of direction for all the policy decisions taken lower down in the government.

The various departments' relations with Parliament, with outside bodies and professions are all governed by the same consideration that the minister is in charge and that he can be attacked (in or out of Parliament) for anything that happens or fails to happen in his department. So civil servants have to establish that negotiations with outside bodies will be in secret or else they will not be able to explain and consider alternatives in case the arguments they deploy in favour of an option, not eventually chosen, may later be quoted against their minister. For the same reason, civil servants above a certain level cannot take an overt or active part in politics in case it could be said that their opinions influenced the minister.

This convention of ministerial responsibility also enforces a vertical organisation on the departments. Everything that is done must be subordinate to some official who reports up to a member of the administrative class, who is under an Assistant Secretary who then puts the matter to the Permanent Secretary, he being the adviser to the minister. It is not possible to take separate sectors of administration, appoint an official to be in charge, give him a budget and let him get on with it, because if anything is raised in the press or in the House about this sector, there must be an immediate channel of communications to and instructions from the top. For these reasons also, it is hard to fit in any check points at intermediate levels in the hierarchy. The position of junior ministers reflects this problem. In amalgamated ministries or multi-purpose ministries, they are relatively happy as they can, in effect, be the minister running a sub-section. In Defence, for example, the Under-Secretaries of State for Defence for the Navy and the Army are virtually ministers in charge of a Department and in the Scottish Office, its sub-sections on Education, on Agriculture and Fisheries and on Development (Housing and Roads), each fall to a separate Under-Secretary. But if there are no such obvious internal divisions or sub-sections, it is hard to fit in these junior ministers. The Permanent Secretary must deal directly with the minister but a junior minister with his own area of discretion can scarcely come between subordinate levels in the hierarchy of officials, so that the problem of what they are supposed to do has never been satisfactorily solved.

Somewhat the same difficulty arises when outside bodies wish to deal with the civil service as such. For instance, when select or specialist committees of the House of Commons have called officials as witnesses, the latter have often been uncomfortable. The older civil servants accept that they can put facts before parliamentary committees and explain the grounds on which ministers took certain decisions but, if asked for their own opinion, they feel they must decline in case their arguments are later used against the minister. Younger officials have tended to feel freer to express opinions and when the Association of First Division officers gave evidence to the Fulton Committee, it noted that officials called before parliamentary committees 'are excused from answering questions on matters of policy, but this does not, in practice, exclude very much'. However, the doubts as to just how far the old practices can be put aside do remain. They arose over the work of the Parliamentary Commissioner (the Ombudsman) when he found that there had been maladministration in certain Foreign Office decisions about compensation due to men kept in Sachsenhausen concentration camp. The Foreign Secretary, Mr George Brown, denied any error but changed the decision to which objection had been taken. The Committee of the House appointed to review the work of the Parliamentary Commissioner wished to interview the official who had taken the decision in order to find out what the Foreign Office had done to prevent such errors recurring. The Foreign Office refused to allow the official to give evidence and sent the Attorney-General who said that to call anyone below the rank of Permanent Secretary was a breach of the collective responsibility of the department. The Committee refused to accept this but the dispute was not resolved and no further case of this kind has as yet arisen. In a milder way, the doctrine of ministerial responsibility also inhibits the mass of able and highly trained and experienced men in the Civil Service from contributing fully in their own professional associations and academic conferences in case their opinions or comments on their own work or methods might catch a headline or embarrass a minister. The doctrine of ministerial responsibility is thus a major explanation for the isolation of Whitehall departments, for their inward looking nature and for their constant emphasis on keeping within the policy bounds set from above.

It may be wondered why this doctrine is retained, but it has great

advantages for both the major groups involved—the ministers and
the civil servants. The original point of the doctrine has disappeared.
It was devised in the mid-nineteenth century, at a time when the
Commons had considerable direct power over the government,
the purpose being to ensure that the Commons could exercise
control over officials by pressing the appropriate minister. Then, this
method was effective, forcing ministers to watch over everything
that might cause trouble and forcing officials to be punctilious
about every major step they took. Since the decline of the Commons'
direct powers to censure ministers, they have not felt obliged to
resign if faults are revealed in their departments. It is true that
Sir Thomas Dugdale insisted on resigning over the Crichel Down
case in 1954 but he was not pressed to go. He had no further parliamentary ambitions and chose to resign in order to increase the
severity of the admonition given to his officials. Once a political
element arises, that is if the opposition takes up the issue, the
Prime Minister may well refuse to let a minister resign even if he
wants to. In 1958 Mr Lennox-Boyd was to some degree censured
by the Devlin Report on Nyasaland disturbances and by the inquiry
into the deaths of eleven men in Hola detention camp, but the
Government were under pressure in the House, so the Prime Minister
would not contemplate his resignation. Similarly when the Lang
Report in 1964 found errors in the costing branch of Mr Julian
Amery's Ministry of Aviation (over profits made by Ferranti), he
was exonerated by the Prime Minister.

Thus ministers no longer feel that the doctrine exposes them to
special risks in the House but, by confining all the advice of the
departments to ministers, it does ensure that they are so much
better informed and briefed than their critics. As a result, the public,
the press and MPs are often starved of the material with which to
make up a counter-argument. The ministries are staffed by very
able men who have spent years on these particular issues. They can
put the case for the minister's decision, copy his style, anticipate
hostile points and leave him feeling at a great advantage in any
conflict. If the doctrine were broken and officials could explain their
views freely in public, then ministers would have the much more
formidable task of making their case against men who were seized
of the key counterpoints and who knew that their arguments were
accepted by many in the ministry. It is clear why ministers, who
lose only a little and gain a great deal from the doctrine, should
want to keep it going.

For civil servants, the advantage is that the doctrine leaves them utterly free of any repercussions arising from their advice and thus greatly adds to their freedom and power. Consider, for instance, the position of the men in the Ministry of Employment and Productivity who advised Mrs Barbara Castle to press for sanctions against unofficial strikers in 1969. If their names were known, large sections of the Labour party would be baying for their blood. Under the working of the doctrine, they can tell the minister what they believe to be proper and still meet the TUC on good terms. The experience of a recent Governor of the Bank of England, Sir Leslie O'Brien, a quasi-civil servant, is a constant reminder to senior Treasury officials of their good fortune. When Sir Leslie commented publicly on policy in a manner disliked by the left in the Labour party, there were immediate motions calling for his removal, yet there is no doubt that some Treasury chiefs said much the same with no unpleasant repercussions. In addition, the doctrine reinforces civil servants' positions as 'insiders'. They know what is going on, their advice is the best informed and they know how difficult it is for ministers to rely on outsiders for other opinions. The outsiders (such as Professor Kaldor or Lord Balogh) are named and known and are therefore the targets for just the kind of attacks which the civil servants escape.

Thus ministerial responsibility is the main principle moulding the structure and outlook of the senior civil service and it is retained because it does much to reinforce the special position and powers both of ministers and of civil servants.

3. The Northcote–Trevelyan principles

The second main body of principles governing the Civil Service derives from the Northcote–Trevelyan Report of 1853 which was put into full operation in 1870. The first idea on which the Report was based was that the Home Civil Service (the Foreign and Colonial Services were not included) should be organised as a single body of men with a common system of recruitment based on academic ability. This latter task was allotted to a semi-independent Civil Service Commission which would conduct examinations for men in two age groups, 19 to 25 and 17 to 21, the one on the level of final examinations at a university, the other at approximately school-leaving standards. Once recruited on this basis, the candidates would be allocated to departments. Though promotion from one class to another was possible, it was across a wide gulf as the distinction between classes was held to be the distinction between mechanical and intellectual activity. It was accepted that some specialists and a class of supplementary clerks would be needed, but they did not fit into the overall scheme.

This system has remained in broad outline, the university entrants being called the administrative grade, the school leavers doing 'mechanical' work the executive grade, with clerks added as a subordinate clerical grade. The unity of the service has been encouraged by the movement of men from one department to another. Training has been 'in-service' rather than before entry and the highest posts have not gone to specialists but to broadly educated men who have specialised only in administration. Thus administrators have tended to live a relatively insulated life of their own lacking close connections with those doing similar work for private organisations or in professional life. As a result the service has produced men with a distinctive approach and outlook. Accustomed to the doctrine of ministerial responsibility, used to the idea that they are the repository of the collective wisdom and experience of their departments, accepting that they must handle outside agencies and pressure groups as well as the vagaries of the politicians and the press, they operate with caution but also with great confidence knowing that they alone are in possession of all the facts and that without their activity the whole machine would come to a halt.

4. Departmental organisation and the Treasury

Besides ministerial responsibility and the Northcote–Trevelyan principles, a third determining feature has been the organisation of the service on a departmental basis. Being highly centralised, the British system has not been to have powerful centres outside London from which groups of services can be conducted for that area but to have each of the important functions of government run from Whitehall for the whole of the country. The exceptions are Northern Ireland, Scotland and Wales, experiments with regional offices and controllers in England having done nothing to alter the fact that both policy and much of the details of administration are still controlled from Whitehall.

The first of the special cases mentioned is Northern Ireland which (until the imposition of direct rule in 1972) had a devolved system based on the 1920 Government of Ireland Act. This Act allocated agriculture, health, home affairs, education, housing, roads and indeed all internal administration to a local executive and civil service responsible to the Stormont Parliament. In Scotland and Wales, there are regional ministries under a Secretary of State, the Scottish Office having four departments (Education, Development,

Home and Health, and Agriculture and Fisheries) while the Welsh
Office has housing, roads, local government and certain aspects of
development.

England is administered by centrally based functional departments
while such functions as the supervision of Employment and Productivity, the work of the Department of Trade and of the Ministry of
Pensions and Social Security also extend over Scotland and Wales.
Given this pattern, the task of controlling and coordinating these
departments at the centre is of major importance. This is undertaken
first by the Cabinet and the Cabinet Secretariat and then by the
Treasury and the Civil Service Department.

The central role of the Treasury dates from a minute of 1860 when
it was decided that all funds for the government should be released
by the Treasury to the various ministries. These ministries had to
ask permission for all major items of expenditure within the total
sum voted and had, at the end of the year, to account to the Treasury
for the detailed expenditure of their allocation of funds. The Permanent Secretary in each ministry became the Accounting Officer
responsible to the Treasury for the expenditure of the money
allocated to his ministry. Besides this control through the finances
of a department, new activity usually means more staff and this
requires the sanction of a special Civil Service department which
was, before 1968, part of the Treasury but has since become a
separate coordinating ministry on its own. The constant oversight
of the Treasury is now maintained not only by its control of the
normal disbursement of money but by the fact that each year forward
estimates of public expenditure have to be put by the departments
before the Treasury and Public Expenditure Survey Committee and
agreed upon there. The Treasury employs sections which monitor
the expenditure of the various departments and go over their estimates, the role of the Treasury being to insist on certain overall
policies and ceilings on expenditure while the spending departments
tend to argue in favour of certain policy objectives or programmes,
hoping that if these are accepted, the necessary funds will be forthcoming. The Treasury never likes to get involved in considerations
of which aspects of departmental policy are more or less desirable
as the only result would be to commit the Treasury to the financial
consequences. Yet in fixing the allocations between departments,
they have to take into consideration the policy of the government
and what each department proposes to do with the money.

F

5. Criticisms of the Civil Service: its relations with ministers

Given this framework and governing principles, the Civil Service has operated without many upheavals over the last century. Recently, however, there has been some criticism and some arguments about its structure in addition to the more long-standing discussion of how far ministers can dominate their departments and how far Civil Service practices and attitudes have proved too much for the politicians. The criticisms have fallen into certain categories, one general line being that the service has failed to adopt modern methods of management, that it has been slow in understanding the use of statistical information and of specialised knowledge of the social services and that it does not think ahead enough or organise its planning on a sufficiently systematic basis, in part because officials spend too much time on routine departmental work. A second theme has been a particular criticism of the Treasury and of its economic policies on the lines that in the 1950s and 1960s the Treasury laid too much emphasis on the balance of payments and too little on growth, that it was absorbed with old economic orthodoxies and that a new approach was needed in this field. Finally, there have been attacks on the 'generalist' or 'all-rounder' in administration combined with the argument that the Civil Service is too isolated, complacent and insulated from outside pressures.

Before considering these, it is worth looking at the older worry dating from the 1930s about the relationship between ministers and civil servants and about the problems of how far the outlook of the departments limits the freedom of action of the political leaders of the country. The worries on this subject began in the 1930s for two reasons. The first was the disappointment felt about the record of the first two Labour Governments and, in particular, the Government of 1929–31. When it was realised that no distinctive 'socialist' or radical policies were emerging from the Labour Cabinet, and in particular that its Chancellor of the Exchequer, Mr Snowden, sounded like the mouthpiece of the Bank of England, many inside and outside the Labour party began to wonder if Labour ministers had been confused, converted or captured by their official advisers. The second was that commentators, exemplified by Mr Ramsay Muir in *How Britain is Governed,* had been brought up on the theory that a minister could watch over all the policy decisions made in his department. When, by the 1930s, it became apparent that this was impossible and that some policy issues were settled by civil servants, they became very alarmed and termed this 'bureaucracy'.

By the 1960s, the cruder uses of this term implying that there might have been some political content in the attitude of civil servants were abandoned. There is now little doubt that the trouble with the first two Labour Governments was not just that in some cases departmental policies prevailed, but that the ministers placed in charge of these departments and the Cabinet as a whole had no coherent alternative or distinctive policies to put forward. The postwar governments, both Labour and Conservative, have shown that a minister with coherent, workable policies and reasonable energy and capacity can get loyal cooperation from his or her civil servants. Moreover, for such a minister, the ideal is not a department without a policy or officials without positive ideas as to what needs to be done. If there is a vacuum of this kind, far from the field being clear for political decision-taking (as Ramsey Muir suggests), the minister is lost because there are no properly prepared and documented alternatives from which he can choose. On the other hand, from the civil servant's angle what is wanted as a minister is not a malleable man who can be moulded or pushed into particular views. The officials want and respect a minister who can pick up a problem quickly, select from among the alternatives the line most in accord with the outlook of his cabinet colleagues and his party, who is courageous and can win any necessary battles with other departments outside or inside the Cabinet, and who can explain the policy well in public. Above all, they want a minister who, having taken a decision, does not constantly alter it every time some pressure is brought to bear.

But though the relationship, when satisfactory, is relatively straightforward and works as would be expected when any large organisation is taken over by a new and competent managing director, there are other cases where problems can arise. For instance, Cabinets are not chosen on grounds of administrative competence. This is a factor in selection and all Cabinets have some first-class administrators, but there are other, political reasons for appointments and it is possible that in any Cabinet of twenty, a half would not have been chosen if the only grounds had been the capacity to run a large department. Secondly parties new to power have on their front bench men selected for their oratory and their critical faculties and these may not be associated with the administrative and constructive capacities needed for government. And the longer a party is in opposition, the fewer of its leaders have had a chance to develop these abilities. After thirteen years in opposition, only two of the Labour front bench in 1964 had had experience of a previous

Cabinet. Finally, the reasons for moving ministers frequently have little to do with ability and the time spent in any particular office is often too short to allow the minister to master the subject and the department. Professor Anthony King has shown that compared with this country before 1914 or other countries today, British ministers have a far shorter average length of stay in one post, in the decade 1956–66 the period being just under two years. It is often said that it takes a man a year to become thoroughly familiar with a new and intricate task and only after three years is he really on top of his job. On that basis, he would be more than ready for a 'reshuffle', as ministerial swop-arounds are now called.

When these situations occur, when the minister lacks ability, experience, knowledge of the particular subject or, perhaps, the time to become confident of his own judgment, then the departmental policy tends to prevail. And this may be desirable, for a country cannot be policyless on major issues. Even when the relationship between a minister and his department is of this kind, there is no conscious usurpation of authority and officials must always act through the minister. What happens is that having to serve on many Cabinet and other committees, anyone other than a top-grade and experienced minister tends to use the brief he has been given. And before most ministerial committees an equivalent official committee meets and goes over the points, so that the meeting can proceed without a hitch to an agreed conclusion, provided none of the ministers wishes to interject a personal note. The author recalls an able Treasury minister who, after resignation, became a convinced and cogent parliamentary reformer explaining that as a minister he had had no time to work out this aspect of policy and therefore, since the Treasury was opposed to more specialist committees of the House of Commons, he used the brief they provided and he had been a formidable opponent of these reforms at the Cabinet Committee level. One source of official strength is to take time. Civil servants are in the same department for many years, if not for life, while the minister lasts only two to three years. It is understandable that a civil servant takes longer to negotiate or work out a solution over which he is unenthusiastic, the result being that by the time the work is complete, there is a new minister who is more ready to see the weaknesses of this line of action. In addition, to argue with able, patriotic, experienced men is tiring and some ministers have found that it is best to reserve their energies for major issues. Finally, a strong departmental philosophy, such as the Foreign Office's conviction from the early 1960s onwards that Britain should join the EEC, is hard for any minister to resist. It can be done. Neville Chamberlain carried through the latter stages of the appeasement policy leading up to Munich and Sir Anthony Eden launched the Suez invasion in 1956 in each case against the almost united opposition of the Foreign Office (which, in consequence, was largely by-passed or kept in the dark because of this known disagreement).

Thus the normal analysis of this question of relative influence has been that if and when a government seriously sets its mind to a change of policy that is within the limits of feasibility, this can be achieved. But whenever ministers fall short of this degree of ability and determination, competent officials are able to offer opinions as to the proper policy, though these can be moulded by ministerial views. And if the ministers do lack opinions or energy, the departments can at least maintain sufficient continuity and activity to keep government going.

6. Criticisms of the Civil Service: its administrative methods

Turning to the criticisms of the administrative machine through which the political leadership operates, the pattern was set in the early 1960s by Professor Brian Chapman's *British Government Observed*. He argued that Britain had failed to make 'a reasonable proportion of right and wise decisions in matters of major policy', and that other nations had done better. The specific weaknesses of British government which Chapman alleged were first that the ministries, though expected to take all key decisions, were not expected to act—to build roads, run hospitals, train teachers and so on. This always had to be done by another agency so that British government became 'a rich Byzantine structure' of boards, local authorities, commissions and joint committees. As a result, he argued, responsibility is hard to pin down, action becomes desperately slow, planning is inadequate and too many wrong decisions are made. In part, this is because the Civil Service is a closed corporation, over-specialised in 'general administration' and London-based to the point of becoming parochial. In part it is because training is in-service and little emphasised and also because so much of government is secret, information being deliberately kept from Parliament and the public. Further evidence of these weaknesses is the way governments, faced with difficult problems, do not turn to the departments (or to the Commons) but set up Commissions and inquiries manned by distinguished outsiders to investigate and pronounce.

This was a formidable catalogue of sins but many of the ideas became generally accepted and to some extent underlay Mr Wilson's thinking in 1963 when he talked of the Conservatives' period in power since 1951 as 'thirteen wasted years' and promised that in the first hundred days of dynamic government after a Labour victory at the polls a new atmosphere would pervade Whitehall.

By the mid-1960s the kind of criticisms being made began to alter, particularly when the Labour Government produced neither a distinctive atmosphere in administration nor a greater number of policy successes. Also, by the mid-1960s, attention was being focused almost entirely on balance of payments problems and attention shifted to the type of criticisms featured in Mr Samuel Brittan's book called originally *The Treasury Under the Tories* (1964) and reissued in 1969 as *Steering the Economy*. He was less critical of the machinery itself saying that 'the British Treasury was ahead of most other Finance ministries over most of the period' (1945–69) and in terms of its readiness to use Keynesian techniques 'it had a lead of many years over most of its European counterparts'. While Mr Brittan had doubts as to whether the ethos and training of the Civil Service was entirely suitable for its contemporary tasks, his chief criticism was of 'the excessive "overseas" orientation among the upper reaches of British policymakers, which gave priority to the maintenance of a world role the country could no longer carry'. This was simply another way of saying that the Treasury and the other key ministries in Whitehall did not accept Mr Brittan's view of the relations of the UK, the US, and Europe with consequent effects on defence, economic and trading policies. But it may have been the case that some senior civil servants objected to these policies and were overruled by the politicians for this kind of overemphasis on Britain's world-wide role until the late 1960s spread far beyond the ranks of the civil servants.

7. The Fulton Committee's proposals

This moderation in the tone of criticism was reversed when the Committee under Lord Fulton, which was appointed in 1966 to 'examine the structure, recruitment and management, including training, of the Home Civil Service', reported in 1968. It asserted that 'the structure and practices of the Service have not kept up with the changing tasks' and found six major faults. The first was the 'cult of the generalist' or 'all-rounder' which the Fulton Committee said was 'obsolete at all levels and in all parts of the Service'. Then the division into classes was held to be an impediment and a cause of frustration. The Report alleged that many scientists, engineers and other specialists were not given the opportunities they should have and too few civil servants were skilled in the techniques of modern management. There was not enough contact between the Service and the world outside Whitehall while, in general, promotion depended too much on seniority and too little on merit.

Before considering the Fulton Committee's proposals to remedy the situation, these assorted criticisms of the public service have to be examined. In general, the Fulton Committee's critique was overdone in that it was attacking a caricature of the Service which was never wholly true and certainly underestimated the changes that had taken place since the late 1950s. The two further major reservations that must be made are first that the Service is moulded chiefly by the doctrine of ministerial responsibility with all that flows from it—anonymity, one collective viewpoint, secrecy and a degree of isolation from the rest of the community. The Fulton Committee was not, by its terms of reference, allowed to look at the relationship with Parliament but, as a result, it blamed the service itself for many characteristics imposed on it by virtue of this relationship. The second was that this was the very difficult period when, as Dean Acheson said, Britain 'had lost an Empire and failed to find a role'. Inevitably policy failures were attributed to the government and its officials when the blame lay more widely with the whole of the community and in particular with the strong British dislike both for re-thinking an entire situation and for the radical changes that might have to follow from such a reconsideration.

Given these two reservations, some of the detailed criticisms contain an element of truth but others are superficial. For instance, the attack on the 'generalist' is overdone and for most specialists, the training that counts is what they learn after they start work. After ten years in a department working, for example, on housing, that one man's undergraduate degree was in philosophy and another's in sociology will make little or no difference; what will matter is the capacity and experience they have developed at the task. It is true that over a decade when the senior Civil Service was moving from being primarily regulatory in outlook to being primarily managerial, there was a lack of research, of assessment of situations before action could be properly planned. It is also true that the service is still obsessed with the idea that it should, if possible, not act itself but should operate through some external agency. Thus when the officials think they must do something to stimulate tourism, plant trees or preserve the countryside, instead of acting themselves, they float a Tourist Board, a Forestry Commission or a Countryside Commission. This has its merits and has been the practice in Sweden, but it is of value only if the central government departments then restrict themselves purely to planning, thinking and regulating. In Britain, however, because of ministerial responsibility and because of the suspicion that the appropriate ministry could do the job much better than a new, inexperienced board (which usually has a lower calibre of staff), the ministries concerned have their own sections on tourism, forestry and the countryside which go over everything the board in question proposes, giving authorisations, suggestions or exercising a veto. The result is delay, duplication and frustration. The ministries become bogged down in detail when their energies and resources should be concentrated more on overall policy and the *ad hoc* commissions grow disillusioned and frustrated because they are not allowed to get on with the job.

To solve the problems it diagnosed, the Fulton Committee recommended a number of changes which amounted to an attempt to introduce the modern (largely American) techniques of business management into the Civil Service. The main principle involved is the delegation of responsibility for budgets and for staff to accountable units each with defined objectives and one person responsible for the performance of the unit. Control is exercised by financial techniques and revision of the objectives set for each unit. This permits both an effective method of assessing ability and achievement with the minimum of day-to-day interference. The weakness of this approach in terms of the British Civil Service is that it ignores the force of ministerial responsibility. At present, no minister could answer a parliamentary question by saying that whatever his views on the matter, responsibility had been allocated for this function to Assistant Secretary Brown and it was up to that official to take whatever course of action he thought best to achieve the set objectives. In addition, two of the continuing aspects of the service accepted or recommended by the Fulton Committee make such delegation of responsibility impossible; these are the continuing financial control of the Treasury and the supervision of all staff by the new Civil Service department.

Thus the aspects of the Fulton recommendations which could be put into practice were those which were compatible with ministerial responsibility, such as the creation of a new Civil Service department, the abolition of classes in favour of a single unified grading structure (the grading of each post to be determined by job evaluation), the foundation of a Civil Service College, the establishment of planning units and of management units and the devotion of greater resources to career management. But all of these simply underlined trends already evident before the Fulton Committee reported and none of them will make any basic difference to the structure or functions of the Service.

8. The Civil Service and Parliament

The fundamental problems, which any proper review of the Service ought to have tackled, are its relationships with Parliament, with the public and with the organised interest groups which constitute so much of what the Civil Service must regard as public opinion. Once the parameters which condition the existence and operation of the Service have been agreed and set out, its internal organisation can be arranged on lines which give the' maximum efficiency compatible with these conditions. First, is it desirable that Civil Service departments should deal directly with the public? If no suitable local elected authority can be found, should the central department run a service itself through officials in the regions? Is it intrinsically more desirable for local nominated hospital boards to run the hospitals or would this be better done by regional sections of the Ministry of Health? In part, the answer depends on the size and capacity of the local government units to be established. But if the principle is accepted that any services not operated by local government should be conducted directly by the central ministries (perhaps through their regional offices), this would lead to a tremendous simplification of administration and probably to much greater efficiency.

Then there is the question of whether the Civil Service should deal directly with pressure groups, reach agreements, embody these in draft legislation and only then tell Parliament or whether Parliament should be brought in at a formative stage so that the pressure groups would be encouraged to lobby MPs as well as departments. If the objective of a democratic legislative process is to inform the public about the issues, to let them know what pressure groups are saying on their behalf and to allow the Civil Service to assess public reaction before rather than after the government is committed to a line of action, then both the pressure groups and the Civil Service ought to explain their proposals to Parliament which, in practice, would mean to committees of the House of Commons.

Finally, if Parliament is to exercise its ancient function of scrutinising both legislation and departmental policy-making, it has to be able to deal directly with the Civil Service because ministers do not, in fact, make all policy decisions. These changes would require the destruction of the principle of ministerial responsibility, a principle which is such a comfort to both officials and ministers. But to do so

F*

would not only help to achieve better relations between the Civil Service on the one hand and Parliament, the public and the pressure groups on the other. It would also make all the Fulton reforms in management possible. If it could be accepted that ministers made overall policy but that the working and effectiveness of sub-sections within departments, which operated under certain policy directives, was not the responsibility of the minister but of the civil servant in charge, this would make an enormous change. The civil servant would cease to be anonymous. He would be allowed to explain and defend his sub-section's conduct in public. The minister would only be blameworthy if the sub-section failed to achieve its objectives or overspent its budget to no purpose and the minister then failed to take the appropriate action.

If this pattern were adopted, Parliament could develop departmental specialist committees which would watch over these sub-sections of the administration and offer their heads a platform for explaining and defending their policies. Because control was being exercised through the investigations and comments of a parliamentary committee, the pressure groups would once again find it worthwhile to spend some of their time pressing their case on MPs, some of whom would be members of the specialist committee concerned while others could raise points in the normal course of debate.

But not until ministerial responsibility has been abandoned will it be possible to end the pyramidical structure of the Civil Service, to diminish anonymity, to decrease secrecy and to open up the processes of public administration to public discussion and accountability. Also it is almost certainly the case that in terms of pure efficiency, it does any administration good to have to explain and defend its policies against every variety of argument and pressure which interest groups and an informed representative assembly can bring to bear.

GOVERNMENT OUTSIDE WHITEHALL

The purpose of this chapter is to describe the rest of the machinery through which the political leadership operates outside Whitehall and this includes more than just the system of local government. In the late nineteenth century, all administration was grouped at two levels—central and local—so that at each level, decisions could be subjected to the scrutiny of an elected body. Since then, central government departments have established regional offices, the government has taken control of industries and agencies, some with their headquarters in London, but mainly operating in the regions. Numerous *ad hoc* bodies have been created to run specific functions such as the Highland Development Board, Ports Authorities, bodies to preserve historic buildings, to run industrial training schemes, and so on. Some regional authorities have been created out of functions taken from the local authorities, an example being the area health boards. Finally, there is the two-tier system of local government established by the Local Government Act of 1972 for England and Wales and by the Scottish Local Government Act of 1973.

The mass of governmental agencies which are strictly speaking neither part of the central Whitehall machine, whose distinctive feature is direct subordination to a particular minister, nor are they part of the elected pattern of local government, have come to be called 'intermediate government'. This description is not very satis- factory as it suggests some sort of geographical location at unknown points between London and the centres of local government. Many of these agencies do operate in the regions but so do some Whitehall ministries with networks of employment bureaux, factory and school inspectors, dockyards and airforce bases. The distinguishing feature of this range of government is not its location but simply that it is outside the normal pattern of direct control by ministers responsible to Parliament or by committees responsible to an elected local council.

1. The nationalised industries

When these various bodies were created, the question of control did arise, most acutely in the case of the nationalised industries. These were created or taken over by the State at various times since the first examples under the 1906–14 Liberal Government, but the largest group of Nationalisation Acts covering coal, road and rail services, gas, electricity and iron and steel came under the 1945–51 Labour Government. At that time the old doctrines of the need for democratic control were still strong and an argument arose between those, such as Mr Aneurin Bevan, who favoured total subordination to Parliament (with a minister for each industry on the lines of the Post Office), and those led by Mr Herbert Morrison, who wanted to leave the industries a measure of independence to operate as fully commercial undertakings. The latter approach prevailed and though the various Nationalisation Acts differ in detail, the main points were the same. A board was nominated to run each industry as a viable commercial enterprise. The minister can change the board and give the board directions of a general character which have to be observed. He has to be consulted on any substantial capital outlays and be provided with a full report of the board's activities. In practice, the minister has only once had to issue such a directive (when the Conservatives after 1951 stopped any further action by the Iron and Steel Board) as these reserve powers are quite sufficient to make the boards listen carefully to any suggestions made in a less formal manner by the minister. Parliament, however, has a far weaker position. It is entitled to see (and debate, if necessary) the annual accounts and report of each industry but it can only question the minister on those aspects of the industry's activities for which the minister is responsible. In practice, this means that censure motions are possible and questions can be tabled on the general issues where it could be held that the minister ought to have issued a directive. But on day-to-day issues or on detailed matters where the minister would not be authorised to intervene by the relevant Act, however much he might discuss these points on an informal basis and influence the actions of the board, Parliament can do nothing.

In practice, the nationalised industries are subject to Whitehall and civil servants often re-examine the major management decisions (and some minor ones) in case points of principle arise, in particular

considering whether investment and pricing policies are satisfactory
from the ministry's point of view. Also ministers are often prepared
to get answers on detailed questions for MPs, though the Commons
decided that such letters were not 'proceedings in Parliament' and
were therefore not protected from actions alleging libel. It is scarcely
surprising that when the Select Committee on Nationalised Industries examined this problem it found a 'lack of clarity and certainty
and purpose' among what it called the sponsoring government
departments. The result was a 'lack of understanding and in some
cases, a breakdown of mutual confidence between boards and
ministries'. The Select Committee then went on to recommend very
much the same principles as the Fulton Committee wanted to see
adopted widely in the Civil Service. It argued that government control
should be 'strategic guidance' and should be exercised as far as
possible in the same way for all the industries by the use of economic
and financial criteria and that this should be done by one minister
and one department. Other aspects which concerned the public
such as the need to retain certain uneconomic railway lines, the use
of coal to prevent too fast a rise in unemployment in areas dependent
on mining or the case for airports on remote islands in Scotland,
could then all be urged from outside on the individual industries and
on the Ministry for Nationalised Industries without confusing these
social objectives with the normal criteria of operation. These recommendations (made in 1968) have not been adopted, but the idea of
control within government being exercised by financial and commercial techniques while the major method of ensuring public
accountability is through a Select Committee of the House of Commons (in this case, the Committee on Nationalised Industries) is
entirely in accordance with a combination of the Fulton proposals
for the Civil Service and the parliamentary reformers' case for more
Select Committees of the House of Commons.

An example of current thinking on the nationalised industries is
the recent reorganisation of the Post Office. This office was a department of the government from 1517 and more particularly from 1840
when Rowland Hill introduced the penny post, but in 1967 the Labour
Government decided that the Post Office would benefit from complete commercial independence with its own career structure separate
from the Civil Service. The reasons were that such a separation would
permit the Post Office to organise its own structure and leave the
government free to rearrange the Civil Service as a purely administrative or supervisory machine. The Chairman could then devote
himself solely to management, leaving the public interest to be

represented by the minister. The latter's control would be considerable, but Parliament would be left merely with general debates on supply days, debates on borrowing powers, Bills, adjournment debates and questions on the broader issues for which the minister would accept responsibility.

Although this has been the drift of official and ministerial thinking and these ideas have been embodied in various acts, the practice has not followed suit. As each government, particularly the Conservative Government since 1970, has encountered economic difficulties, there has been a tendency to use the immediate control available over the nationalised industries to try and influence the economy. Thus Mr Heath's Government intervened in labour disputes forbidding more than a certain level of pay increases, intervened in the Coal Board's policy of closing uneconomic pits, imposed price ceilings and altered investment plans. With these industries so far drawn into the area of political management, it will be hard ever to give them the degree of independence that modern commercial practice demands.

2. Local government before the 1972 Act; its structure and weaknesses

At the time of writing (late 1973) local government is in the process of transition from a system with historic origins which assumed its present form in the late nineteenth century to a new system embodied in the 1972 Local Government Act. In order to appreciate some of the present problems and the need for a reform, it is necessary to examine the pattern of local government as it stood before the 1972 Act. This pattern dated originally from the Middle Ages when the towns were able to purchase their right to self-government by paying an impecunious Crown for a charter. The latter gave the right to self-government and self-taxation to all living within the town walls or boundary, leaving the surrounding rural area under the control of the aristocracy. This division between town and country became hardened by the end of the nineteenth century into 58 County Councils and 82 County Boroughs in England and Wales. While these County Boroughs looked after all their own local government, in the counties there were subordinate partially self-governing bodies; namely 270 non-County Boroughs, 535 Urban District Councils and 473 Rural District Councils, these last being further subdivided into some 7500 Parish Councils. Thus the administrative map of England and Wales looked like a cloth with patches on it, the patches being towns governed by Borough or Urban District Councils with the entire surrounding area administered by a County

Council. County Boroughs totally opted out of the surrounding County Council's affairs, but for the other types of subordinate authorities the situation was complicated because they performed some functions for themselves while other functions in their areas, such as education, were run by the County Council. Thus the councillors for non-County Boroughs who were nominated to attend the County Council could deliberate and vote on certain parts of the agenda but had to withdraw for others. Similarly the rates paid by the citizens in these areas had to be shared between the two levels of local authority.

In Scotland, the structure was very much the same except that the number of people resident in the various categories of local authorities tended, on average, to be smaller and there was no third tier equivalent to the Parish Council. The actual structure consisted of 31 counties and 4 cities, with the counties divided into 21 large Burghs, 176 small Burghs and 198 District Councils.

This system of local government had much fine work to its credit but it was generally accepted that its structure had not changed enough to keep pace with the changing social patterns of travel to work, shopping and holiday areas. Nor were the levels of resources available enough to pay for the increased skills needed for the more complex requirements of local administration. These weaknesses appeared in many forms. Perhaps the most fundamental was the great variation in the size and resources of units all supposed to perform the same tasks at roughly the same standards. Thus Rutland and Westmorland were counties with 27 940 and 67 410 inhabitants and a penny added to the local rates yielded £3401 and £9420 respectively, yet these two units were supposed to provide the same standard of education and welfare services as Lancashire with 2·3 million people where a penny rate raised £325 741. The range among boroughs was equally great from Birmingham with 1·1 million citizens and a penny rate producing £204 450 to Canterbury where 32 770 people paying an extra penny provided £6350. (In Scotland the discrepancies were even greater.)

The results of these variations and the fact that there were so few boundary changes over the last century were that most authorities were too small and too poor financially to provide the highest standard of services, to hire the requisite staff and provide the necessary specialised units, while some were simply far too small and weak. For example, the Department of Education and Science estimated that a proper education service is difficult to organise when there are fewer than 300 000 people but they would prefer authorities with

500 000 inhabitants. In this case 13 of the 45 English counties, 11 of the 13 Welsh counties and 27 of the 31 Scottish counties fell below the minimum figure as did 70 of the 78 English boroughs, all 4 Welsh boroughs and 2 of the 4 Scottish cities. The Home Office has argued that adequate children's services cannot be organised for units with less than 250 000 people while the Ministry of Health indicated (in evidence to the Redcliffe-Maud Commission) that the optimum would be between 200 000 and 250 000 inhabitants.

For proper administration, the problem was not just being too small. There was also the difficulty of inappropriate areas. Glasgow was big enough, with a million people, to have an adequate planning unit but the city is part of the single conurbation of the Clyde Valley where there were in fact 14 separate planning authorities. In general, the division between the town and the countryside caused many problems, residential suburbs were built outside city boundaries so that many who worked in the city and used its facilities contributed nothing to the cost of these services. The counties naturally resented the extension of borough boundaries but the failure to do so led to constant quarrels and prevented the cities from controlling their water supplies or planning their transport systems in a sensible way.

Besides these limitations of area and size, finance added another dimension. Traditionally, local government provided services for property owners—paved streets, lighting, water, sewerage and police—and so the main local government tax has always been a rate levied on property values. But this meant that the areas with most problems are usually those where property values are low and where there are therefore fewest resources available to pay for remedial services. Secondly, while many other tax sources are buoyant, property assessments only rise slowly and so more revenue means raising the tax rate and this always causes trouble as the tax is regressive, weighing more heavily as a percentage of total income on those in the lower income ranges.

A combination of these difficulties of area, population and finance meant that local authorities could not always gather a proper level of staff to operate their services. There were many vacancies and many posts were filled with persons lacking the proper qualifications. In particular, it was hard to recruit the necessary planners, architects, engineers and medical officers. For instance, of the 2341 child-care officers in England and Wales in 1968, only 28 per cent were professionally qualified and 40 per cent had no qualification at all. Forty seven per cent of authorities said they experienced 'extreme difficulty' in filling these posts and 7 per cent of the posts had to be left vacant. When residential child-care staff are considered, of the 5035 in employment, 10 per cent held the appropriate certificate and 82 per cent were without any qualification. Part of the problem is that in many of the smaller authorities, proper salaries, a career structure and a sufficiently varied and interesting job cannot be offered. Also there were simply not enough planners and probably not enough work to make all the 175 planning departments outside London attractive to the relatively thin flow of newly trained men.

These weaknesses as administrative agencies partly explain the suspicion of local government in the central departments and among many politicians and others in all walks of life. In part, these feelings sprang from the tremendously centralised tradition of British society and administration. It was felt by many politicians and officials that local government, in its recent form, was slow and inept so that the departments dealing with local authorities either developed a mass of controls to enable them to watch over local authorities or actually withdraw services from the local authorities. They also developed a series of financial controls through the grants made to local government. All was underpinned by the widespread belief that local councillors were not likely to take a progressive view on educational policy, such matters as the arts or the preservation of historic buildings, and that local authority officials were less competent than their counterparts in Whitehall.

The results were evident at many levels. One was the withdrawal of such functions as running hospitals, manufacturing gas and electricity and the distribution of national assistance (now known as supplementary benefits) from local government. A second was the elaborate controls over the remaining functions which typically began with the duty to lay a scheme before the appropriate minister. Then approval was required for the aquisition of land and for any capital investment, for the plans of buildings, and for the detailed reorganisation of the service. The qualifications and superannuation of staff were laid down as were the standards of service so that, for instance, the Housing (Scotland) Act, 1966, contains more than one hundred separate provisions in which the local authority's housing function was subject to the consent or direction of the minister or his officials. In finance, local authorities were left tied to an unpopular and regressive tax so that their dependence on central government grants steadily increased (by 1970 over 40 per cent of their total revenue). This money was either earmarked specifically for certain services or was a block grant calculated by an extremely elaborate formula set out in the Local Government Act of 1966. There was also control over borrowing and through the audit of local authority accounts.

The total result of this level of central management was that one local authority could not be so very different in its policies from the next; citizens could travel from one part of the country to another under different party control without detecting any very noticeable differences in the quality of local services. This and the fact that local authority work was organised on the time-consuming basis of a committee to watch over each function meant that only about half of the seats open to election were contested, vacant places on committees being filled by cooption. It also meant that councillors tended to be drawn largely from those businesses, trade unions or professions which were in any case involved in municipal affairs and public interest was extremely low, elections often failing to draw more than a third of the voters to the polls.

The central government was partly responsible for this situation and its actions tended to reinforce these trends. When tasks arose which Whitehall could not perform either because of the volume of the work (e.g. planning appeals) or because of the desire to keep the Civil Service in a supervisory role, there was seldom any sug-gestion that local government should be asked to do the job. Occa-sionally this was tried, an example being when the Scottish City and County Councils were asked to produce plans for the preservation and development of the countryside. After ten years only two out of the thirty-five authorities had responded so that the moral once again was that the local authorities were not up to it. In recent times, the reaction of the central government has been to create an *ad hoc* body or series of bodies to take over the task in question or to push the local authorities into forming joint committees. Examples of the former were the hospital boards set up in 1948 or the Country-side Commissions for England, Wales and Scotland created in 1968, the Tourist Boards and River Pollution Boards, the Water Boards, Nature Conservancy, Arts Council, Forestry Commission, Sports Council, Ancient Monuments Commission and the Passenger Transport Authorities proposed in the 1968 Transport Act. Examples of the latter, that is of local authority joint committees, occurred in such functions as public health, port health, water supply, sewerage, burial, police, fire services, harbours, tunnels and airports.

3. Regional government: Northern Ireland, Scotland, Wales. Is there a case for England?

Another approach to this problem which recognised the value of some decentralisation and the fact that local conditions could differ came after the Second World War when the Government asked any Whitehall departments with regional offices to adopt the wartime 'standard Treasury regions'. Later, in 1956, when regional planning was extended from Scotland and the North-East to the rest of the country, England was divided into eight economic planning regions. In each, a board of civil servants was established bringing together the local representatives of the central departments involved in economic development. To this was added a nominated council of prominent local figures. The task of the Board and the Council in each region was to draw together the planning and administration of the area, to produce comprehensive studies setting out the regional priorities and to link the efforts of central government and the local authorities.

In three cases, this problem of regional administration has been met with special machinery. Northern Ireland was governed under the provisions of the 1920 Government of Ireland Act supplemented by several conventional arrangements. The Act established a bi-cameral parliament at Stormont near Belfast and gave it control of agriculture, health, education, roads, indeed of all internal adminis-tration that did not affect other parts of the UK or external relations. The Act also reduced Northern Irish representation at Westminster to 13 seats. The financial arrangements were that the Northern Ireland government received 2·5 per cent of whatever was raised by UK taxation and could raise a very limited amount in taxation on its own account. Out of this it was agreed that services (unemploy-ment relief, pensions, education, etc.) were provided at a similar level to those in Britain and if there was any money left, an 'imperial contribution' was paid towards the cost of common services such as the armed forces and the cost of conducting foreign policy. In return for the element of subsidy in this system, the Treasury was consulted about any expenditure which was abnormal by British standards. Thus Northern Ireland enjoyed the same standard of services and endured no greater taxation than the rest of the UK. In most fields, the Stormont government aimed to follow British practice in as far as this benefited its citizens but to act separately when special local conditions required separate treatment. Normally London left Stormont to get on with these policies, only intervening in 1969 when there was a clear danger of a collapse of law and order due to disputes between Catholics and Protestants over local government, over the allocation of houses and of jobs and over the conduct of the Royal Ulster Constabulary and of the 'B' special reserves.

From 1969, the British government pressed certain reforms on the Stormont Government while the British army was deployed in Northern Ireland to try and preserve law and order. As the situation deteriorated, it was felt that some further evidence of the British government's determination not to allow the majority to lean on the minority was needed. In March 1972, the Stormont Parliament and executive were abolished and direct rule was applied. After much discussion but no evident diminution in the communal struggle, the British government brought out a White Paper in March 1973 proposing a return to a modified Stormont system. The modifications were proportional representation with 'power-sharing' in the Cabinet and in the committees of the Assembly which would run the departments, the powers of the Assembly being similar to those of Stormont except that control of security and law and order remained with the UK government. Whether this system will be acceptable to those elected to the Assembly, whether it will then begin to operate and whether the result will be to help reduce communal strife cannot (in late 1973) be forecast.

In Scotland and Wales, there is no devolved subordinate legislature but exceptions have been made by the creation of regional ministries under Secretaries of State for Scotland and for Wales, each with some junior ministers. In the case of Scotland, the regional ministry consists of four Departments covering Development (economic planning, housing and power), Home and Health (hospitals, child care, police and probation), Agriculture and Fisheries, and Education. The Scottish Office, often known from the name of its Edinburgh offices as St Andrews House, deals with the work of nine English ministries in Scotland leaving the rest of Scottish administration to the remaining UK departments. These cover the functions which it was felt required uniform standards throughout the country, such as the work of the Departments of Employment and Environment, the Department of Trade and Industry, Defence and Social Security. The Welsh Office is similar except that it has considerably fewer devolved powers, lacking, for instance, education, health and home office affairs.

These regional ministries operate as a normal part of the Whitehall machine except that they are located in Scotland and Wales and they have the normal right to membership of any cabinet committees dealing with matters for which they take responsibility in their areas. Although one object of having such ministries is that they can deal with problems in a manner specially suited to conditions in Scotland and Wales, the fact that the ministers belong to the UK Cabinet and are responsible to the UK Parliament means that there is considerable pressure for uniformity. In the case of Northern Ireland, the pressure for uniformity came from the electorate who want to be as well treated as British citizens are in England or Scotland and who can, in the last resort, leave if conditions are much less satisfactory in Northern Ireland. In Scotland and Wales there is the same pressure for equal treatment but it comes in the first instance from MPs who will pounce on any discrepancies and ask why England (or Scotland or Wales) is receiving special treatment. As a result, it is an established convention that the Scottish and Welsh Offices consult their Whitehall opposite numbers (and vice versa) before proposing any action which could be the thin end of an undesirable wedge for the other ministry. In financial arrangements, neither of these Offices approaches the Treasury with a request for a single budget for all their functions. They allow the English ministries to make a case for an overall allocation for housing, health, roads and so on, the Scottish (and, where relevant, the Welsh) Departments putting in a bid for a share of these functional budgets based on the special needs of Scots or Welsh housing, roads or water resources. The reason for accepting this approach rather than asking for a 'block allocation' is simply the conviction that the summation of functional budgets produces a larger and more defensible total.

In England it has often been disputed whether there is any regional feeling and obviously there is nothing of the quasi-nationalism evident in Scotland and Wales. There may be some sense of cohesion in the North-East, Yorkshire, Lancashire or the South-West but even if this sentiment is totally lacking in the rest of England, it can be argued that these areas would be better administered by a series of regional ministries. However, most of those in politics and in the Civil Service clearly prefer the functional and centralised system based in Whitehall.

Yet there is an administrative case for certain functions, particularly those concerned with land use and economic planning, being organised on a regional basis as the creation of the Planning Boards and Councils has indicated. The effect of policies which appear reasonable and desirable for the whole country may be quite different and seriously damaging in specific areas—for instance, if a valley loses its industry, finds its railway closed and a new town in the next valley attracts all the new firms coming to the area. Similarly the planning of transport systems may require different local priorities with more emphasis being placed on a motorway or on the retention of a commuter railway line.

The case for elected authorities at the regional level is that if these functions are best administered by such large units, then it might be possible to arouse the electors' interest in playing a part in the process. Land-use planning, transport and all the environmental tasks of government do excite great local concern. Also elected bodies at this level would make possible an element of democratic control over the many *ad hoc* or intermediate government agencies that have been described. A final consideration is that this form of organisation would permit considerable devolution of categories of decisions so that the over-loading of central government (for example, when the Ministry of Housing and Local Government used to take all planning appeals) could be eased. On the other hand, to do this would permit an element of regional diversity and this would be disliked by those who prefer central control and uniform standards and methods.

4. The reform of local government

This question of the reform and rationalisation of government outside Whitehall, of the size and powers of regional and local authorities was discussed and examined for many years and by many committees. But the lack of any popular interest in the subject, and the opposition of the local authority associations and of councillors who often hold posts in the constituency organisations of their parties, prevented any action. Ultimately the pressure for reform came from the Whitehall ministries because they had to use local government to execute many of their plans, particularly for local economic development and urban renewal and they found that the machinery was simply ineffective. Local Government Commissions for England and for Wales set up in 1958 were able to produce only local boundary review proposals, so the case for local government reform was put to ministers. Scotland led the way with a White Paper, *The Modernisation of Local Government in Scotland* in 1963 (Cmd 2067). Then came a White Paper called *Local Government in Wales* (Cmd 3340) in July 1967. The spate of reports on English local government began with the Report by Professor Allen of *The Committee of Inquiry into the Impact of Rates on Households* (Cmd 2582) in 1965. The Report on the *Management of Local Government* chaired by Sir John Maud came out in 1967 as did the Report on

Staffing of Local Government prepared by a Committee under Sir George Mallaby. Then in 1969, the two Royal Commissions reported, the Scottish Commission presided over by Lord Wheatley and the English by Lord Redcliffe-Maud. The Government followed this with its own response, the *Reform of Local Government in England* (Cmd 4276), a paper called *Local Government Reorganisation in Glamorgan and Monmouthshire* (Cmd 4310) and a second Green Paper on *The Future Structure of the National Health Service*. (Two green papers on the Structure of the Health Service had already been produced in 1968, one for England and one for Scotland.) None of these local government papers dealt with London whose government had been considered by a Royal Commission under Sir Edwin Herbert between 1957 and 1960, the main proposals being enacted in the London Government Act of 1963.

The chief weakness of all this work was that the fundamental questions were not tackled first. It was assumed rather than argued that all government should be under some form of democratic control. But, having made this decision, the two Royal Commissions on local government were not allowed to consider how the vast range of central, local and intermediate government agencies could be supervised or scrutinised in a democratic way. Rather than face this, the Royal Commissions were limited to 'the structure of local government . . . in relation to its existing functions' so that there was no serious discussion of what should or should not fall to local government as opposed to central government or of the financial problems facing local government.

Given these limitations, the two Commissions proceeded in a very similar manner. The Redcliffe-Maud Commission began by considering each of the existing functions of local government in turn. Evidence was heard from many sources but great weight was placed on the views of the central government departments. They gave minimum population figures arguing that below these there were not the financial resources or flow of work to permit the employment of a highly specialised staff and thus a proper service could not be run. Some departments gave estimates of optimum figures but most of the evidence merely tried to fix a minimum. The result was a broad agreement that the major services required a unit consisting of at least 250 000 people and, without much evidence, Redcliffe-Maud fixed a ceiling of a million beyond which, it was said, administration would cease to be local.

Then each service was examined and it was found that there were clear interconnections. Planning involved transport and the wider aspects of urban redevelopment but all these were tied up with housing. Then the social services of health, education and welfare were best administered together but these also had close connections with housing. The result was that the Redcliffe-Maud Commission found itself turning towards unitary authorities of between 250 000 and a million in size performing all these functions and the Commission finally recommended 58 such bodies in England. This excluded London and the Commission also named three metropolitan areas where, it argued, planning and the environmental services would have to stretch over an area including far more than one million people, the result being that the personal services would be too remote. For this reason a second tier administering education, housing, social and health services was recommended in these metropolitan areas. The Commission accepted that there were broader aspects of physical planning which the 58 unitary authorities could not handle and, for this purpose, they recommended provincial councils but these were to be indirectly elected and were to have no executive powers. The provincial councils were simply to coordinate planning for the unitary authorities and it was thought that they might also undertake the preparation of wider schemes in the fields of further education, the education of handicapped children and in cultural and recreational matters. Finally, the Commission proposed local councils with no powers but with the right to put forward the views of local communities (the boundaries probably being the same as those of the present unreformed local government units) to the unitary authorities.

The Wheatley Commission on Scottish local government proceeded in a similar way but concluded that there was sufficient difference between the sizes of authority needed for the broader services and the more immediate local functions to merit the retention of a two-tier system. However the second tier proposed by Wheatley had nothing like the powers recommended for the second tier in the English metropolitan areas, being confined to local planning, local amenities and minor regulations. In fact, the distribution of population in Scotland would have made two unitary authorities possible, one based on Aberdeen and the other on Dundee, but the Clyde Valley is a major conurbation while the Highlands and Borders both lacked any appropriate urban centre. As a result, Wheatley proposed seven regional authorities with an average of 755 000 people and a second tier of 37 district authorities averaging 143 000 inhabitants. There was a similar suggestion to that made by Redcliffe-Maud that local councils without statutory powers could be used wherever wanted to put the views of electors to the new local authorities.

As one of the major principles of both Commissions was that the division between town and country should be abolished in local government terms, the White Paper *Local Government in Wales* (Cmd 3340), which in 1967 had proposed five enlarged counties and three county boroughs, had to be revised. The eleven counties of mid- and north-Wales were still to be reorganised on a two-tier, four-county and twenty-council basis. But in Glamorgan and Monmouthshire, the new White Paper *Local Government Reorganisation in Glamorgan and Monmouthshire* (Cmd 4310), published in 1970, proposed three unitary authorities based on Cardiff, Newport and Swansea. This last White Paper also withdrew the earlier White Paper's proposals for an all-Welsh Council with some powers in the fields of land use and economic planning and with power to advise on the administration of transport, the national parks and the countryside, the arts and the promotion of tourism. This, it was said, was too critical an issue for any pronouncements prior to the report of the Commission on the Constitution (see below pp. 189–90).

Despite this attempt to revitalise local government, the Government decided to abandon any idea of restoring the hospital service to local government and therefore to democratic control. It also found it very hard to propose the unification of the three arms of the service, the hospital, the general practitioner and local authority services, as had long been advocated by reformers. A new Green Paper, *The Future Structure of the Health Service*, published in 1970, proposed area health authorities which would coincide with the unitary authorities and metropolitan authorities of Redcliffe-Maud and with groups of London boroughs. These health authorities would be responsible for services that are primarily medical, taking over, for example, the school health service from local government. On the other hand, the home help service would be left to the local councils. Thus the divisions within the health service would remain, though the shares would be altered, the area health authorities administering the hospital and general practitioner services and taking over from local authorities ambulances, family planning, health centres, health visiting, home nursing, maternity and child care and preventive medicine. The new unitary local councils would retain the services dealing with the elderly, handicapped and homeless, the children's services, family case work, day centres, residential accommodation for those needing care, unsupported mothers and the home help service. The Green Paper made proposals for sharing staff in an effort to bridge this gap between the health authorities and the local councils. Also the area health authorities are regarded as too small to plan overall hospital and specialist services, to organise postgraduate medical and dental education, to deploy senior staff or to run training schemes or the blood transfusion service. To supervise these functions, fourteen or more regional health councils are recommended to follow the areas of the present Regional Hospital Boards.

Thus it is clear that the Labour Government barely tackled the problem of how to reorganise the diverse sectors of government outside the main Whitehall departments in order either to rationalise the system or to provide for democratic supervision and control. The various Royal Commissions were only allowed to examine the present powers of the existing structure of local government, and at the end, the degree of devolution of power intended by the Government was not clear. The Redcliffe-Maud Commission did suggest that once the new structure had been created, many of the controls maintained by central government should be reviewed and relaxed. The Wheatley Report was much more definite saying that 'the opportunity should be taken to build into the statutes a new kind of relationship between the central government and the local authorities'. But on this, the White Paper giving the Government's views on Redcliffe-Maud, called *Reform of Local Government in England* (Cmd 4276), was not explicit. It quoted Mr Harold Wilson's speech to the Association of Municipal Corporations in September 1969, in which he hoped for greater freedom for local authorities but gave little concrete evidence of how this was to be achieved. Meanwhile, the White Paper on Public Expenditure 1969–74 (Cmd 4234) set out the totals, year by year, of local authority expenditure that would be acceptable to the Treasury indicating that a strong central grip on such expenditure would be retained.

There is an impression in parts of Whitehall that the purpose of local government reform is not to create new centres of local democratic initiative but to produce a more efficient set of agencies for carrying out central government policies and that some departments have no intention of devolving any significant group of decisions to the reformed councils. Even on the structural side, the aspects of the Redcliffe-Maud proposals endorsed by the Labour Government in their White Paper (Cmd 4276) did not produce a coherent system or one that looked like lasting for any period of time. The White Paper added two metropolitan areas to the three proposed by the Royal Commission—West Yorkshire and South Hampshire—and these, with Greater London, mean that 42 per cent of the population of England would have been living under a two-tier system. Thus the simplicity and universality of Redcliffe-Maud's unitary principle was destroyed from the outset. In addition, there was an almost open invitation to other unitary authorities to put a case for amalgamation into metropolitan areas. The Royal Commission itself recognised that the remaining unitary authorities would be too small not merely for additional services but for some existing local authority functions, examples being the police, fire, further education, child care and cultural and recreational services. However, despite this, the Labour Government decided to postpone any consideration of the proposal for an upper tier of provincial councils.

The Conservatives, in opposition, had objected to the unitary authorities and came out for a two-tier system which was explained, after they had won office, in a White Paper, *Local Government in England* (Cmd 4584) published in February 1971. Their scheme was for 38 counties and six metropolitan areas. The counties were divided into about 300 second-tier districts which were to handle housing, aspects of planning and development and local amenities. The six metropolitan areas contained 34 districts. This plan was put into the Local Government Act (39 counties with 296 districts; 6 metropolitan areas with 36 districts), the only change being a slight increase in district powers. Wales was divided into eight counties and 37 districts.

This scheme was far from the Redcliffe-Maud proposals and solved few of the weaknesses noted earlier in this chapter. The authorities are still too many and too small and it is ironical that while land-use planning had been in the hands of some 150 authorities, it is now shared among 380 while there is no one (except Whitehall) to look at planning at the regional level. In the metropolitan areas, the districts are often too weak and it will be hard to establish rate equalisation schemes, whereby the richer districts aid the poorer, as the consent of every district is necessary. Also the boundaries of the metropolitan areas have been tightly drawn so that there is no room for expansion and the unsatisfactory separation between the town and the country is preserved. Some district boundaries are highly artificial and the split between the functions of the two tiers is by no means clear; it will still be necessary to have joint committees. Although the Act was supposed to bolster the strength of local government, in the process of reform, water, sewage disposal and some sewerage functions are removed and given to new regional water authorities while the local authority health services were allocated to the new area health boards.

As a result, the relations between central and local government have not been materially altered and the system of detailed central government controls remains virtually intact. The Conservatives, like the Labour party, had condemned too much dictation to local councils on local issues but their Housing Finance Act of 1972 gave Whitehall the power to determine and enforce local authority rents and, by other legislation, councils were not allowed to give free milk to children over seven. There will continue to be conflicts between authorities and overlaps of jurisdiction with some agencies of intermediate government so that the central government will still have to authorise, plan, adjudicate and audit as before.

It is interesting that this Act was pushed through in 1972 (and later in 1973 a similar Bill with a two-tier system based on the Wheatley Report for Scotland) just when the Government was about to get the report of the one Commission which was asked to take an overall look at the state of government outside Whitehall. This was the Commission on the Constitution under Lord Crowther (then, when he died, under Lord Kilbrandon) which was appointed in 1968 because of direct political pressure. In July 1966, the Welsh Nationalists won a by-election at Carmarthen and in November 1967 the Scottish National Party overturned a 16 000 Labour majority to win a by-election at Hamilton. These results were backed by solid gains at local elections and it became clear that the Nationalists had made substantial inroads into the Labour vote at any rate between general elections. Until this point, the structure of government outside Whitehall had been merely a matter which worried civil servants who wished to see their departmental policies executed more rapidly and efficiently, though some Liberals, some academics and sections of the 'quality press' had shown a passing interest in the subject. For most of those in political life, the existing pattern of local government (through which numbers of politicians, particularly in the Labour party, had graduated) was quite satisfactory and there seemed to be little point in tinkering with it. Most politicians, in any case, are not interested in the machinery of government; their absorption is with the end product, the pensions, houses, levels of income and foreign policies that come out of the machine. Added to this, MPs and ministers have in a special degree the conviction that central government knows best and that any devolution from London must mean giving powers to authorities that are poorer, weaker, slower, perhaps corrupt, perhaps more reactionary (for Labour members) or perhaps more reckless with public funds (for Conservative members).

But the advent of the Nationalists, though hard to analyse, did suggest that there were votes to be won or lost, at least in Scotland and Wales, on the public's sense of remoteness from decision-taking or its lack of knowledge of the existing degree of devolution to the Scottish and Welsh offices and on the general confusion as to which body was responsible for what. Both major parties were seriously worried by the situation. The Labour party saw its strongholds in Scotland and Wales endangered and some of the younger members elected in 1964 and 1966, who had been interested in devolution and governmental reform long before the nationalist challenge arose, saw this as their chance to press for a degree of devolution to an elected all-Welsh or all-Scottish Council. But the older MPs from these areas saw these efforts as merely concessions to the Nationalists. On the Labour side, these members were the products of the 1930s when the main issue in politics was insufficiency. For them, the task was to win power at the centre and then to distribute wealth more fairly. Talk of regional governmental or elected assemblies seemed pointless eyewash, a sign of weakness in the face of the nationalist challenge; a policy designed to lead either to a call for total independence for Scotland and Wales or to a permanent loss of authority by Whitehall and therefore a diminution in the competence of Scottish and Welsh MPs.

The Conservatives likewise were aroused by the prospect of a weakening of Labour's hold on Scotland and Wales as the Conservatives had had a constant majority at every post-1945 general election in England; it was the Celtic fringe that tilted the balance in favour of Labour. Also some Conservatives were genuinely interested in decentralisation. In August 1968, the Conservatives established a Scottish Constitutional Committee, which behaved like a royal commission, under Sir Alec Douglas-Home. It reported in early 1970 recommending a Scottish elected Assembly of some 125 members which would take all but the last or third reading stage of Scottish Bills and would debate the Scottish estimates and general topics. The flaw in this idea was that the Assembly was to have no executive powers and no powers to make or unmake ministers. It would be expected to advise the Secretary of State for Scotland who would still be in the UK Cabinet and responsible to the UK House of Commons, a situation which would be intolerable to its members, resented by Scots MPs and bound to lead to conflict.

Inside the Labour party the conflict as to how to react was acute, those opposed to any concessions finally triumphing with the well-known formula of putting the matter to a Royal Commission which could not report till after the forthcoming general election. This was the Commission on the Constitution asked to look at 'the present functions of the central legislature and government in relation to the several countries, nations and regions of the United Kingdom'.

When the Nationalists won only one seat at the general election of 1970, the tension went out of the argument. At the same time it made it easier for members of the main parties to discuss the issue without being labelled as crypto-nationalists. British entry into the European Community led to some stress on regional needs and problems but, despite this better atmosphere, it is hard to see a government which has just reformed local government turning to rearrange the entire structure of government outside Whitehall. The probability is that the report of the Commission on the Constitution, due to be published in the autumn of 1973 will simply be shelved.

Meanwhile, the new local government Acts, with all their imperfections, will come into operation. There is no doubt that this machinery can and will function and produce results but there is no evidence that it has remedied the weaknesses in administration or in democratic control that beset the old system or that it will do anything to make British government a less centralised and rigid system.

THE DIRECTION OF CHANGE:
THE ATTITUDES OF THE PARTIES

1. Away from the Westminster Model towards what?

At the end of Chapter 3 it was pointed out that the 1960s had seen a series of reform proposals in British government and that by 1973 most of these had been carried out in some form though the Commission on the Constitution had still to report. But these reforms failed to coalesce into a coherent system because there was no prevailing political doctrine which could provide answers to such questions as, how much power or influence should the House of Commons exercise or how far is it desirable to have some democratic control over local and regional administration? The doctrine that is usually referred to in the opening pages of these Royal Commission or Ministerial Committee Reports is a watered-down version of the late-nineteenth-century belief in democracy which inspired the system described above as 'the Westminster Model'. Genuflections are still made towards these old gods. Thus every time a nominated board is established to perform some administrative function, it is felt that some sort of democratic check is necessary and as elections cannot be run for each *ad hoc* board, another nominated body is created called an 'advisory council', the idea being that this acts in lieu of democratic control. In fact, these advisory councils neither have the strength conferred by expert knowledge, nor the experience of full-time work in the field, nor the responsibility conferred by direct election, but they cover up for the assumed need for some outside, popular supervision of these administrative agencies. At the same time, this adherence to the remnants of old political beliefs can add to the complication of government. For example, in the interests of efficiency, there should be amalgamations of the many regional and local authorities responsible for planning, development and the major environmental services. One solution, to do all this from Whitehall, which is allegedly under the scrutiny of the House of Commons, is impossible because of the extent and variety of the work. To hand the work over to elected local authorities covering an extensive area would be to set up bodies with a genuine degree of independence and power and this is suspect. The result is the present multiplicity of bodies producing confusion both at the administrative level and on the part of the electorate who are left wondering where and by whom decisions are actually taken. The same problems inhibit reform of the Commons. If it were possible to be clear about what power or general role the House should have, the relations between MPs and the executive could be adjusted accordingly. At present the fiction that each MP acts on his own judgment and takes a discriminating part in legislation is preserved by insisting that members must be present and pass through the lobbies night after night, though in fact such activity makes no material difference, but seriously impedes MPs in their task of keeping up to date with their special interests and with their constituency work.

It would be perfectly possible to recast the system of democratic supervision so as to restore a considerable part of the power of the Commons and to provide a devolved system of regional and local elected councils which would mean that every important administrative body was subject to checks and examination at one or other of the three levels—national, regional or local. At the same time, the doctrine of ministerial responsibility could be limited, the degree of independent influence already existing in the Civil Service openly recognised, the Fulton reforms on management implemented and the Commons given powers of direct scrutiny of these sub-sections of the public service. The reason all this has not happened has not been because of technical problems but because there is no clear view of how government should be organised or controlled. The public are not very interested in such issues. They are used to politicians listening with some care to their demands and the evidence of this attention and the obvious impact of general elections is usually sufficient to make them feel that the old maxims of the Westminster Model still have some meaning.

If the present drift in ideas and in practice was recognised and accepted, the British political system could openly be established on a popular plebiscitary basis, with a quinquennial election to put one party or the other in power checked only by 'advisory committees' at certain levels—the Commons in the centre and similar nominated or elected bodies at suitable subordinate points in the administration.

But though the machinery of government is developing in this direction, there is insufficient willingness to face the facts, to give up some of the pretences left over from the old period of vigorous, participatory democracy in order to remove the anomalies and rationalise the system.

2. The political parties and the community

If some clarity of purpose and coherence of action is to take the place of this drift, the ideas and energy ought to come from the political parties because, in theory, they are supposed to provide the driving force in political development. Yet the parties are rooted in the community. The old view of the party organisations dating from Ostrogorski's great work, *Democracy and the Organisation of Political Parties* (translated by F. Clarke in 1902), was that these bodies had a life of their own. They were organisations which could operate on the one hand on the electorate and on the other on the MPs, thus directly influencing policy. In fact, this is to elevate a small group of officials or 'caucus', as Ostrogorski called them, into a prominence they do not deserve. In Britain, the party machines are relatively weak and only hold meetings, choose candidates, run election campaigns and hold conferences. But the parties are also deeply influenced by the two ends of their operations, the one end being in the constituencies and the other in the Cabinet or Shadow Cabinet. The parties' greatest area of freedom and influence lies in the local constituency activists' power to choose the candidate for a parliamentary election. This is a once and for all choice as it is quite exceptional for the sitting MP to be refused renomination. But in making the choice, the selection conference in the case of the Labour party, and the constituency executive in the case of the Conservative party, are not easily moved by pressure from outside and even the leaders of the parties have found it hard to get close friends and political associates nominated. Senior party figures (such as Creech Jones on the Labour side after 1951 or Christopher Soames on the Conservative side after 1966) have found it almost impossible to be selected. Thus this is one important way in which the parties must reflect the opinion of the more active local members, a necessity which keeps the parties tied fairly closely to their local connections.

At the other end, the parties are tied to putting out the views of the parliamentary leadership. In the Conservative party, the organisation is directly under the control of the leader while in the Labour party, the organisation serves the National Executive which is elected by the annual conference. In practice, being elected to the

G

National Executive does give its members a degree of power and position. Some are elected because of their independent standing in the party and because of specific positions they have adopted on certain issues. But a combination of the loyalty of trade union members, of the distribution of ministerial posts among MPs on the Executive, of personal persuasion by the Prime Minister and senior colleagues and of the fact that the Executive would not want to weaken the overall standing of the party, normally preserves unity between the Executive and the party leadership.

These two ends of the parties, in the constituencies and in the Cabinet, are brought together at regional and national conferences where the activists meet and exchange views with their leaders in the company of their MPs. On such occasions, there is a process of mutual education and stimulation which can at times descend to mere manipulation of the delegates by the leadership and can also rise to a high level of discourse about the basic problems confronting the nation. The activists are usually to the left, in the case of the Labour party, and to the right, in the case of the Conservatives, of their parliamentary leaders. But there is a recognition by both activists and leaders that the party's task is to win an election and this means carrying the less opinionated sectors of the electorate with them. On the other hand, the leadership appreciates that it cannot indefinitely trample upon the deeper convictions of the solid party supporters.

Rooted in this way in the community, the parties are not organisations apart from British society which can, as it were, operate on society from outside. The parties are collections of those most actively concerned with the political aspects of government and, by long association, these groups of activists develop their own slogans, atmosphere, myths and methods. While Professor R. T. McKenzie is right to argue that the common purpose of winning elections and of maintaining a government in power imposes or produces an almost identical power structure in the parties, it is wrong to infer from this that the atmosphere within the parties is the same. A visit to the annual conferences of the two major parties should convince any observer of the deep contrasts and this is as evident in the case of the minority parties such as the Liberals and the Scottish and Welsh Nationalists.

The question that remains is whether any of these parties is likely to impose some pattern on the development of British institutions in the foreseeable future. Will there be an attempt to restore more complete democratic control? Is there a preference for efficiency as a criterion? And what, if any, are the parties' attitudes to the specific problems of government that have not been resolved? The answers are confused.

3. The Labour party

Looking first at the Labour party, its doctrine or beliefs are, in 1973, by no means as clear cut as when the party constitution was adopted in 1918. Clause Four declared that the objective of the party was 'to secure for the producers by hand or by brain the full fruits of their industry, and the most equitable distribution thereof that may be possible, upon the basis of the common ownership of the means of production and the best obtainable system of popular administration and control of each industry and service'.

Underlying this was a mixture of beliefs and of desires to remedy particular situations. British society was condemned by the early Labour leaders as being selfish and cruel. There was too much poverty, and hardship fell on those with the fewest reserves and resources. The accepted explanation was that the capitalist system of production was based on selfishness since only some in the community could prosper as their prosperity had to be at the expense of others. This was because these capitalists lived in part or in whole out of the profits which should have been shared with all those who had helped in the process of production. The solution was to end the capitalist system by turning to public ownership, where community interests could be considered first, where profit would be eliminated and where work and reasonable prosperity could be guaranteed to all. But there was also a strong democratic element in the doctrine. The early Labour leaders supported votes for women, home rule not merely for Ireland but for Scotland and Wales, and were deeply concerned about the respect that should be paid to individuals, about the sense of freedom that was lacking in the nineteenth-century employer–employee relationship.

In the 1930s, the emphasis changed. The misery of the interwar years in the areas of declining heavy industry left their mark, while the intractable nature of the problem was revealed by the failure of the first two Labour Governments. As a result, Labour thinking began to lay more stress on state control, on the need to take over at the centre and then to redistribute wealth and plan for the whole country. This drift of thought was emphasised in the 1940s by the Beveridge Report recommending a comprehensive pattern of welfare organised on a national basis, by the new emphasis on Keynesian planning and by Herbert Morrison's concept of the large national corporation as the best method of organising nationalised industries. The populist element in the party's thinking remained but focused more on the party conference than on the degree of scope to be given to the House of Commons or to local government. On the whole, the Labour party took the old radical view that the task of Parliament was to enact the legislation foreshadowed or promised in the party's election manifesto. A Labour majority in the House of Commons should rally round the executive and protect it against the array of hostile capitalist forces, the Conservative Opposition being merely the front-line troops for the captains of industry, the financiers and the press barons.

These ideas came together and were put into operation by the 1945–51 Labour Government. Some of its politicians were backward-looking in that their major objectives were to remedy interwar problems. The older declining industries were nationalised, the Beveridge plans enacted, a National Health Service started and full employment maintained, the emphasis all being on the results of these policies, on their effects on people's lives. Little attention was paid to the machinery of government and Aneurin Bevan abandoned any attempt to reform local government. There was a considerable growth in the size of the central government, many *ad hoc* organisations were created and there were complaints about bureaucracy and controls. The tendency was to dismiss these as Conservative propaganda, since for many Labour activists, controls and rationing were what had brought fair shares during and after the war. At the same time, the Government had to grapple with newer or less anticipated problems of regional development, of a weakness in the overall balance of payments and of a rapid change in Britain's international position, all of which combined to prevent any basic rethinking of socialist doctrine.

When the Conservatives, after 1951, managed to retain most of the benefits of Labour rule with fewer controls, no rationing and an increasing standard of living, this helped to precipitate a flare-up inside the Labour party. The dispute was over a mixture of issues, the left or Bevanites being somewhat anti-American, opposed to rearmament, opposed to charges being introduced into the Health Service and, it was assumed, in favour of the traditional public ownership approach of the party. Later some of the Bevanites, though not Mr Bevan himself, added opposition to nuclear weapons to their list of policies.

The right, or Gaitskellites, were committed to a balance of power approach in foreign affairs which came to include a defence of nuclear weapons. They doubted whether there was any intrinsic value in public ownership, believing that the main object of the party was to reduce class barriers. This was best achieved by accelerating the rate of economic growth which meant creating confidence in industry, though this was not incompatible with financial controls, the power to influence the location of industry and perhaps some newer forms of intervention and of public ownership. It was also, according to the Gaitskellites, important to increase the proportion of money spent on the public and social services and to make the educational system more egalitarian. At one stage, the dispute between the left and the right concentrated upon a proposal to repeal Clause Four of the 1918 constitution of the party, at others on the demand that Britain should renounce her nuclear weapons, but the struggle was really a wider one over the basic aims of the party at a time when its ideal of a reasonable standard of life for all seemed to be being achieved under a mixed economy managed by the Conservatives.

When Mr Wilson was elected to the leadership in 1963, these doctrinal disputes were smoothed over and the Labour party entered office in 1964 committed to a more rapid rate of growth, improved welfare benefits, more expenditure on schools, houses, roads and health and one major measure of public ownership—the renationalisation of the steel industry. Mr Wilson had also said a good deal about modernising the machinery of government. He had proposed a more extensive No. 10 staff, a smaller Cabinet and many of the modern techniques of business management in the Civil Service which were later elaborated in the Fulton Report. In 1966, he went further and proposed two new select or investigatory committees in the House of Commons. But after four years of difficulty and unpopularity, the attitudes of the Labour party were more mixed. In economic affairs, fiscal controls were being practised by the Treasury to try and maximise the advantages gained by the 1967 devaluation of the pound. The new Ministry of Technology, on the other hand, was using more positive methods of intervention, injecting public money into industry, encouraging mergers and pushing technological innovation. At the same time, welfare benefits were increased but this did produce complaints about 'idlers' and 'scroungers', across-the-board welfare payments were becoming increasingly expensive and some Labour party members began to press for more selective methods of eliminating poverty.

By the early 1970s, it remained true that the Labour party was identified with the interests of the working classes, with the need for a reduction in class barriers and for the maintenance of the welfare system. But there was less confidence that rapid growth could be ensured and less assurance that the gaps between the really poor and the better-off workers could be narrowed by the traditional remedies. There was some evidence that Labour's emphasis on regional development had reduced the contrast between the prosperous Midlands and South-East and the older industrial areas. But it would be hard to identify a coherent or clear-cut Labour or socialist philosophy in the sense in which such philosophies had existed before 1914. The democratic element in the party's thinking was mainly a conviction that 'the people must be right' but popular views were indicated by the act of choosing every four or five years between the two major parties. The Labour Government had tried small items of parliamentary reform, experimenting with morning sittings and with a limited number of select or 'specialist' committees. But these experiments had come at a time of internal tensions in the party and were associated with more relaxed attitudes to party discipline in the House, tendencies which angered the older, loyalist backbenchers. In the Labour strongholds of Scotland and Wales, there had been challenges from the Nationalist parties which won by-elections in 1966 and 1967. For a while these sections of the Labour party considered possible forms of devolution or regional assemblies but when the Labour Cabinet decided to postpone the issue by setting up the Commission on the Constitution, the Scottish section of the party set its face against any change, though the Welsh Council still advocated an elected all-Wales assembly.

On the whole, by 1973, the experience of six years of government and three of opposition had weakened those in the Labour party interested in institutional reform both at the Westminster and at the local levels. There was some talk of referenda and participatory democracy but this was in the rather specialised context of opposition to British entry to the European Community. On the central issue of prices and incomes, the voters' reactions to attempts to hold back wage increases between 1966 and 1969 and the contrast between the hopes of rapid growth and the economic restraints actually experienced, all strengthened those who believed that what mattered in politics, what moved Labour voters, was the end-product—higher wages, better houses, more adequate pensions and full employment. The style of government, the quality of public discussion, the way in which and the degree to which people were consulted and the protection of individual rights seemed vague and relatively unimportant. It was true that there were reactions against politicians as a profession, against excessive bureaucracy, against men who said one thing in government and another in opposition and against 'remoteness' among decision-takers. After the 1970 defeat, the division over British entry into the European Community caused a deep split, though in part this was because it epitomised the old Gaitskellite versus the left division, though on this issue the left won over the centre of the party and had strong trade union support. The anti-market stance, particularly of the left, showed up what had always been a rather hollow internationalism and revealed a conservatism, especially over the maintenance of parliamentary sovereignty, and a touch of xenophobia that was deep in the Labour Movement. Nevertheless, by 1973 this issue was declining as prices, rents and the basic economic issues came to the fore again. Although the class divisions in British society are weakening or blurring at the edges, with the approach of a general election in 1974–5, the parties and the public have tended to fall back on these divisions as the only touch-stone they have in politics.

4. The Conservative party

The Conservatives, in contrast, have always been a party more accustomed to government and less interested in theories but they have been equally class identified. Although the party had a strong aristocratic and agricultural interest, by the 1930s it was becoming closely connected with industry. Conservatives strongly held the Victorian belief that there were large areas of social organisation in which it was simply improper for government to meddle. The government did not have to concern itself with the balance of payments (which was always expected to be favourable or self-adjusting), free trade meant that there was no need for elaborate connections with industry, the level of employment had to be left to the supply and demand for labour and all that the government should do was elementary regulation in the interests of those sections of the community unable to defend themselves. With this view, the Conservatives in the interwar period were for small-scale government and low taxes—the less done by government, the better and cheaper. At the same time, those public health, welfare and property protection services which the central or local government did provide, should be efficiently administered. Thus, though Neville Chamberlain personified the Conservatives' connection with industry and with these *laissez-faire* ideas, he was a most effective and efficient Minister of Health from 1924 to 1929. In addition, the Conservative party was closely identified with Britain's overseas empire, with the armed forces and with a foreign policy resting on a balance of power in

Europe and elsewhere on the use of appropriate force to defend British interests.

In the 1930s, this Conservative outlook (rather than philosophy) did not face any very serious challenge from the Labour party's ideas but events did inflict certain serious blows. The first was the pressure for independence or at least for a measure of internal self-government in India. But more serious was the alarm and despondency caused by the 1929–33 slump in which the confidence of British industrialists, already sapped by the doldrums of the 1920s, was seriously shaken. Some of the beliefs in the limited nature of government activity were abandoned. The Conservatives turned to protection disguised as imperial preference in 1933 and adopted a series of State measures to aid the reduction and consolidation of the declining heavy industries. This whole experience was so shaking that though the Labour party had failed in both its minority governments and had shown no sign of making radical changes when it was in office, the Conservatives were seriously worried by the possibility and consequences of losing office. This sense of self-doubt also had some part in convincing Conservative leaders that neither Britain nor Western society could survive another trauma of the seriousness of the First World War and thus, for the only time in its history, the party abandoned its usual reliance on strong defences and the balance of power in Europe, adopting a policy towards Nazi Germany known as appeasement.

Although Conservative morale rallied under the pressures of the Second World War and first accepted and later was thrilled by the leadership of Winston Churchill, some of the other aspects of the War constituted a serious challenge to Conservative ideas. Wartime experience seemed to show that the government could control industry, produce full employment and higher output and then share the available produce more fairly. Also the movement of people involved in wartime adjustments, the identification of the Conservatives with appeasement and the 'fair shares' aspect of rationing all helped to undermine *laissez-faire* doctrines. As a result, the Conservatives found themselves badly defeated in 1945.

In response to the early activities and enthusiasm of the Attlee Government, the Conservatives mounted little challenge. Their older emotional attachments suffered with the decision to grant independence to India, Burma and Ceylon but the new postwar MPs who came into the party (particularly at the 1950 election) were more exclusively concerned with domestic policy. In part, they developed the traditional Conservative view that government was inherently inefficient and undesirable, particularly fastening on the record of the nationalised industries. Also, because they were continually looking to see whether a service or a subsidy could be removed, the Conservatives were less interested in any machinery which might have been set up to permit some element of popular control or consumer representation in these industries and services.

However, the thoughts that did occur went in two directions. At first Conservatives suggested that the regional hospital boards should be directly elected. They were also protagonists of greater parliamentary supervision of the nationalised industries and supported the creation of the Select Committee on these industries against Labour resistance in the mid-1950s. But the Conservatives are also by tradition believers in a strong executive. They have felt this was necessary to conduct proper policy and, while in power, they trusted their own leaders. For most Conservatives, there was no need for elaborate control systems built into Parliament. Normally, having chosen a leader, they were prepared to leave everything to him. If there was trouble and they became unhappy, a direct visit to the leader or the Chief Whip would usually suffice. So there was no need for specialist committees, or reformed local government. As for the Civil Service, it has to be cut down to the lowest level necessary. But if a service was necessary, for example at the Ministry of Defence, then it should be supported against interference, particularly by a parliamentary committee which might well contain several busybodies, ultra left-wingers or just cranks. Thus the Conservatives wanted a smaller, efficient and cheap executive but were then ready for a strong executive. And each time there was a surge forward in governmental activity, for instance during the war or under the postwar Labour Government, they were prepared to extend their view of what was necessary to cover some if not all the machinery which had been established.

Thus, after their return to power in 1951, the Conservatives made a 'dash for freedom' with a 'bonfire of controls'. Coming into office just at the time of the post-Korean War boom with the terms of trade swinging in Britain's favour, the Conservatives presided over a period of rising living standards and felt that they were able to stabilise the degree and pattern of government intervention so that free market forces were able to operate in the rest of the economy. This allowed normal Conservative instincts with their dubiety about institutional innovation to be confirmed and there was little talk of change. The entire policy appeared to be vindicated in 1959 when the Conservatives increased their hold on the Commons for the third successive general election as a result of a short boom, the party's policy becoming characterised by the phrase 'you never had it so good'.

But by the end of the decade and into the early 1960s, new problems appeared which required a more positive approach on the part of the Government and this threw the Conservatives into some disarray. One issue was 'the two Britains', the problem of regional discrepancies in the different levels of wages, unemployment and emigration north and south of a line drawn across England at about York. Gradually this forced the Conservatives into ideas of planning and influencing the location of industry, special plans being brought out for Scotland and for the North-East of England. Then the effort to locate industry in new areas and to build new towns showed up the weakness of local government as an executive agency and the first talk of reform began in Whitehall. In the early 1960s, it became fashionable to criticise British institutions and to say that this country was lagging behind its European competitors in many aspects of modern life from trade union structure to central heating, from the capacity to sell and provide after-sales service abroad to playing football. Devising and enacting appropriate remedies fitted more easily into the Labour party's outlook than into that of the Conservatives and they produced few very positive ideas for reform or change. On the other hand, the disengagement from empire was completed then the Conservatives decided to apply to join the European Common Market in 1961.

After Labour won the general elections of 1964 and 1966, the Conservatives were on the defensive until the consequences following on the deflation of July 1966 began to make the Labour Government unpopular. But, unlike the last years of the Attlee Government, the Conservatives developed no critique of the form or extent of government. Rather, they called for tax reductions, firmer enforcement of law and order and legislation to reduce the number of unofficial strikes. At the same time, the Conservatives looked on the possibility of decentralisation a little more favourably than the Labour party. The Conservative ex-Prime Minister, Sir Alex Douglas-Home, chaired a committee which proposed an elected assembly to debate the early stages of purely Scottish legislation, the estimates and general Scottish questions. The difficulty for the Conservatives was that while they were prepared to look with some favour on proposals which reduced the size of the central government machine, the particular solutions of elected assemblies in Scotland and Wales would produce Labour-dominated authorities with considerable power even when Britain was under a Conservative Government in Westminster. The Conservatives also appeared to be prepared to devolve more powers in any local government reform in England.

Thus Conservative views were very much the same as in the 1950s. There was a willingness to accept most of the new social and economic measures but to administer them as tightly as possible and to cut the cost of government. Within this framework, the Conservatives wanted to retain a strong executive and to strengthen similarly the hands of private authorities, particularly the employer in dealing with the unions. Some Conservative leaders have said that they would like to improve the Commons' capacity to scrutinise public expenditure and to appoint some more select or specialist committees but this is neither an agreed nor an emphasised aspect of party policy.

A new feature in moulding the Conservative outlook was the presence of a powerful ideologist in the person of Mr Enoch Powell. An ex-Minister of Health, he was opposed to the accretions of central government interventionism and wanted to return to the more clear-cut ideas of the 1920s whereby the limits of government action were clearly defined and fixed on theoretical rather than on pragmatic grounds. Also, while accepting the end of empire and the lack of any national interest in maintaining a world-wide defence system, Powell believed that there was a lack of a national sense of purpose and identity and he felt this could only be re-created by taking a strong line against immigrants, coloured and Irish, a strong line against the European Common Market and against Scottish and Welsh separatism. Powell carried far further than the Conservative leadership the case for ending regional planning and aid to industry, the case for increased selectivity in the social services and for ending all subsidies for public housing. Such policies, he argued, would make possible a very considerable reduction in taxation and a great stride forward in personal initiative and activity. The effect of Powellite doctrine, which had considerable public support, was not to alter official Conservative doctrine but to widen the gap between it and Labour party practice and to suggest that the application of Conservative principles would be more vigorous if and when they won power. In practice, after 1970, the Heath Government pursued its policies with vigour for over a year. Taxes were cut, 'lame duck' industries left on their own, entry to the European Community was pressed, legislation to curb the unions was passed and regional policies scaled down. Then, with unemployment in 1971 reaching the million mark, the Government kept its key policies on

Europe and on inflation but to cut unemployment, it pushed public expenditure up £700 million a year beyond Labour's target, baled out Upper Clyde Shipbuilders, the Mersey Docks and Harbour Board, Rolls-Royce and BSA and then applied a statutory prices and incomes policy.

All this goes to show that both major parties are chiefly concerned with the product of government, the level of taxes, welfare benefits and wages, the degree of unemployment and the standards of the public services and are less interested in the machinery of government, the ideas behind it or the quality of public life and debate. Nor is this surprising. All this means is that the parties reflect the attitudes of the public. The voters are only interested in the machinery of government if the existing institutions fail to do what they want, if there is serious inefficiency or injustice, in short if their lives are disrupted. And the politicians are only interested in these subjects if the voters are reacting strongly. Nothing has demonstrated this more than the major parties' retreat from any interest in devolution once it became apparent in late 1969 and early 1970 that electoral support for the Scottish and Welsh National parties was rapidly declining.

5. Liberals and Nationalists

The Liberals are much less interested in the major class-based attitudes that distinguish the Conservative and Labour parties. They have no distinctive economic policies and are not identified with the interests of any specific social groups. But the Liberals are deeply concerned about the institutional structure of British government, about parliamentary reform and the rights of individuals. They advocate a type of federalism for Scotland and Wales, England being divided into a number of large provinces with a second tier for immediate local government. In practice, the Liberal party draws most of its support from the rural areas of the Celtic fringe in Scotland, Wales and the West country where the normal British class divisions are weaker. In these areas, there is a remnant of the old anti-landlord, anti-aristocratic feeling which has been the basis of historic Liberalism. Also there is no industrial base for the Labour party, the Liberals thus reaping the benefit of these older social cleavages. The whole experience of the Liberal party shows that the distinctive institutional reforms and causes which that party has espoused are of interest only to a small, largely middle-class minority and probably the Liberals do not in this sense represent majority opinion even in the seats which they hold.

Unlike the Liberals, in the period between the 1966 and 1970 general elections, the Scottish and Welsh National parties did make major inroads in the industrial and urban areas which were normally the preserve of the two main parties. This may appear curious in that the main plank of these parties is basically a solution to the problem of local government, albeit an extreme one in that they advocate total independence. But in practice, the appeal of these parties was a combination of impatience at remote or impersonal bureaucracy and disappointment at the economic performance of the Labour Government, coming at a time between general elections when the traditional loyalties could safely be relaxed to permit a protest. Only some 20 per cent of those voting nationalist wanted total independence though over 60 per cent declared a desire 'for more say over our own affairs'. Thus the rise of these parties is a symptom of the element of alienation from 'the system' which does exist and of the weakening of class loyalties, while their decline as a general election approached showed that class loyalties, even in their weakened state, are still the major factor in determining British voting behaviour.

6. Conclusion: no clear direction

This survey of party attitudes to the problems of government in Britain both helps to explain and confirm why the situation is as it is. The major parties reflect the public's concern with their own conditions and in this, the chief determinant is still the social structure. The fact that the cleavages are not deep also reflects the large measure of agreement over the major problems affecting the society at any one time. Those who regard the division between the parties as bogus are merely asserting that they feel that other issues which cut across both parties, rather than between the parties, are more important to them. This may be true for them but it is clearly not true for the majority whom the parties represent. Nor is there much evidence that the present basis of social and political divisions is disappearing. Butler and Stokes have argued, almost certainly correctly, that it is weakening but it still remains as the principal guide to and determination of political loyalties.

The result of this investigation does not, however, help answer the question of how British government is likely to develop in the next decade. It shows that the community has not gone through dramatic experiences (of rapid industrialisation, defeat in war, or class or race conflict) which would produce a powerful political philosophy, a philosophy which would then provide the answers to the major problems of political organisation. There are remnants of old beliefs, a new hedonism, an interest largely in the outcome of government, an impatience with authority, a dislike of élite assumptions, all mixed together. As a result it is likely that the solutions adopted will be mixed but will, on the whole, confirm the present drift towards centralised executive power controlled only by the reference of the government and the Prime Minister's overall record to the voters at infrequent general elections.

BIBLIOGRAPHY

There is now an enormous literature on this subject, ranging from primary sources such as Hansard (the verbatim record of the proceedings of the two Houses of Parliament), the documents issued by the government (Acts, White Papers, innumerable reports) and the memoirs of politicians to secondary sources in the form of commentaries in the press, in learned journals and in many studies by observers and academics. It is hard to arrange this material in a form which runs parallel to the treatment in this book because so many of these sources are relevant to several chapters and ought not to be neglected by anyone wishing to pursue the subject of the chapter.

On the other hand, it would be repetitive to keep listing certain basic historical works and contemporary analyses just because they had material relevant to four or five chapters. As a result, this bibliography has been confined to an alphabetical list of the major works in the field. There are also many useful articles in the *British Journal of Sociology, Government and Opposition, Parliamentary Affairs, Public Law, Political Quarterly, Political Studies* and *Public Administration.*

L. Abraham and S. C. A. Hawtrey, *A Parliamentary Dictionary* (London 1964)

M. Abrams and R. Rose, *Must Labour Lose?* (London 1960)

Action Society Trust, *Regionalism in England*, 3 vols (London 1966)

R. K. Alderman and J. A. Cross, *The Tactics of Resignation* (London 1967)

R. R. Alford, *Party and Society* (London 1964)

A. J. Allen, *The English Voter* (London 1964)

Sir C. K. Allen, *Law and Orders* (London 1964)

Sir C. K. Allen, *Administrative Jurisdiction* (London 1956)

Sir C. K. Allen, *Law in the Making* (London 1951)

V. L. Allen, *Trade Unions and the Government* (London 1960)

V. L. Allen, *Power in the Trade Unions* (London 1954)

V. L. Allen, *Trade Union Leadership* (London 1957)

L. S. Amery, *Thoughts on the Constitution* (London 1964)

Sir J. Anderson (Ed.), *British Government since 1918* (London 1950)
C. R. Attlee, *The Labour Party in Perspective: and Twelve Years Later* (London 1949)

Walter Bagehot, *The English Constitution* (Fontana ed. London 1963)
S. D. Bailey, *British Parliamentary Democracy* (London 1962)
S. D. Bailey (Ed.), *The Future of the House of Lords* (London 1954)
S. D. Bailey, *The British Party System* (London 1953)
R. J. S. Baker, *The Management of Capital Projects* (London 1962)
G. B. Baldwin, *Beyond Nationalisation* (London 1955)
E. E. Barry, *Nationalisation in British Politics* (London 1966)
R. Bassett, *The Essentials of Parliamentary Democracy* (London 1962)
R. Bassett, *1931 Political Crisis* (London 1958)
BBC, *Whitehall and Beyond* (London 1964)
F. Bealey, J. Blondel and W. P. McCann, *Constituency Politics* (London 1965)
S. H. Beer, *Modern British Politics* (London 1965)
S. H. Beer and A. B. Ulam, *Patterns of Government* (New York 1962)
S. H. Beer, *Treasury Control* (London 1957)
M. Beloff, *The Party System* (London 1958)
H. Benham, *Two Cheers for the Town Hall* (London 1964)
M. Benney, A. P. Gray and R. H. Pear, *How People Vote* (London 1956)
A. H. Birch, *Small Town Politics* (London 1959)
A. H. Birch, *Representative and Responsible Government* (London 1964)
J. Blondel, *Voters, Parties and Leaders* (London 1963)
H. Boardman, *The Glory of Parliament* (London 1960)
J. Bonham, *The Middle Class Vote* (London 1954)
F. Boyd, *British Politics in Transition 1945–63* (London 1964)
J. Boyd-Carpenter, *The Conservative Case* (London 1950)
H. J. Boyden, *Councils and their Public* (London 1961)
C. F. Brand, *The British Labour Party* (London 1965)
F. H. Brasher, *Studies in British Government* (London 1965)
Lord Bridges, *Treasury Control* (London 1959)
Lord Bridges, *The Treasury* (London 1964)
Lord Bridges, *Portrait of a Profession* (London 1959)
Sir H. Brittain, *The British Budgetary System* (London 1959)
S. Brittan, *Steering the Economy* (London 1969)
P. A. Bromhead, *Private Members' Bills* (London 1956)
P. A. Bromhead, *The House of Lords and Contemporary Politics* (London 1958)
R. D. Brown, *The Battle of Crichel Down* (London 1955)
W. P. Buck, *Amateurs and Professionals in British Politics 1918–59* (London and Chicago 1963)
I. Budge and D. W. Urwin, *Scottish Political Behaviour* (London 1966)
J. G. Bulpitt, *Party Politics in English Local Government* (London 1967)
D. E. Butler, *The British Electoral System Since 1918* (London 1963)

D. E. Butler, *The British General Election of 1951* (London 1952)

D. E. Butler, *The British General Election of 1955* (London 1955)

D. E. Butler and R. Rose, *The British General Election of 1959* (London 1960)

D. E. Butler and A. King, *The British General Election of 1964* (London 1965)

D. E. Butler and A. King, *The British General Election of 1966* (London 1966)

D. E. Butler and J. Freeman, *British Political Facts 1900–60* (London 1963)

R. Butt, *The Power of Parliament* (London 1967)

G. A. Campbell, *The Civil Service in Britain* (London 1965)

Lord Campion, *Parliament: a survey* (London 1963)

Lord Campion, *Introduction to the Procedure of the House of Commons* (London 1958)

Sir C. Carr, *Concerning English Administrative Law* (London 1941)

A. M. Carr Saunders, D. Caradog-Jones and C. Moser, *Social Conditions in England and Wales* (London 1958)

B. E. Carter, *The Office of Prime Minister* (London 1956)

T. Cauter and J. S. Downham, *The Communications of Ideas* (London 1954)

Central Office of Information, *Local Government in Scotland* (Edinburgh 1959)

B. Chapman, *The Profession of Government* (London 1959)

B. Chapman, *British Government Observed* (London 1963)

D. N. Chester and N. Bowring, *Questions in Parliament* (London 1962)

D. N. Chester, *Central and Local Government* (London 1951)

Lord Chorley, B. Crick and B. Chapman, *Reform of the Lords* (London 1954)

J. B. Christoph, *Capital Punishment and British Politics* (London 1962)

B. Chubb, *The Control of Public Expenditure* (London 1952)

R. S. Churchill, *The Fight for the Tory Leadership* (London 1964)

J. J. Clarke, *Outlines of Central Government* (London 1961)

J. J. Clarke, *The Local Government of the United Kindgom* (London 1955)

J. J. Clarke, *Outlines of the Local Government of the United Kingdom* (London 1960)

J. J. Clarke, *A History of Local Government in the United Kingdom* (London 1955)

H. A. Clegg, J. Killick and R. Adams, *Trade Union Officers* (London 1961)

H. A. Clegg, *Industrial Democracy and Nationalisation* (London 1955)

H. A. Clegg and T. E. Chester, *The future of Nationalisation* (London 1955)

E. W. Cohen, *The Growth of the Civil Service* (London 1965)

G. D. H. Cole, *The Post-War Conditions of Britain* (London 1956)

G. D. H. Cole, *A Short History of the British Working Class Movement* (London 1948)

G. D. H. Cole, *Studies in Class Structure* (London 1955)

M. Cole, *Servant of the County* (London 1956)

G. O. Comfort, *Professional Politicians, a Study of the British Party Agents* (Washington 1958)

D. Coombes, *The MP and the Administration* (London 1966)

W. C. Costin and J. S. Watson, *The Law and Working of the Constitution: Documents 1660–1914*, 2 vols (London 1961–4)

D. Corbett, *Politics and the Airlines* (London 1966)

H. Cowie, *Why Liberal?* (London 1964)

C. A. Cross, *Principles of Local Government Law* (London 1966)

G. Cross, *The Fascists in Britain* (London 1961)

H. Daalder, *Cabinet Reform in Britain, 1914–63* (London 1964)

Daily Telegraph, 'Election '66' (London 1966)

H. E. Dale, *The Higher Civil Service* (London 1941)

H. Dalton, *The Principles of Public Finance* (London 1954)

H. Daudt, *Floating Voters and the Floating Vote* (Leiden 1961)

R. Day, *The Case for Televising Parliament* (London 1966)

P. Deane and W. A. Cole, *British Economic Growth* (London 1964)

A. V. Dicey, *Introduction to the Study of the Law of the Constitution* (London 1959)

Dod's Parliamentary Companion (London, published annually)

J. C. R. Dow, *The Management of the British Economy* (London 1964)

R. E. Dowse, *Left in the Centre* (London 1966)

G. Drain, *The Organisation and Practice of Local Government* (London 1966)

C. Driver, *The Disarmers* (London 1964)

J. M. Drummond, *The Finance of Local Government* (London 1962)

F. Dunnill, *The Civil Service: Some Human Aspects* (London 1956)

Sir H. Dunnico, *Mother of Parliament* (London 1951)

M. Duverger, *Political Parties* (London 1964)

J. Eaves, *Parliament and the Executive in Great Britain 1939–51* (London 1957)

H. Eckstein, *Pressure Group Politics* (London 1900)

H. C. Edey, A. T. Peacock and R. A. Cooper, *National Income and Social Accounting* (London 1967)

H. W. Ehrmann, *Interest Groups on Four Continents* (Pittsburgh 1958)

J. Ehrmann, *Cabinet Government and War 1890–1940* (London 1958)

P. Einzig, *The Control of the Purse* (London 1959)

S. J. Eldersveld, *Political Parties* (Chicago 1964)

C. S. Emsden, *The People and the Constitution* (London 1962)

I. Epstein, *British Politics in the Suez Crisis* (London 1964)

H. J. Eysenck, *The Psychology of Politics* (London 1954)

Fabian Group, *The Future of Public Ownership* (London 1963)

H. Fairlie, *The Life of Politics* (London 1968)

H. Finer, *The Major Governments of Modern Europe* (London 1960)

H. Finer, *English Local Government* (London 1950)

S. E. Finer, H. B. Berrington and D. J. Bartholomew, *Backbench Opinion in the House of Commons, 1955–9* (London 1961)

S. E. Finer, *Anonymous Empire* (London 1965)

S. E. Finer, *Private Industry and Political Power* (London 1958)

A. Flanders and H. A. Clegg, *The System of Industrial Relations in Great Britain* (London 1956)

J. E. Floud, A. H. Halsey and F. M. Martin, *Social Class and Educational Opportunities* (London 1957)

M. Foot, *Parliament in Danger* (London 1965)

C. D. Foster, *The Transport Problem* (London 1963)

D. Foulkes, *Introduction to Administrative Law* (London 1964)

W. G. Freidmann (Ed.), *The Public Corporation* (London 1954)

R. Fulford, *The Liberal Case* (London 1959)

R. Fulford, *Votes for Women* (London 1957)

R. Fulford, *The Member and his Constituency* (London 1957)

Hugh Gaitskell, *Socialism and Nationalization* (London 1956)

J. F. Garner, *Administrative Law* (London 1963)

I. Gilmour, *The Body Politic* (London 1969)

E. N. Gladden, *British Public Service Administration* (London 1961)

E. N. Gladden, *Civil Service or Bureaucracy?* (London 1956)

E. N. Gladden, *The Essentials of Public Administration* (London 1964)

E. N. Gladden, *An Introduction in Public Administration* (London 1966)

D. V. Glass (Ed.), *Social Mobility in Britain* (London 1954)

Louis Golding, *Dictionary of Local Government in England and Wales* (London 1962)

J. Gollan, *The British Political System* (London 1954)

S. Gordon, *Our Parliament* (London 1964)

H. R. G. Greaves, *The Civil Service in the Changing State* (London 1948)

H. R. G. Greaves, *The British Constitution* (London 1955)

L. P. Green, *Provincial Metropolis: The Future of Local Government* (London 1959)

J. A. G. Griffith, *Central Departments and Local Authorities* (London 1966)

J. A. G. Griffith and H. Street, *A Casebook of Administrative Law* (London 1965)

J. A. G. Griffith and H. Street, *Principles of Administrative Law* (London 1967)

John Grigg, *Is the Monarchy Perfect?* (London 1958)

J. Grimond, *The Liberal Challenge* (London 1963)

J. W. Grove, *Government and Industry in Britain* (London 1962)

W. L. Guttman, *The British Political Elite* (London 1963)

K. M. Gwillian, *Transport and Public Policy* (London 1964)

W. B. Gwyn, *Democracy and the Cost of Politics in Britain* (London 1962)

Lord Hailsham, *The Conservative Case* (London 1959)
C. J. Hamson, *Executive Discretion and Judicial Control* (London 1954)
Lord Hankey, *Diplomacy by Conference* (London 1946)
Lord Hankey, *Government Control in War* (London 1945)
Hansard Society, *Parliamentary Reform 1933–60* (London 1961)
A. H. Hanson and H. V. Wiseman, *Parliament at Work* (London 1962)
A. H. Hanson, *Public Enterprise and Economic Development* (London 1959)
A. H. Hanson (Ed.), *Nationalization: A Book of Readings* (London 1963)
A. H. Hanson, *Parliament and Public Ownership* (London 1962)
A. H. Hanson, *Managerial Problems in Public Enterprise* (London 1962)
J. S. Harris, *British Government Inspection: The Local Services and the Central Department* (London 1955)
M. Harrison, *Trade Unions and the Labour Party Since 1945* (London 1960)
J. Harvey and L. Bather, *The British Constitution* (London 1963)
W. O. Hart, *Introduction to the Law of Local Government and Administration* (London 1962)
J. Harvey and K. Hood, *The British State* (London 1958)
W. W. Hayes, *Nationalisation in Practice* (London 1953)
T. E. Headrick, *The Town Clerk in English Local Government* (London 1962)
E. G. Henderson, *Foundations of English Administrative Law* (London 1963)
Sir A. P. Herbert, *Anything But Action?* (London 1961)
Sir A. P. Herbert, *Independent Member* (London 1958)
Sir A. P. Herbert, *The Ayes Have It* (London 1937)
Sir A. P. Herbert, *I Object!* (London 1958)
R. F. V. Heuston, *Essays in Constitutional Law* (London 1964)
Lord Hewart, *The New Despotism* (London 1929)
U. K. Hicks, *Public Finance* (London 1955)
A. Hill and A. Whichelow, *What's Wrong with Parliament?* (London 1964)
J. D. Hoffman, *The Conservative Party in Opposition 1945–51* (London 1964)
C. Hollis, *Can Parliament Survive?* (London 1949)
H. Hopkins, *The New Look: A Social History of the Forties and Fifties in Britain* (London 1963)
O. Hood Phillips, *Constitutional and Administrative Law* (London 1962)
A. Howard and R. West, *The Making of a Prime Minister* (London 1965)
P. Howarth, *Questions in the House* (London 1956)
E. Hughes, *Parliament and Mumbo Jumbo* (London 1966)
J. H. Humphreys, *Proportional Representation* (London 1911)

Sir C. Ilbert, *Parliament* (London 1960)
Institute of Electoral Research, *Parliaments and Electoral Systems* (London 1962)

Institute of Race Relations, *Colour and the British Electorate* (London 1965)
Inter-Parliamentary Union, *Parliaments* (London 1962)
C. Irving, *Scandal '63* (London 1963)

B. Jackson and D. Marsden, *Education and the Working Class* (London 1962)
R. M. Jackson, *The Machinery of Local Government* (London 1958)
R. M. Jackson, *Machinery of Justice* (London 1960)
W. E. Jackson, *The Structure of Local Government in England and Wales* (London 1966)
W. E. Jackson, *Local Government in England and Wales* (London 1959)
C. Jenkins, *Power at the Top* (London 1959)
R. Jenkins, *Mr Balfour's Poodle* (London 1954)
R. Jenkins, *The Labour Case* (London 1959)
Sir I. Jennings, *Parliamentary Reform* (London 1934)
Sir I. Jennings, *Parliament* (London 1957)
Sir I. Jennings, *Principles of Local Government Law* (London 1960)
Sir I. Jennings, *Party Politics*, 3 vols (London 1960–2)
Sir I. Jennings, *The Law and the Constitution* (London 1959)
Sir I. Jennings, *Cabinet Government* (London 1959)
Sir I. Jennings, *The Queen's Government* (London 1954)
Sir I. Jennings, *The British Constitution* (London 1966)
J. Jewkes, *Public and Private Enterprise* (London 1965)
D. Johnson, *On Being an Independent MP* (London 1964)
F. A. Johnson, *Defence by Committee* (London 1960)
M. Johnson, *Parliament and Administration* (London 1966)
J. E. A. Jolliffe, *The Constitutional History of Medieval England* (London 1937)

H. R. Kahn, *Salaries in the Public Service in England and Wales* (London 1962)
K. Katzarov, *The Theory of Nationalisation* (The Hague 1965)
C. Kaufmann, *The Left* (London 1966)
G. W. Keeton, *The Passing of Parliament* (London 1952)
D. L. Keir, *The Constitutional History of Modern Britain* (London 1964)
B. Keith-Lucas, *The English Government Franchise* (London 1952)
R. Kelf-Cohen, *Nationalisation in Britain* (London 1961)
R. K. Kelsall, *Higher Civil Servants in Britain* (London 1955)
J. E. Kersell, *Parliamentary Supervision of Delegated Legislation* (London 1960)
Lord Kilmuir, *The Law of Parliamentary Privilege* (London 1959)
A. King, *British Politics* (Boston 1966)
H. King, *Parliament and Freedom* (London 1962)

E. Lakeman and J. D. Lambert, *Voting in Democracies* (London 1959)

H. J. Laski, *Parliamentary Government in England* (London 1938)
H. J. Laski, *Reflections on the Constitution* (London 1962)
R. J. Lawrence, *The Government of Northern Ireland* (London 1965)
E. Layton, *Building by Local Authorities* (London 1961)
P. Laundy, *The Office of Speaker* (London 1964)
J. M. Lee, *Social Leaders and Public Persons* (London 1963)
G. H. Le May, *British Government 1914–53, Select Documents* (London 1955)
R. Lewis and A. Maude, *Professional People* (London 1952)
R. Lewis and A. Maude, *The English Middle Classes* (London 1953)
E. Liggett, *British Political Issues*, 2 vols (London 1964)
V. D. Lipman, *Local Government Areas, 1834–1945* (London 1949)
K. Loewenstein, *British Cabinet Government* (London 1967)
D. Lofts (Ed.), *Local Government Today and Tomorrow* (London 1963)
S. Low, *The Governors of England* (London 1904)
A. L. Lowell, *The Government of England*, 2 vols (New York 1912)

R. E. McCallum and A. Readman, *The British General Election of 1945* (London 1947)
L. J. Macfarlane, *The British Communist Party* (London 1966)
L. J. Macfarlane, *British Politics 1918–64* (London 1965)
K. R. Mackenzie, *The English Parliament* (London 1959)
R. T. McKenzie, *British Political Parties* (London 1963)
W. J. M. Mackenzie, *Free Elections* (London 1958)
W. J. M. Mackenzie and J. W. Grove, *Central Administration in Britain* (London 1957)
J. P. Mackintosh, *The British Cabinet* (London 1968)
J. P. Mackintosh, *The Devolution of Power* (London 1968)
F. W. Maitland, *Constitutional History of England* (London 1961)
D. C. Marsh, *The Changing Social Structure of England and Wales* (London 1965)
A. H. Marshall, *Financial Administration in Local Government* (London 1960)
G. Marshall and G. C. Moodie, *Some Problems of the Constitution* (London 1961)
K. Martin, *The Crown and the Establishment* (London 1963)
A. Mathiot, *The British Political System* (London 1958)
D. R. Matthews, *The Social Background of Political Decision Makers* (New York 1964)
Sir J. Maud and S. E. Finer, *Local Government in England and Wales* (London 1953)
Sir T. E. May, *The Law, Privileges, Proceedings and Usage of Parliament* (London 1964)
R. Michels, *Political Parties* (London 1911)
R. Miliband, *Parliamentary Socialism: A Study in the Politics of Labour* (London 1961)

R. Millar, *The New Classes* (London 1966)
R. S. Milne and H. C. Mackenzie, *Straight Fight* (London 1958)
R. S. Milne and H. C. Mackenzie, *Marginal Seat* (London 1958)
B. R. Mitchell and K. Boehm, *British Parliamentary Election Results 1951–64* (London 1966)
J. Mitchell, *Groundwork to Economic Planning* (London 1966)
G. C. Moodie, *The Government of Great Britain* (London 1964)
J. H. Morris, *Local Government Areas* (London 1960)
Lord Morrison, *Government and Parliament* (London 1964)
C. L. Mowat, *Britain Between the Wars* (London 1956)

S. Neumann, *Modern Political Parties* (London 1956)
H. G. Nichols, *The British General Election of 1950* (London 1951)
Sir H. Nicholson, *George V* (London 1952)
M. Nicholson, *The System* (London 1967)
N. Nicolson, *People and Parliament* (London 1958)
E. A. Nordlinger, *The Working Class Tories* (London 1967)
E. L. Normanton, *The Accountability and Audit of Governments* (London 1967)

T. H. O'Brien, *British Experiments in Public Ownership and Control* (London 1937)
M. Ogilvy Webb, *The Government Explains* (London 1965)
G. N. Ostergaard and A. H. Halsey, *Power in Cooperation* (London 1965)
M. I. Ostrogorski, *Democracy and the Organisation of Political Parties*, 2 vols (London 1962)

P. Paterson, *The Selectorate* (London 1967)
A. T. Peacock and D. J. Robertson, *Public Expenditure: Appraisal and Control* (London 1962)
A. T. Peacock and J. Wiseman, *The Growth of Public Expenditure in the United Kingdom* (London 1961)
H. Pear, *English Social Difference* (London 1955)
A. J. Pearson, *The Railways and the Nation* (London 1964)
H. Pelling, *A Short History of the Labour Party* (London 1965)
H. Pelling, *A History of British Trade Unionism* (London 1963)
H. Pelling, *The British Communist Party* (London 1958)
Political and Economic Planning, *Advisory Committees in British Government* (London 1960)
S. Pollard, *The Development of the British Economy, 1914–50* (London 1962)
A. R. Prest, *Public Finance in Theory and Practice* (London 1960)
D. N. Pritt, *The Labour Government 1945–51* (London 1963)

T. Raison, *Why Conservative?* (London 1964)
A. Ranney, *Pathways to Parliament* (London 1965)

J. Rasmusson, *The Liberal Party: A Study of Retrenchment and Revival* (London 1965)

J. Redlich, *The Procedure of the House of Common,* 3 vols (London 1908)

J. Redlich and F. W. Hirst, *The History of Local Government in England* (London 1958)

A. M. Rees and T. Smith, *Town Councillors* (London 1964)

G. Reid, *The Politics of Financial Control* (London 1967)

G. Rhodes, *Administrators in Action,* vol. 2 (London 1965)

P. G. Richards, *Honourable Members* (London 1964)

P. G. Richards, *Patronage in British Government* (London 1963)

P. G. Richards, *Delegation in Local Government* (London 1956)

B. C. Roberts, *Trade Union Government and Administration in Great Britain* (London 1957)

W. A. Robson, *The Development of Local Government* (London 1954)

W. A. Robson (Ed.), *Great Cities of the World* (London 1957)

W. A. Robson, *The Government and Mis-Government of London* (London 1948)

W. A. Robson, *Local Government in Crisis* (London 1966)

W. A. Robson, *The Civil Service in Britain and France* (London 1956)

W. A. Robson, *The Governors and the Governed* (London 1964)

W. A. Robson, *Justice and Administrative Law* (London 1951)

W. A. Robson, *Nationalized Industry and Public Ownership* (London 1962)

W. A. Robson (Ed.), *Problems of Nationalized Industries* (London 1952)

W. A. Robson (Ed.), *Public Ownership* (London 1937)

A. A. Rogow, *The Labour Government and British Industry* (London 1955)

G. Rose, *The Struggle for Penal Reform* (London 1962)

R. Rose (Ed.), *Studies in British Politics* (London 1966)

G. W. Ross, *The Nationalisation of Steel* (London 1965)

J. F. S. Ross, *Parliamentary Representation* (London 1948)

A. Roth, *Business Background of MPs* (London 1967)

D. C. Rowat, *The Ombudsman* (London 1965)

Royal Institute of Public Administration, *New Sources of Local Revenue* (London 1956)

Royal Institute of Public Administration, *Budgeting in Public Authorities* (London 1959)

S. K. Ruck, *London Government and the Welfare Service* (London 1963)

A. Sampson, *The Anatomy of Britain Today* (London 1965)

J. R. Sargent, *British Transport Policy* (London 1958)

G. Sawyer, *Ombudsman* (London 1964)

A. N. Schofield, *Local Government Elections* (London 1954)

A. N. Schofield, *Parliamentary Elections* (London 1959)

B. Schwartz, *Law and the Executive in Britain* (London 1949)

P. Self and H. Storing, *The State and the Farmer* (London 1962)

M. Shanks (Ed.), *The Lessons of Public Enterprise* (London 1963)

L. J. Sharpe, *A Metropolis Votes* (London 1962)

K. Shinwell, *The Labour Story* (London 1963)

C. H. Sisson, *The Spirit of Public Administration and some European Comparisons* (London 1966)

F. Smallwood, *Greater London: the Politics of Metropolitan Reform* (Indianapolis 1965)

K. B. Smellie, *A History of Local Government* (London 1957)

K. B. Smellie, *A Hundred Years of English Government* (London 1950)

B. C. Smith, *Regional Institutions* (London 1964)

B. Smith and G. N. Ostergaard, *Constitutional Relations: Between the Labour and Cooperative Parties* (London 1960)

S. A. deSmith, *Judicial Review of Administrative Action* (London 1959)

Diana Spearman, *Democracy in England* (London 1957)

M. Stacey, *Tradition and Change* (London 1960)

W. J. Stankiewicz, *Crisis in British Government* (New York 1967)

J. D. Stewart, *British Pressure Groups* (London 1958)

M. Stewart, *The British Approach to Politics* (London 1966)

H. B. Stout, *British Government* (London 1953)

E. Strauss, *The Ruling Servants: Bureaucracy in Russia, France and Britain* (London 1961)

A. J. P. Taylor, *English History 1914–45* (London 1965)

E. Taylor, *The House of Commons at Work* (London 1965)

G. Thayer, *The British Political Fringe* (London 1965)

E. P. Thompson, *Out of Apathy* (London 1960)

D. Thomson, *England in the Twentieth Century* (London 1965)

H. Thomson, *The Establishment* (London 1959)

The Times, 'House of Commons 1966', published after each general election (London 1966)

J. Treneman and D. McQuail, *Television and the Political Image* (London 1961)

E. O. Tuttle, *The Crusade Against Capital Punishment in Great Britain* (London 1962)

T. E. Utley, *Occasion for Ombudsman* (London 1961)

Sir G. Vickers, *The Art of Judgement: A Study of Policy Making* (London 1969)

J. Vincent, *Pollbooks: How the Victorians Voted* (London 1967)

J. Vincent, *The Formation of the Liberal Party 1857–68* (London 1968)

E. C. S. Wade and G. C. Phillips, *Constitutional Law* (Longman 1957)

H. W. R. Wade, *Towards Administrative Justice* (Michigan 1963)

H. W. R. Wade, *Administrative Law* (London 1961)

Graham Wallas, *Human Nature in Politics* (London 1908)

J. H. Warren, *The English Local Government System* (London 1963)

J. H. Warren, *The Local Government Service* (London 1952)

A. Watkins, *The Liberal Dilemma* (London 1961)

G. Watson (Ed.), *The Radical Alternative* (London 1962)

A. Wedgwood Benn, *The Privy Council as a Second Chamber* (London 1957)

W. E. Weiner, *British Labour and Public Ownership* (London 1960)

West Midland Group, *Local Government and Central Control* (London 1956)

G. C. Weston, *English Constitutional Theory and the House of Lords* (London 1965)

K. C. Wheare, *Government by Committee* (London 1955)

K. C. Wheare, *Legislation* (London 1963)

Sir J. Wheeler-Bennett, *George VI* (London 1958)

C. W. White and W. D. Hussey, *Government in Great Britain* (London 1961)

Sir J. Whyatt, *The Citizen and the Administration* (London 1962)

N. Wilding and P. Laundy, *An Encyclopaedia of Parliament* (London 1961)

R. Wilkinson, *The Prefects* (London 1964)

A. Williams, *Public Finance and Budgetary Policy* (London 1963)

F. Williams, *Fifty Years March: the Rise of the Labour Party* (London 1949)

F. M. G. Willson, *Administrators in Action: British Case Studies* (London 1961)

F. M. G. Willson and D. N. Chester, *The Organisation of British Central Government* (London 1957)

C. Wilson, *Cases and Materials on Constitutional and Administrative Law* (London 1966)

H. H. Wilson, *Pressure Group* (London 1961)

J. Wilson, *Public Schools and Private Practice* (London 1962)

N. Wilson, *The British System of Government* (London 1963)

T. Wilson, *Policies for Regional Development* (London 1966)

Duke of Windsor, *Crown and People 1902–53* (London 1953)

H. V. Wiseman, *Parliament and the Executive* (London 1966)

N. Wood, *Communism and British Intellectuals* (New York 1959)

G. Wootton, *Workers' Unions and the State* (London 1966)

D. C. M. Yardley, *Introduction to British Constitutional Law* (London 1964)

W. Young, *The Profumo Affair, Aspects of Conservatism* (London 1963)

INDEX